Mel Bay presents

HARMONIC MECHANISMS
FOR GUITAR

George Van Eps

I wish to dedicate these books with love and respect to my late wife Jo—

1 2 3 4 5 6 7 8 9 0

GEORGE VAN EPS ... *In Admiration*

by Charlie Menees

Charlie Menees, for decades a jazz observer, writer, teacher, record collector, lives in St. Louis, hosts "Jazz Under the Arch" every Saturday night on KMOX radio, the Voice of St. Louis.

Rich rewards from this book were mine considerably before knowledge began to unfold from its pages. Title and content were unknowns as anxiously I awaited my first opportunity to meet, now also an author, a musician I had admired from afar for decades.

The phone jingled and Mel Bay said George Van Eps was coming to St. Louis to finalize publishing of a guitar book Van Eps had written. Would I like lunch, later dinner, with the visitor? The heart of a veteran music buff and record collector beat faster at the thought of shaking hands for the first time with a longtime idol. Anticipation repeated later at a second similar invitation.

In those two meetings I got better than casually acquainted with both George Van Eps, the guitarist, and the person. Now I feel so at ease with this talented, articulate, warm, and gentle person that I beg permission to henceforth refer to him on most occasions in these paragraphs, but always respectfully, by his first name.

I suspected, but now know for sure, that George is more than the jazz guitarist that prior reading and recordings had mainly emphasized. I discovered that he is no less capable, knowledgeable, and concerned in classical and other schools of guitar.

His knowledge and defense of many musics brought realization that my own limited musical abilities and knowledge are insufficient qualification for the indepth expert appraisal that George's writings deserve. Therefore, I unashamedly admit that some of the judgments, insights, and forecasts, even to some exact phrases, evolve from discussion with Mel Bay, and his son Bill.

But before any of that, it is high priority to cite the zeal and devotion George has devoted to this guitar text writings in the recent several years. Concert and recording performances politely turned down, hopefully only temporarily, he had labored almost exclusively on this and companion volumes to follow. The overall project has become something of a mission, the zenith of a dedicated artist-creator's hopes to bestow a worthy and abiding legacy to the ages. Perhaps "life's work" is apt. Rest assured that not forgotten for a moment is the George Van Eps legion of already indelible guitar legacies etched on recordings.

Guitar and guitarist are George's constant concerns. Guitar playing, to him, is never less than an art. Evolving fresh insights into the guitar and its playing are based, of course, on his many years of study, creation, and performance. Enhancing this recurring freshness is unflagging enthusiasm.

George's concepts transcend any one particular style of music; they are applicable to anyone who has ever played guitar, whether by pick or finger. His text challenges both diligent work and that enriching type of concentration described as "thinking through." George probably didn't realize that his writings, to borrow from an old expression, both "light a candle" and "fill the bucket."

These pages encourage regard of the guitar in new light, as vehicle for harmonic expression rather than just a medium for concern with chord forms and inversions as block entities. Ever on surface are the author's hopes that the guitarist will view each note and voice in every chordal structure as one independent entity leading to another independent entity.

The text is chromatically oriented, and explores infinite harmonic possibilities, both factors necessary in developing the ear that hears the remarkably unusual in chordal movement.

Exposed are growing respect for the guitar, and constant striving for mastery of what the author feels are the instrument's still unattained potentials. Dedication to techniques, he emphasizes, is the guaranteed path to future guitar creativity and achievement. Guitarists unaware of the unexplored and unattained can hopefully be convinced that only years of study and impervious dedication will open the windows of this exciting new guitar world.

George's text outlines exceptional and multi-perspective working knowledge of the guitar fingerboard in all positions. The guitarist completing this, and succeeding volumes, will have worked arduously up and down the guitar neck through countless harmonic possibilities, with hands accustomed to moving in new and independently creative possibilities.

Developed is an extraordinary degree of independence in both left and right hand, mastery of which will catapult the guitarist to a lofty level of coordination between the two. The ultimate, of course, is George's "thinking" approach to guitar. No room therein for routine and redundant ideas of chordal formations.

A work of this magnitude, from such a virtuoso, should be sought by guitarists of countless generations. These timeless concepts will remain fresh and viable in the twenty-first century.

George belongs to that famous Van Eps plectrist family that eminated from Plainfield, New Jersey. Fred Van Eps, the famous banjoist, headed that remarkable family that produced four sons who became leading professional musicians, Bobby, Fred, John and George.

From banjo, young George switched to guitar, became best known to the wide public for stellar work in the bands of Harry Reser, Smith Ballew, Freddy Martin, Benny Goodman and Ray Noble, and for work with Paul Weston, Matty Matlock, and many others. For years he was one of Hollywood's top studio players. Stars with whom he appeared and accompanied are now super stars in show biz history.

Guitar followers are aware, of course, that George has long been distinguished as designer of the 7-string guitar—the added one being a bass string. He performs on this instrument on several Capitol and Columbia recordings which, though now out of print, can be located for study in libraries and private collections. Titles include "My Guitar," "George Van Eps and His Seven-String Guitar," and "Soliloquy." Contents reveal several original works preserved as evidence of George's gifts as composer.

If George Van Eps were not so modest about his truly remarkable and creative musical talents and accomplishments, and about his equally impressive abilities to talk with enviable articulation, humor, honesty and accuracy about his illustrious guitar chapters in American musical history, I'd like to do my own book . . . about him.

FOREWORD

The material in this series of books represents some of the more important findings of my research over the years concerning harmonics and fingerboard gymnastics.

The playing of keyboard and fingerboard instruments is highly physical, therefore, knowledge of harmony becomes quite useless without the mechanical means to produce the necessary notes—naturally, each depends on the other.

These studies help to build discipline, independent finger control, multi-thought control, and independent harmonic chromatic notational selectivity. These, I believe, are the foremost objectives in order to play an instrument well.

My books contain no single voice studies as such. All of the studies employ two or more voices, however, single voices will stand out in most of the various harmonic structures.

Each book contains some of my concepts and principles which may or may not appear to be exactly new to the reader, but, I believe some of the fresh viewpoints may perhaps add to one's concepts; my intention being to provide a little food for thought and add to familiar perspectives, thus showing some of the various harmonics in a slightly different light.

This material is intended to add to ones present knowledge. It's meant to blend with it, not denounce it, or take its place, because, all schooling and experience is valuable. In other words, for those with previous schooling this material can be supplemental information.

In creating any musical composition, harmony must begin somewhere, it must go somewhere, and it must end somewhere; therefore, it is of utmost importance to know where the voices have been, where they are at the moment, where they are going logically, and where they can go by creative free choice and surprise. This material can help provide the mental and physical tools for accomplishing this goal.

Some of the studies may appear to be redundant and identical at first glance, but careful scrutiny will show that they are not identical, they are different—bear in mind that "similar" is not "identical". The study of subtle mechanical and notational differences is more than just desirable, it is absolutely necessary. The hands can never be too mechanical, agile, or well trained—nor can the mind ever know too much about harmony.

I do not claim that these books, in any way, cover all of the facets of playing, nor all of the multi-millions of harmonic possibilities. However, the mechanics, devices, and thought lines are presented that will enable those who are interested to pursue them as far as desire and time will allow.

In the many years that I have spent researching and developing fingerboard gymnastics and harmonic devices of this nature, I have, quite naturally, delved mainly into the areas that greatly fascinated me, and my most sincere hope is that they will be of some interest and benefit to others.

GENERAL REMARKS

The world of harmony is a most gratifying place to dwell—there is nothing more satisfying than the wonderful audio pictures that gradually take shape by manipulating lines of voices within chordal structures.

As Segovia so aptly put it: "The guitar to me is like looking at a full orchestra through the wrong end of the binoculars."

In order to be able to play the guitar well one must be an athlete; it takes athletic endeavor in the form of a vast variety of hand and mental gymnastics. This is why the diligent practice of awkward, difficult, and unusual hand positions, stretches, formations and finger combinations are of utmost importance.

The hand must be well-trained to be ready for all attitudes, and as many different fingering situations as possible. Practicing just what lies under the fingers is not enough—the ideal is for the hand not to be surprised by the unusual.

The ideal technique must be able to handle the uncomfortable unusual situations that occur when improvising, within the limits of the hand, of course.

Physically, exercises have many purposes. Some are designed to train the hand to walk smoothly on the fingers. Some are designed to be awkward and difficult, to teach the hand how to be ready for the nearly impossible. Others are designed to fill the degrees in between. All are necessary—it is important to keep this in mind.

Of course, one should keep what has been accomplished in the past, but we must never shy away from the new—the perhaps uncomfortable areas of more advanced material.

It is understandably human to want to sound good to ourselves when we practice, and therefore play what we already know well. However, real advancement comes from tackling new things; coming to grips with work that is more advanced, work that is out of reach unless one really tries to accomplish the seemingly impossible—after all, they're only impossible for a while.

Progress comes from working with material that elevates—material that is always a little above and out of reach.

Acquiring harmonic fingerboard knowledge and technique is a gradual progressive climb; one must not expect to jump from first to eighth grade material, for that is the sure path to disappointment.

About all work material can hope to do is to create an incentive or desire, whet the appetite for knowledge, then provide the necessary information and path to follow for further investigation and experiment.

ACKNOWLEDGEMENT

I wish to thank my daughter Kay (Van Eps) Adikes for her able assistance in preparing this work.

GENERAL REMARKS

The areas of harmonic/mechanical investigation are so vast that it would take tons of manuscript to show just a small portion of them in detail. Since time and space will not permit following every facet to any kind of finality, the understanding of the basic principles and formulas that can provide the tools for further pursuit seem most important. After the principles are understood, they can be carried as far as desired and used in any direction; they can be applied at any time to any situation in any phase of development. Therefore, I deemed it necessary to present the basic principles and rules pertaining to my findings that will make further investigation possible. I believe enough written material is presented in these books to establish the thought lines.

I have been known for verbal redundancy for many years—however, there is a very good reason: through many years of teaching, I have found that directives, explanations, rules, warnings, etc. must be repeated periodically over and over to make absolutely certain that they not only are understood, but that they become firmly implanted in the mind—so firmly embedded that they are ever present. They must become habitual. Particularly in text books, periodic repetition is necessary because so many people open books in the middle, the end, or any place.

Fundamentals don't teach one how to compose. Composing by fundamentals would be by rote, (parrot fashion). However, they do tell you what not to do.

> All laws and rules of music can be warped, twisted, distorted, and still make sense if the principles are clearly understood in the first place. As I have said before, "Luck won't do it, and ignorance can't."

A person cannot be taught to compose. The creative spark must be there. Taste cannot be taught, it must be there. Fundamentals don't teach taste—"influence-by-association" affects taste, but it does not create it. Listening to, and analyzing good music of all types, be it classical or jazz, is the real teacher. In other words, it can rub off.

A painter doesn't paint with a book on the technique of painting in one hand and a color chart in the other. Writers learn to write by reading the works of great authors, not books on how to write. All a teacher can do is provide the necessary tools and show the student how they work. The teacher can't be by the student's side constantly to tell him when and where to use the tools—his judgment, sense of taste, balance, and proportion must do that.

Music is inspirational in concept, but mechanical in reproduction. Therefore, mechanisms are necessary to enable voices to move freely. When the technique level is achieved that allows voices this freedom, ideas flow like water.

Scales, arpeggio's and exercises are the instrumentalist's tools. One cannot play without these tools. The knowledge and physical dexterity that comes from working with these tools is absolutely necessary to the instrumentalist; without the disciplined practice of these tools, one cannot play.

I would like to talk about the word "exercise" for a moment. An exercise can be quite long or very short; it can have many forms. A long exercise can embody many notes and mechanisms, or, it can be just the reverse and contain just one or two notes.

> Here is a one note example:
>
> Drop the left arm down by your side, relaxed. Now bring your hand up to the fingerboard and try to hit any predetermined note immediately; let's say a "G" on the third string. As you know now, it is not easy to do; your average is pretty bad. Now, try it with your eyes closed. Now, your average is awful. What good is an exercise like this; what does it do? It helps quite a few basically important things such as judgment of distance, orientation and the general feeling for the instrument.

It is impossible to play anything without using parts of scales, because all melodic/harmonic lines come from the chromatic scale, and since the chromatic scale is an exercise, this "exercise" produces all music.

A young man once told me that "he didn't want to play scales or exercises." I just told him that he might try concentrating on "watching grass grow" for he could not play music, ever.

All scales and arpeggios are exercises—but not all exercises are scales and arpeggios.

Going back and forth from "C" to "B" repeatedly is exercising. Playing a B seventh chord to E major repeatedly becomes an exercise. They are very basic examples but they are exercises.

What I'm leading up to is this: make exercises out of all musical situations by taking one or two steps of any scale, arepggio, or progression, and repeat them over and over until they are very smooth. Then go on to the next step and repeat the process. Select a scale that contains many notes and gradually eliminate notes until down to just a few. In other words, reduce these stations down to their smallest part. Practice them forward and backward, inside out, upside down, outside in, etc. Apply this format to all of this material, no matter how simple or complicated the form.

Take all studies apart note by note to analyze them. Select sections of different variations and blend them together to make other variations etc. Compound them as far as possible.

Don't just run scales up and down, break up the regular continuity by skipping some of the intervals to make short and long arpeggios out of them. Skip intervals and insert them some place else. Change the order by rearranging the stations of the scales. Work with them using as many different variations as possible. Here are just a few suggestions for scale patterns:

> 1-2-8—1-3-8—1-4-8—etc.   1-7-8—2-7-8—3-7-8—etc.   7-8-1—6-7-1—5-6-1—etc.
>
> 1-2-7-8—1-2-3-7-8—1-2-3-4-7-8—etc.   1-3—2-4—3-5—etc.   1-4—2-5—3-6—etc.
>
> *TRY CONTRARY MOTION:*
> 1-8—2-7—3-6—4-5—5-4—6-3—7-2—8-1—etc.
>
> These are just a few of the vast possibilities. This kind of work helps one's judgment of distance. It is good practice gymnastically also.

It is very important to know where harmonic duplicates are located on the fingerboard whether they be two note chords, four note chords, or larger. There isn't enough space to indicate all of the duplicates for all of the steps and stations of the material in these books. However, enough of them are shown to indicate the vast potential. Knowing where duplicate voicings are located is essential to the overall understanding of the instrument—I cannot stress this point enough.

Good technique is based on common sense. Hands must become machines and be trained to work with the greatest precision possible. A sloppy machine lacks precision. Eliminate all lost motion and try to be as accurate as possible. Keep fingers above and close to the fingerboard where they will be ready to function when needed. Keep the thumb of the left hand logically placed on the back of the neck (not around it) so that it doesn't have to change attitude every time the hand moves.

Don't depress more strings than are being used because of the "fatigue factor." When three strings are depressed, but only two sounding, the result endurancewise is a 1/3 waste of energy, and over the long haul this becomes a sizable loss—when the hand is fatigued it makes mistakes.

We know that using four fingers to play four chromatic tones is smoother and more logical than using one finger—that is common sense. One can travel just so fast hopping on one leg; use two legs and the speed more than doubles. Compare hopping to a fast run and you have the answer.

"Alternation"—common sense, therefore, tells us that we should copy this walking action with our fingers as much as possible; shifting the balance from one finger to the other just as in walking. But in doing this, we must think four instead of two because we have four fingers. Now, just as two more than doubled the effectiveness of one, four will more than double two.

This "walking" action principle applies to more than just single notes, it can be applied to many harmonic intervals from 2nds to two octaves. Here are a few examples:

GENERAL REMARKS

FOREWORD

SEE PAGE 13 FOR STRING CHART

MULTIPLE ALTERNATE FINGERING:

Multiple alternate fingering may seem a little difficult at first - It must be practiced slowly - ease and velocity will come later.

As I mentioned before, the articulating teams of fingers must be precise, but the end result is well worth the work.

This type of finger team work is one of the logical mechanisms that is necessary for good overall technique.

There are times when alternate fingering can't be used because the other fingers are busy - and then there are times when it is desirable to repeat with the fingers because the notes lie well and it is comfortable and smooth to repeat, particularly when the repeat is on the same string or strings - Here are a few Examples:

MULTIPLE ALTERNATE AND REPEAT FINGERING -

alternate fingering for right hand also

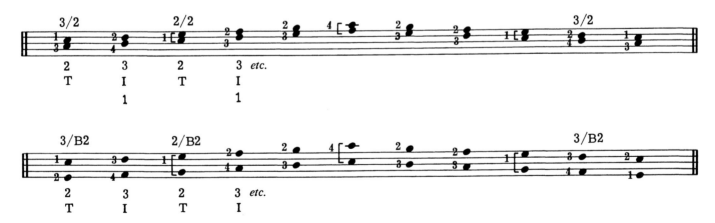

It is desirable to alternate with the right hand fingers whenever possible as in the above examples. For the very same reasons just mentioned - there will be times when fingers have to repeat, or comfortable to repeat, but, usually, a good rule to follow is:

Don't repeat fingers on either hand unless you must do so.

GENERAL REMARKS

FOREWORD

Alternation can be employed with the barre's, From double stops to the small, medium, and large barre's - When a player has developed a powerful hand, even the "GRANDE" Barre can be played this way, as the following Examples show:

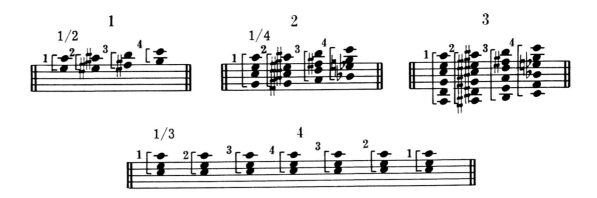

The last example shows alternate fingering while the notation remains the same - this is very good practise - apply it to others ---

Alternation applies to barring as well as to single and multiple notations as has been shown. Using the arched Finger technique (finger tips) and the barre in combination is necessary for overall technique -It's also necessary to be able to (lock down) sustain notes while other Fingers are in motion- I refer to this as "standing on notes".
The first example shows the fourth Finger standing on the note "E" for the full count of four while the other Fingers sound the quarter notes.

The pressure of the sustaining Fingers must be constant and very even for the entire measure while the articulating Fingers are busy applying and releasing pressure -When this is done properly the sustaining notes will not buzz or die.
Each Finger must be able to function independantly and responsibly--

When exercises are similar notationwise but employ different Fingering, They should be correlated -In other words, the differences should be applied to each other for a more rounded picture of the Fingering possibilities---

GENERAL REMARKS
SIMILIES

The example below shows a few basic similarities between writing, painting, and music:

	Writing	Painting	Music
	Letters	Colors	Notes
	Words	Mixed colors	Chords
	Sentences	Subjects	Progressions
Result =	Composition	Composition	Composition

The chromatic scale is very similar to the alphabet and color spectrum in this way:
The twelve tone scale is used in the same manner that letters are used in writing and colors are used in painting. Notes are "audio" letters and colors. Writers use combinations of letters to make words—painters use combinations of colors to make hues—musicians use combinations of notes to make harmony. This line of thought applies to numbers also.

GENERAL REMARKS
CHEMISTRY

TONAL CHEMISTRY:

The blending of notes is not only Harmonic, for it affects the quality of sound - It affects the tonal "Timbre", the density of sound --

FOR INSTANCE:

Middle "C" or "E" when struck separately produce their very own sound color - but when struck together they produce a different sound color due to blending the tonal frequencies.

By placing the "C" one octave lower to form a tenth, another sound color is produced even tho the notes are still "C" and "E" -- The tenth generates a much heavier sound color because of Exciting more overtones.

Because of this tonal chemistry a bass line can be above a light harmonic structure and stand out with authority if it has enough weight/density, not louder, but richer in "Timbre"- Sound color.

EXAMPLE:

HEAVIER BASS TONE   LIGHTER BASS TONE

HOLLOW NOTES = BASS

The increased weight mass of the strings add to the density of Tone quality as shown below:

GENERAL REMARKS
Chemistry

Music is made of three basic ingredients which are:
Scales
Arpeggios
Time

Scales provide all of the voice motion; arpeggios come from scales. When some of the notes of a scale are deleted, an arpeggio is produced. In other words, an arpeggio is part of one or more scales.

Arpeggios are broken chords—chords are frozen arpeggios.

Time is rhythm, meter, syncopation, etc.

When these three ingredients are blended intelligently, music is produced . . .

GENERAL REMARKS
CHEMISTRY

The fingering and string set markings in many of the studies in these books are varied and may at times skip around the fingerboard purposely because, the intent is to present as many different fingering combinations as space will permit. There are many more than shown of course, and one must endeavor to find as many as possible.

Fingerboard chemistry is not only tonal, for mechanical chemistry is also involved. A chain of combined mechanisms to produce notes, is necessary to complete any harmonic scale, phrase, passage, progression, etc. A blending of all these different chemistrys results in: "combined tones," plus "mixed mechanics," of which the sum total is: "music."

Except for special articulation, very little right hand fingering is indicated for the following reasons: the majority of people interested in studying these books are already familiar with the various right hand styles, and will govern themselves accordingly.

There are many ways of sounding the strings—the most common are: the plectrum (pick)—alternation is best for velocity—(up and down strokes) the fingers (classic) —again, alternation is best for velocity—(taking turns) the fingers and pick combined—usually a mixture, with both alternating.

The classic finger style offers the greatest advantage because of being able to utilize all five fingers.

The material presented in this series of books is most suited to the classic right hand and the combination of fingers and plectrum.

Instrumental chemistry embodies these three basic elements:

Mechanics—Sound—Music

Mechanical/physical actions produce notes—
Notes produce sound—sound produces music—

In other words, it is the blending of notes and tone qualities, coupled with combinations of various physical mechanisms, plus the notational harmonic melodic chemistry of the music itself.

For lack of a better description, the term "chemistry" was chosen because it describes the blending of all of these variables so well.

CHEMISTRY

This "C" could belong to any key and any harmonic/melodic pattern, as could the "G" below it— and the "E" below the "G". When sounded singly they suggest many things, but actually nothing concrete.

When the "C" and "G" are sounded together a harmonic picture begins to form, but is the relationship major or minor? Not until the "E" (third) is added does its true intention become clear.

The "E" makes a "C" major triad—the lowering of the "E" would make a "C" minor chord.

An "A" in the bass would make it an "A" minor 7th—an "A flat" bass makes it an "A" flat major 7th with a raised 5th. When the fourth voice is introduced the "C" major triad can become many other things. A "B" natural in the bass makes it a "B" eleventh-sharp 5th flat 9th—also a "C" major 7th with the 7th in the bass etc. etc.

Let's say that the "C" is number 1—alone it is just number 1—but as other notes are added the picture changes. Is the number 1 first—somewhere in the middle—maybe last? Or: 123-321-132-231-312-213—

It may seem endless and boring to have to wade through all the various triad studies—but, they must be clearly understood and must be handy before they can be used properly and intelligently.

This material is not presented in the enharmonic keys because it would be redundant. The fingering for the Key of "A" flat is physically the same as it is for the key of "G" sharp, and since these studies were not meant to be sight reading material, it was deemed unnecessary.

STEMLESS NOTES

When there are just whole notes, quarter notes, or half notes, eighth notes, etc. stems are not necessary for time values. Therefore, in many of these studies the stems have been eliminated for the purpose of lessening the congestion . . . for the sake of clarity.

THE IMPORTANCE OF CHROMATICS WILL BE STRESSED THROUGHOUT THESE BOOKS—CHROMATICS, CHROMATICS, AND MORE CHROMATICS—

BASIC VOICING CHART FOR TONIC - THIRD - FIFTH - C-E-G-- "C" MAJOR -

Seperate intervals are indicated on the left of triads - overall intervals on the right.
The angled lines between the triads indicate the repositioning of "THAT" particular note
up or down, Thus changing the voicing and sound while still employing the same three notes.

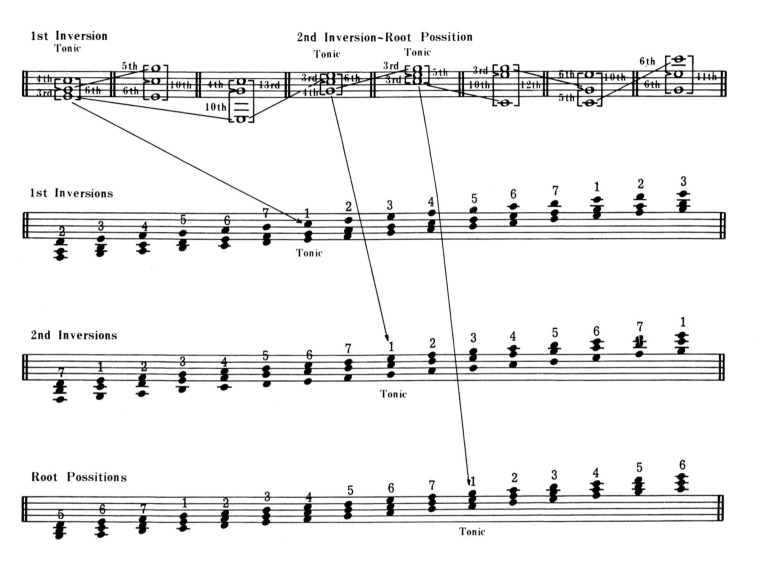

Numbers above the staff indicate steps of the scale - note that the 7th steps contain imperfect
4th's and 5th's

1st Inversion	2nd Inversion	Root Possition
The 4th is perfect	The 3rd is major	The upper 3rd is minor
The 3rd is minor	The 4th is perfect	The lower 3rd is major
The 6th is minor	The 6th is major	The 5th is perfect

These studies are meant to be tools to build musical structures. How to use them must be dictated by one's ear and taste, sense of proportion and balance. The ear knows pleasing sounds, and the combinations of sound.

It must never be said that "this" is the only way to do it. However, I do feel that with careful study these books can provide many of the ways to play difficult, complicated harmonics.

STRING CHART

EXPLANATION OF THE STRING SET SYMBOLS:

A vertical or angled line thus– / –means "Set"—
The number in front of it is the set number—
The number after it indicates the number of strings employed—
Example:
When the 1st-2nd-3rd-strings are employed the symbol is:
1/3—The first set of three–etc.
When the 1st-2nd-3rd-4th-strings are employed the symbol is:
1/4—The 1st set of four–etc.

THE BROKEN AND THE DIVIDED SETS:

Example:
When the 1st-2nd-4th-strings are employed (skipping the 3rd string) it is termed a broken set—the symbol is:
1/B3—The first set of broken three–etc.
When the order is reversed, (skipping the 2nd instead of the 3rd string) the word "broken" is used first, thus:
B1/3—The broken first set of three–etc.

When the 1st-2nd-4th-5th-strings are employed it is termed a divided set—the symbol is:
D1/4—The divided first set of four–etc.
When the 1st-3rd-5th-strings are employed the symbol is:
1/D3—The first set of divided three—and so on—
When the 1st-4th-strings are employed the symbol is:
A 1—
When the 2nd-5th-strings are employed the symbol is:
A 2—etc.
When the 1st-5th-strings are employed the symbol is:
B 1—etc.

NOTE
A symbol for the 1st-3rd-4th-6th-strings is not necessary because it would encompass all of the strings, therefore, the very notation dictates where and on what strings the notes are located.

STRING SET CHART

SYMBOLS:—STRINGS EMPLOYED—

1/2—1st-2nd-
2/2—2nd-3rd-
3/2—3rd-4th-
4/2—4th-5th-
5/2—5th-6th-

1/3—1st-2nd-3rd-
2/3—2nd-3rd-4th-
3/3—3rd-4th-5th-
4/3—4th-5th-6th-

1/4—1st-2nd-3rd-4th-
2/4—2nd-3rd-4th-5th-
3/4—3rd-4th-5th-6th-

1/5—1st-2nd-3rd-4th-5th-
2/5—2nd-3rd-4th-5th-6th-

THE BROKEN AND DIVIDED SETS:

1/B2—1st-3rd-
2/B2—2nd-4th-
3/B2—3rd-5th-
4/B2—4th-6th-

1/B3—1st-2nd-4th-
2/B3—2nd-3rd-5th-
3/B3—3rd-4th-6th-

B1/3—1st-3rd-4th-
B2/3—2nd-4th-5th-
B3/3—3rd-5th-6th-

1/B4—1st-2nd-3rd-5th-
2/B4—2nd-3rd-4th-6th-

B1/4—1st-3rd-4th-5th-
B2/4—2nd-4th-5th-6th-
1D/3—1st-2nd-5th-
2D/3—2nd-3rd-6th-

1/D3—1st-3rd-5th-
2/D3—2nd-4th-6th-

D1/3—1st-4th-5th-
D2/3—2nd-5th-6th-

D1/4—1st-2nd-4th-5th-
D2/4—2nd-3rd-5th-6th-

A1—1st-4th-
A2—2nd-5th-
A3—3rd-6th-

B1—1st-5th-
B2—2nd-6th-

01—1st-6th-

13

GENERAL REMARKS
SELECTIVITY

The term "selectivity" is stressed throughout these books—it has two meanings, the first being:

Good technique demands complete, selective, chromatic control of the instrument. It means having chromatic harmonic knowledge of the fingerboard plus the mechanisms and agility to be able to cope with any harmonic situation within the physical limits of the hands. It means not having to stay within the "well worn" comfortable boundaries of old habits and paths. It means being able to venture into other harmonic areas. It means having the mind dictate to the hands, not the hands to the mind.

An instrumentalist must strive to be able to play in all keys, full range, with as near perfect chromatic control as possible. Working with the many varied mechanisms in all of these subtleties will help build the necessary finger control and dexterity to achieve this goal.

A writer must have complete selective control of the alphabet—
A painter must have complete selective control of colors—
A musician must have complete selective control of notes—

Instrumentalists have a compounded problem in that they must overcome the physical gymnastic aspects of their instruments—they must endeavor to remove as many of the handicaps as possible.

The second meaning of the term "selectivity" is this:
Being able to select the preferred notes in a given harmonic situation—the following example is very basic, but clearly demonstrates the idea.

GENERAL REMARKS

(Selectivity)

These examples employ just open strings - example one = the first four strings-example two = the first five strings --

When a fourth note is added to a triad it is amplified by more than just one note -- It now becomes four triads -- All having a different sound and harmonic meaning thus:

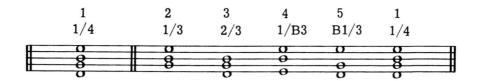

The addition of one note has produced four triads - (trios) numbers 2-3-4-5 and of course one four note chord number 1 - (quartet) which makes five different sounding (but related) chords -- In other words, three notes make a trio -- Four notes makes a group of trios plus one quartet.

Add just one more note and it becomes sixteen chords - they are:

Ten trios - (2 thru 11)

Five Quartets - (12 thru 16)

One Quintet - (1)

Example below

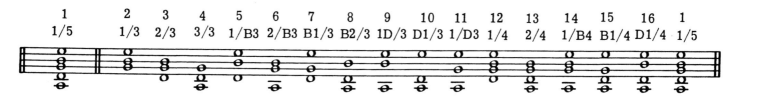

NOTE

When in doubt about a string set symbol used in any exercise, check with the string set chart - however, most of the time the strings employed are quite obvious because of the type of fingering indicated -- Where there are choices - be practical.

GENERAL REMARKS
SELECTIVITY

The following examples show a few of the many voice lines hiding in basic triad work.

By deleting some of the notes the lines become isolated and recognizable and all kinds of patterns result - Many different melodic, harmonic lines are in there just waiting to be selected and heard.

Analyze the line of thought—experiment with this device.

Depress all of the notes at first for orientation but don't sound the x'd notes - then without changing the fingering depress just the selected notes.

This is a device that can lead the mind - and that's important.

Pursue this principle as far as possible.

There are thousands of combinations to experiment with.

As we know, the art of composing and improvising is mostly knowing what notes to leave in and what notes to leave out - being highly selective usually results in a listenable composition.

I'm not implying that composing be done this way - what I am implying is that there is a lot of linear activity hiding in the triads that can be isolated and utilized, instead of mostly being sounded in block form - take the triads apart note by note - place them so they form all kinds of combinations - the lines are there, take advantage of them.

Devices such as this are meant to suggest, to stimulate, they are meant to trigger creative action.

GENERAL REMARKS
SELECTIVITY

If 6 objects are placed side by side, then rearranged one at a time so that they are always in a new position and relationship to each other, it will require 720 moves to complete the cycle. In other words, the number of distinct linear arrangements of six is: 720—

$$5 \times 6 = 30$$
$$4 \times 30 = 120$$
$$3 \times 120 = 360$$
$$2 \times 360 = 720$$

If the 6 objects were the open strings of the guitar there would be 720 different ways to sound them before repeating.

Now, when this arithmetic form is applied to 12 consecutive tones of the chromatic scale the number of moves required in order to complete the cycle is: 479,001,600

The huge difference between the 6 and 12 figure is of course due to geometric progression.

$$11 \times 12 = 132$$
$$10 \times 132 = 1320$$
$$9 \times 1320 = 11880$$
$$8 \times 11880 = 95,040$$
$$7 \times 95,040 = 665,280$$
$$6 \times 665,280 = 3,991,680$$
$$5 \times 3,991,680 = 19,958,400$$
$$4 \times 19,958,400 = 79,833,600$$
$$3 \times 79,833,600 = 239,500,800$$
$$2 \times 239,500,800 = 479,001,600$$

479,001,600 = the possible combinations of 12—when multiplied by 720 totals:

$$
\begin{array}{r}
479,001,600 \\
\times 720 \\
\hline
00 \\
9\ 580\ 032\ 00 \\
335\ 301\ 120\ 0 \\
\hline
344,881,152,000
\end{array}
$$

344 billion, 881 million, 152 thousand, combinations—

Spending one second on each one of the possible combinations 24 hours a day—7 days a week—52 weeks a year—to reach the end of the order would take: 11,036 years (eleven thousand, thirty six years). This gives one a small idea of the many choices available—this is "selectivity"—music as we know it today is less than 400 years old. This means that we have not even scratched the surface yet, not even near the surface.

The meager use of notes does not mean a lack of quality or sound. The lightness or heaviness of sound depends more on the choice of notes, register, voicing, the timber of the tones, etc. rather than the quantity of notes.

Closing a voicing, or opening and thinning a voicing is an audio equivalent of letting in fresh air.

Moving lines must have space. In order for an inner voice to be able to stand out in any harmonic situation it must be given room to be heard. If all the notes on an organ were sounded simultaneously, all motion would be smothered—buried.

In this simple little notation there are four
Different lines - Then the original makes five -   =Five

1   2   3   4   5

Except for the chromatic scale, scales are actually arpeggios. In other words, they are notes selected from the twelve tone scale.

The very life line of music is chromatics, for without it you can't have complete selectivity.

"THE MIGHTY TRIADS"

THE THREE BASIC TRIADS, FIRST, SECOND, AND ROOT POSITION IN DIATONIC SCALE FORM, MAJOR AND MINORS THROUGH THE CYCLE OF FIFTHS—12 KEYS, FULL RANGE——

TRIAD ARPEGGIOS—MAJOR AND MINOR—12 KEYS, FULL RANGE——

CONTRARY MOTION—EXPLANATION OF THE TRIAD NAMES—MIXED MINORS——

"THE MIGHTY TRIADS"

THE IMPORTANCE

OF THE CYCLE OF FIFTHS

Most of the studies in these books go through the keys employing the descending cycle of fifths (up a fourth or down a fifth) in preference to changing keys chromatically. The reason being that it provides more variety and change of fingering then just moving everything up or down a half tone at a time.

Another very important reason is that our whole system of harmonics is heavily based on gravitational/descending harmony in fifths. Therefore, it is very practical to study the cycle by working with it in practice.

A very basic example is, that by just moving from the dominant seventh to the major/minor chord is, in fact, employing two steps of the cycle of fifths—G seventh to C— C seventh to F, etc.

When changing keys one half tone at a time the fingering remains too much the same. In other words taking notational patterns through the cycle of fifths provides better physical exercise plus the fact that it requires much more agility and accuracy—good technique demands both.

The cycle of fifths also demands a higher degree of concentration because the intervals of the various keys must be kept in mind at all times which is very good mental exercise.

GENERAL REMARKS ABOUT THE MIGHTY TRIADS

The recognition, identification, relationships, and understanding of the various triads (major–minor–diminished–augmented, etc.) is very important to all of these studies and music in general.

One must try to evaluate the many possibilities they afford, for they are endless. Most of the studies in these books are based on, and relate to the "triad" in one form or another. Closed and open voicings in all stages of separation are interesting and informative.

More than one triad can occupy the same geographic area at the same time with a compounding effect, and result to form another chord for example, when the sixth step of the first inversion major scale and the third step are sounded together the result is a major sixth chord containing the natural seventh which is commonly called a major seventh with an added sixth, the symbols are: CMAJ.76— Also: C♮7——the compounding of two triads will of course produce six voices which is rarely possible to play if they're in the same general area. Fortunately, most of the time duplicated notes, eliminated, reduce the number of notes required for the desired result.

Careful deletion of notes of least importance to the structure also helps in reducing the size of chords. The upper and lower notes of first inversion triads are major and minor sixth intervals apart. The sixth makes a very powerful two note chord and because of this power, the middle notes can be deleted without spoiling the chordal result. (in many instances, therefore, reducing the number of notes from six to four to achieve the effect of compounding two triads). Naturally, the middle note should not be eliminated when involved with a moving line, and of course this applies to the upper and lower voices also.

(Examples on next page.)

"THE MIGHTY TRIADS"

EXAMPLES

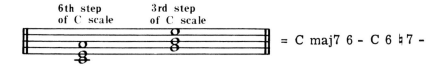

= C maj7 6 - C 6 ♮7 -

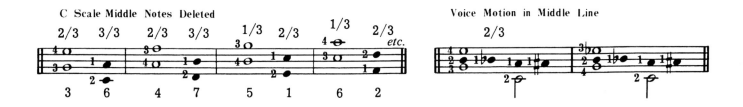

Many of the larger chords can be reduced for they almost always contain doubles, for example the grande F Major chord - There are but three notes in this chord, the other three are doubles:

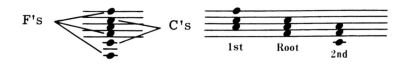

When the doubles are deleted three notes remain - and they make the basic triad - (the notes=F-C-A)

Selectivity is of utmost importance in compounding triads or any chords.

THE MIGHTY "TRIAD"

A very useful tool in harmonic voicing (for all instruments) is: the "hint/suggestion" of a tone. A note can be inferred but not actually sounded, yet its presence is felt to the point where it's almost heard. Example:

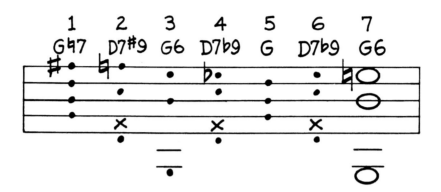

There is no F♯ in 2-4-6- but the inference is there. It is only a hint—but that is enough. In other words, it has been suggested to the ear. X's denote inferred F♯ when the whole passage is played.

"Overtones" also play a very important part in harmonic voicing. Every note contains and excites its primary overtones, which are the fifth—third—and unison to a greater or lesser degree, depending on the register of the tone. The lower notes produce more overtones in the human audio range. They are present in the higher notes but harder to hear and many times are above the human audio range.

When two strings are the same pitch either one can excite the other thus starting it to vibrate in sympathy—it's known as "sympathetic vibration." This happens even when they are many octaves apart. Sympathetic vibration also excites the third and the fifth overtones causing them to ring—here is the proof:

When a first inversion major triad is depressed (but not sounded) all three overtones can be heard clearly by striking the tonic bass note, but not holding it. The overtones will be rearranged forming a second inversion triad—For Example:: If the first inversion triad reads: F– C– A– from the top down and an F bass is struck the result is: A– F– C–. If the bass note didn't contain the third and fifth overtones they could not be excited by sympathetic vibration. In other words, the bass note, because it contains all the notes of the triad, causes the overtones to ring through sympathetic vibration therefore unquestionably proving the claim to be factual.

"THE MIGHTY TRIADS"

In essence, every note contains a trio of strong overtones that can be utilized to good advantage - There are many more than three overtones, But the perfect fifth, the Major third, the tonic unison are the Strongest -- The most easily excited by sympathetic vibration.

Another effective method to Experiment with in the illusionary art of compounding triads or any chords that contain more notes than can be sounded Simultaneously is by a delayed type of coupling - To achieve this effect the chords must be struck fairly close together timewise-

The ear will remember the first notes sounded and automatically couple them to the next notes thus forming an overall harmonic picture.
here are a few very basic Examples of the ears ability to remember tones and sounds- (residual sound) -

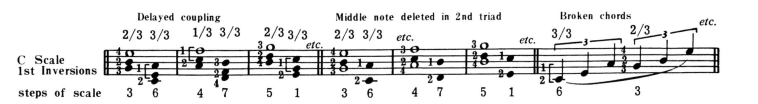

An Arpeggio is a broken Chord -

A Chord is a frozen Arpeggio -

Melodic intervals equal Harmony -

Harmonic intervals equal Chords -

MIGHTY TRIADS
RECAPITULATION

"Inference" is the art of hinting and suggesting that notes not sounded in harmonic structures are present in a mental audio sense. The notes surrounding the inferred notes must be selected very carefully in order to create the effect of boxing these notes in, thereby, identifying them in a subtle way.

"Overtones" are harmonics set in motion by sympathetic vibration. The uses are many and quite obvious—for example: A low "G" and a "B" natural placed one octave and a third above will excite the fifth overtone, thus producing a "D" in the middle, resulting in an open triad, from just two notes. There are many many more examples . . . too many to list.

"Delayed coupling" demands a fair amount of agility because it relies on and utilizes the residual capability and memory of the ear to join smaller harmonic structures together in order to create the effect of larger harmonic situations.

The mind dictates the depth of improvisational involvement and gears it to the available knowledge and technique. If we enjoyed the availability of notes that a three manual organ provides, the guitarist's problem would lessen, but, we have to cope with the fact that we possess but one handful of fingers that can't stray very far away from each other, that must cover a vast fingerboard that at times seems to extend far beyond its actual dimensions. Therefore, the aforementioned principles and techniques are useful and necessary.

GENERAL REMARKS

Notice that the major triads make minor sevenths—
Minor triads make major sevenths—
Three note diminished triads make dominant sevenths—
Three note dominant seventh triads make diminished chords—
Diminished chords make dominant seventh flat nine chords—
The major sixth interval is present in the outside notes of any first inversion minor triad—
The minor sixth interval is present in the outside notes of any first inversion major triad—

THE TRIAD NAMES

In these books the term "triad " is applied to any three note chord voicing whether it be closed or open voicing

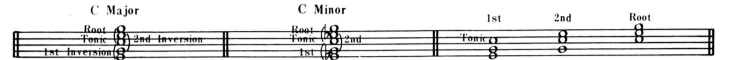

It takes one of the three minor triads to make a major seventh - the C bass note makes them all C major 7ths-all three inversions are the first steps of the E minor scale-they are also the third steps of the C major scale

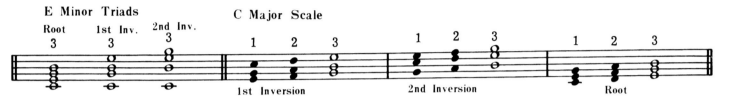

It takes one of the three major triads to make a minor seventh chord - the a bass makes them all "a" minor sevenths - all three inversions are the first steps of the C major scale

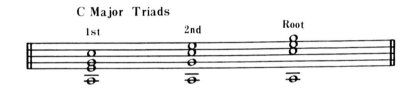

In other words the major triad contains the minor, and the minor contains the major = both are bichordal

THE TRIAD NAMES

In the 1st inversion the tonic is on top, in other words it is first from the top down - in the 2nd inversion the tonic is second - in the root voicing the tonic is the lowest note - "the root" - hence the terms 1st - 2nd root.

The above thought line applied to the augmented triads—all major triads become aug. when the 5th is raised

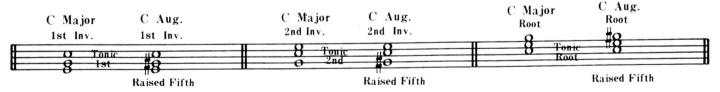

All 3 minor triads become augmented chords when the tonic is lowered a semitone

The same thought line applied to the diminished triads—all major triads become dim. when the 3rd & 5th are lowered

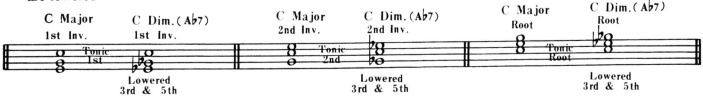

The major and minor triads are very closely related to the dominant seventh chords - all of the closed voicing 4 note dominant 7th chords contain a major triad as the examples below show

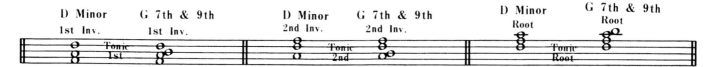

The examples below show the basic close relationship of the minor triads to the dominant seventh chord - all triads are basically bichordal - multichordal

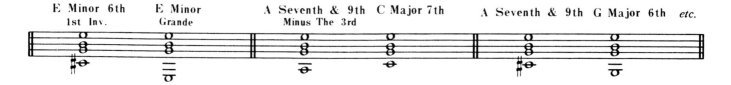

Example of a triad being multichordal: for this example the 3rd step of the C major 1st inversion scale is used

The voices in the examples below are all describing the same scale-they just start on different intervals

C scale in second inversion triads - they are all 2nd inversions-upper voice is 3rd to 3rd-middle voice is tonic to tonic - lower voice is 5th to 5th

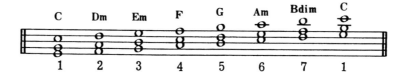

C scale in first inversion triads - they are all 1st inversions - upper voice is tonic to tonic-middle voice is 5th to 5th - lower voice is 3rd to 3rd

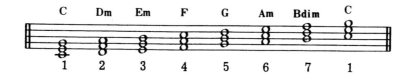

C scale in root position triads - they are all root triads - upper voice is **5th to 5th** - middle voice is **3rd to 3rd**-lower voice is tonic to tonic

FIRST INVERSION TRIADS MAJOR, MINOR, DIMINISHED, TAKEN THRU THE DESCENDING CYCLE OF FIFTHS KEY BY KEY—FULL RANGE

When studying the triad scales taken through the cycle of fifths, note that many of the triads appear in other keys, for instance: the C major scale contains four triads that appear in the first key above C which is the Key of G (one sharp)—they are steps 1-3-5-6-

The second key above C is the Key of D (two sharps) which contains two triads belonging to the central key scale of C— They are steps 3 and 5—This duplication of triads happens in the flat keys also, For Example: the first flat key in the cycle below the Key of C is the Key of F (one flat) which contains four triads found in the C scale—they are steps 1-2-4-6.

The second key below C is B flat (two flats) which (like the D scale) contains two triads found in the central key scale— they are steps 2 and 4.

The reason for pointing out these duplications is that all of the keys are surrounded by these satellite keys—two above and two below—that always contain exact duplicates and always on the same steps as is indicated here—(see graphic example.)

The significance is that this relationship of keys does not change. It can be relied upon to always be there—always in the same place.

FIRST INVERSION TRIADS THRU THE CYCLE OF FIFTHS

If E flat were the central key two triads would appear in the Key of F—which is two keys above E flat; four in the Key of B flat—which is one key above E flat; four in the Key of A flat—which is one key below E flat; and two appear in D flat—which is two keys below E flat.

Become aware of these relationships for they never change, and keep in mind the fact that these satellite keys also have their own satellite keys that automatically includes their own triad relationships, etc.

Graphic example of triad duplication in the keys surrounding any and all keys --

Numbers above the staff represent steps of the signature keys

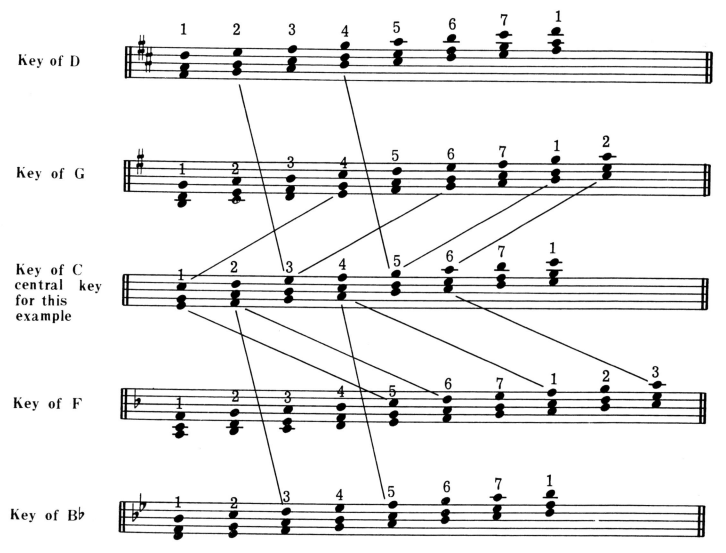

25

"THE MIGHTY TRIADS"

FIRST INVERSIONS
SECOND INVERSIONS
ROOT POSITION
SCALES IN:

MAJOR / HARMONIC MINOR / MELODIC MINOR

Some of the fingerings are intentionally awkward in these and other studies throughout these books. They are good practice for agility and finger discipline/manipulation. There are smoother more ligical fingerings also shown that quite naturally should be used for more flowing continuity.

Each key has been given a slightly different fingering pattern/mixture of fingerings. Certain sections of each key scale may contain flowing fingering while other parts of the same key scale may show awkward gymnastic fingering. In other words, each of the three inversions in each key have been marked with a mixture of varied fingerings thereby offering a wide variety of fingerings from which to choose.

When improvising/composing, performing, there is no absolute way to do things. There is no such thing as: "That's the way it must be done" or "It's the only way." Sometimes a very awkward, hard, fingering will be selected because it has the particular sound that is desired.

Certain fingering combinations allow the hand to travel down the neck (towards the nut) while going up the scale (ascending). This type of articulation has many uses, one being that when playing something in the upper register the next phrase may be down near the nut by choosing one of these fingerings, the connecting phrase will allow the hand to move in the required direction, thereby resulting in a smoother overall effect—in other words: setting up an easier shot.

It is not possible to use completely alternate fingering when working with three voices because usually three fourths of the fingers must repeat - but a solid, positive sound can be achieved by alternating between any two fingers when three voices are in motion - here are a few examples:

No Alternation

Fingers 2 & 4 Alternate

Fingers 3 & 4 Alternate

Fingers 3 & 4 Alternate

To fully appreciate the difference between the above examples, repeat each one a dozen or more times - Notice how much more accurate the alternate fingerings are --- Complete alternation would be possible if we had two more fingers -- We could then sound one triad with fingers 1-2-3 And the next with 4-5-6-- But we lack five and six --- We alternate between two legs when running because it's faster and more accurate than hopping on one leg --- The principles are the same. There are many more examples - such as:

Fingers 1 & 2 Alternate

Fingers 1 & 4 Alternate

"THE MIGHTY TRIADS"

Normally, when successive chords and harmonic situations employ the same fingering, only the first will be marked, and that marking remains good until another fingering appears. However, this does not apply to these scale studies because many of them are shown ascending only and therefore must be read in reverse in order to descend. Marking all of them greatly simplifies this process.

STRING CHART
EXPLANATION OF THE STRING SET SYMBOLS:

A vertical or angled line thus— / —means "Set"—
The number in front of it is the set number—
The number after it indicates the number of strings employed—

EXAMPLE:
When the 1st-2nd-3rd-strings are employed the symbol is:
1/3—The first set of three—etc.
When the 1st-2nd-3rd-4th-strings are employed the symbol is:
1/4—The 1st set of four—etc.

THE BROKEN AND THE DIVIDED SETS:
Example:
When the 1st-2nd-4th-strings are employed (skipping the 3rd string) it is termed a broken set —the symbol is:
1/B3—The first set of broken three—etc.
When the order is reversed, (skipping the 2nd instead of the 3rd string) the word "broken" is used first, thus:
B1/3—The broken first set of three—etc.

When the 1st-2nd-4th-5th-strings are employed it is termed a divided set—the symbol is:
D1/4—The divided first set of four—etc.
When the 1st-3rd-5th-strings are employed the symbol is:
1/D3—The first set of divided three—and so on—
When the 1st-4th-strings are employed the symbol is:
A 1—
When the 2nd-5th-strings are employed the symbol is:
A 2—etc.
When the 1st-5th-strings are employed the symbol is:
B 1—etc.

NOTE
A symbol for the 1st-3rd-4th-6th-strings is not necessary because it would encompass all of the strings, therefore, the very notation dictates where and on what strings the notes are located.

STRING SET CHART

SYMBOLS:—STRINGS EMPLOYED—

1/2	1st-2nd-
2/2	2nd-3rd-
3/2	3rd-4th-
4/2	4th-5th-
5/2	5th-6th-
1/3	1st-2nd-3rd-
2/3	2nd-3rd-4th-
3/3	3rd-4th-5th-
4/3	4th-5th-6th-
1/4	1st-2nd-3rd-4th-
2/4	2nd-3rd-4th-5th-
3/4	3rd-4th-5th-6th-
1/5	1st-2nd-3rd-4th-5th-
2/5	2nd-3rd-4th-5th-6th-

THE BROKEN AND DIVIDED SETS:

1/B2	1st-3rd-
2/B2	2nd-4th-
3/B2	3rd-5th-
4/B2	4th-6th-
1/B3	1st-2nd-4th-
2/B3	2nd-3rd-5th-
3/B3	3rd-4th-6th-
B1/3	1st-3rd-4th-
B2/3	2nd-4th-5th-
B3/3	3rd-5th-6th-
1/B4	1st-2nd-3rd-5th-
2/B4	2nd-3rd-4th-6th-
B1/4	1st-3rd-4th-5th-
B2/4	2nd-4th-5th-6th-
1D/3	1st-2nd-5th-
2D/3	2nd-3rd-6th-
1/D3	1st-3rd-5th-
2/D3	2nd-4th-6th-
D1/3	1st-4th-5th-
D2/3	2nd-5th-6th-
D1/4	1st-2nd-4th-5th-
D2/4	2nd-3rd-5th-6th-
A1	1st-4th-
A2	2nd-5th-
A3	3rd-6th-
B1	1st-5th-
B2	2nd-6th-
01	1st-6th-

28

Scale in first inversion triads taken thru the descending cycle of fifths - 12 keys - full range - triads named for one octave - then they repeat-Upper voice is the tonic of each triad-Numbers above notation denote steps of scale

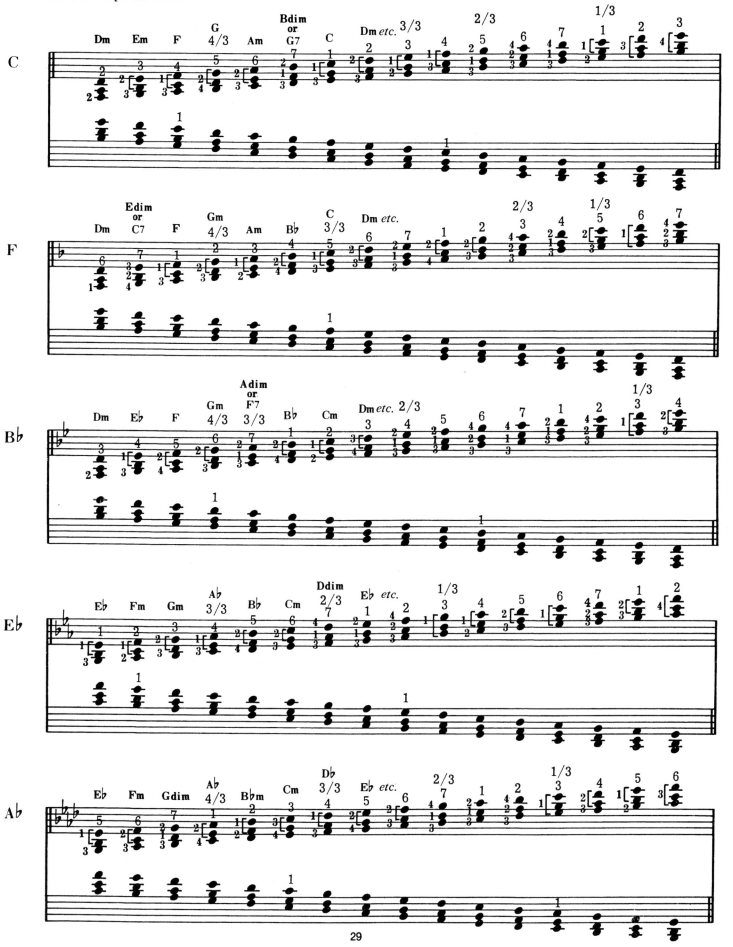

Scale in first inversion triads - Cycle of fifths -

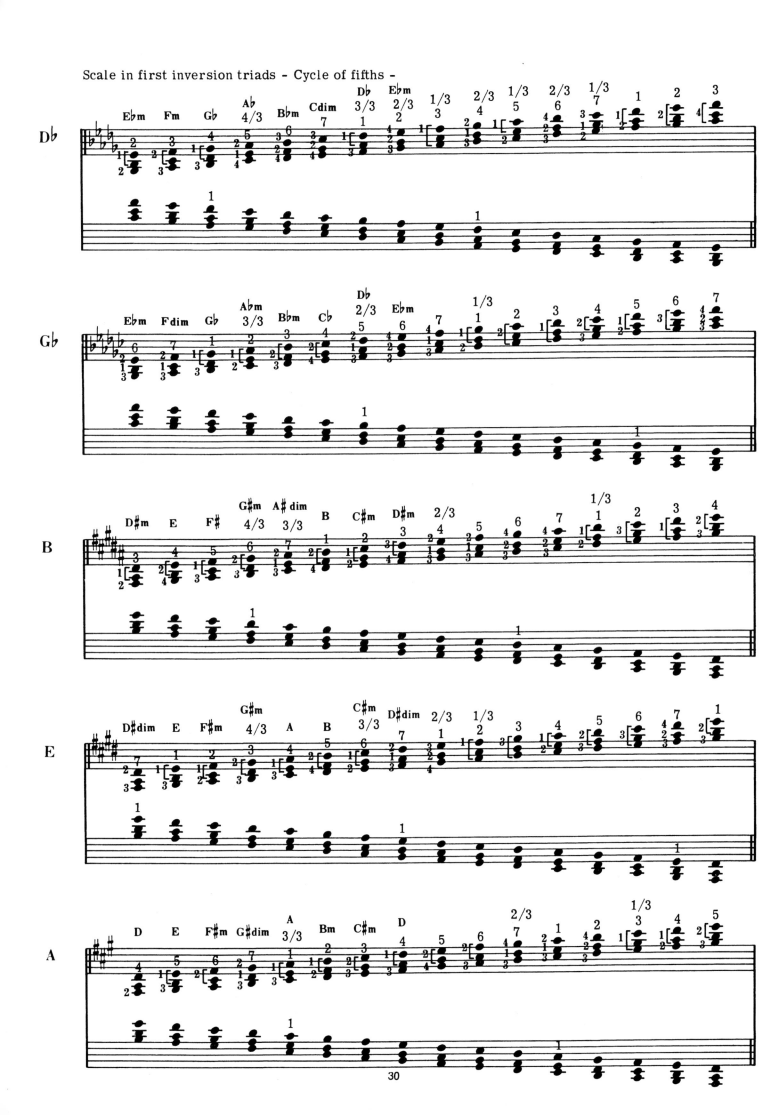

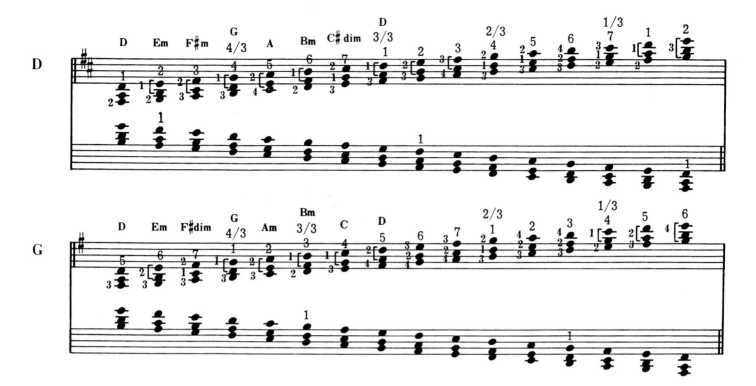

These Examples explain the reason for using 3 fingers on triads (open or closed voicing) that can be played with 1 or 2 fingers - this type mechanism is a very necessary part of good harmonic technique - A moving voice can not go below barred sustained notes

The voice can move lower when the barre is not employed - as in bars = A-B-

The moving voice in bar "C" cant go below "G" because the 1st finger is barring it - in 'D" and 'E" the voices can continue down because of not using the small barre - (double stop)

HARMONIC MINOR
Scale in first inversion triads taken thru the descending cycle of fifths-12 keys - full range - only the ascension is shown; descend using same notation

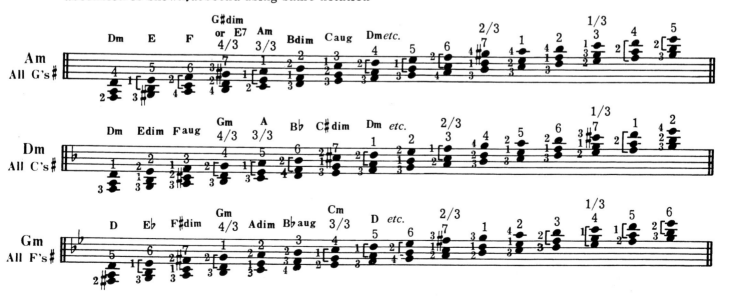

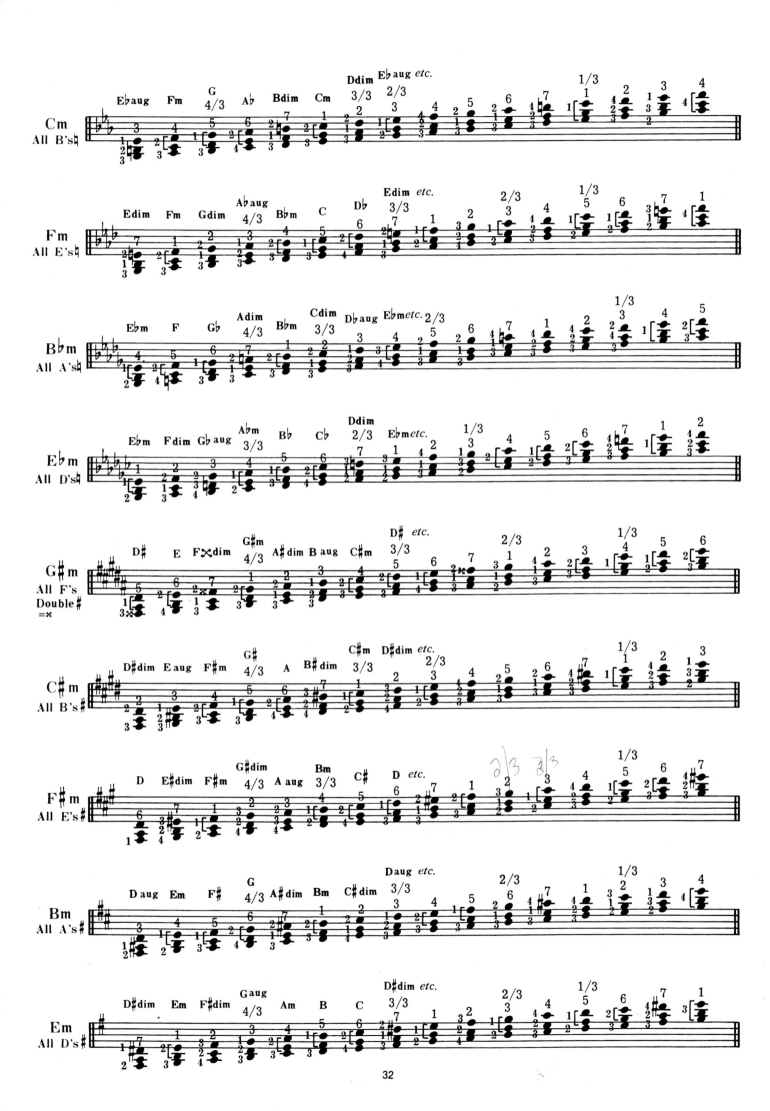

32

Scale in first inversion triads taken thru the descending cycle of fifths-12 keys-full range-descensions are in relative major keys-employ major scale fingering

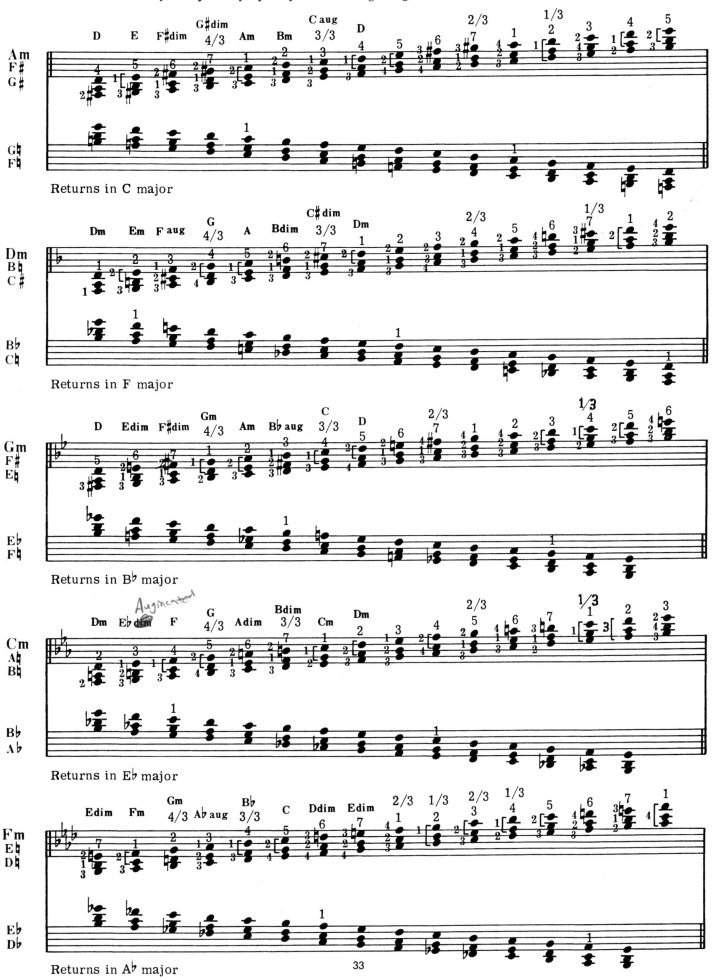

Returns in C major

Returns in F major

Returns in B♭ major

Returns in E♭ major

Returns in A♭ major

Scale in first inversion triads - cycle of fifths

MELODIC MINOR

Returns in Db major

Returns in Gb major

Returns in B major

Returns in E major

Returns in A major

Scale in first inversion triads - cycle of fifths

Returns in D major

Returns in G major

To descend in the relative major key merely cancel the accidentals but not the key signature

NOTE

Every 7th step is a diminished chord - they are also dominant 7ths of the keys

VARIATION

A very interesting "Mixed" minor scale is: ascend using the melodic notation - descend using the harmonic notation - example below

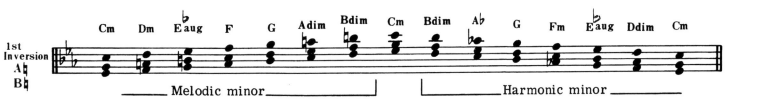

Also, ascend using harmonic notation - descend using ascending melodic minor notation - just reverse the above

The examples below show various plucking orders for all 3 note chords - employ each one separately full range - apply them to the 2nd inversion and root position triads also - apply to open voicings also 1st inversion - 1st station

35

Scale in Second Inversion Triads - Cycle of fifths key by key - 12 keys - full range-middle voice is tonic of each triad

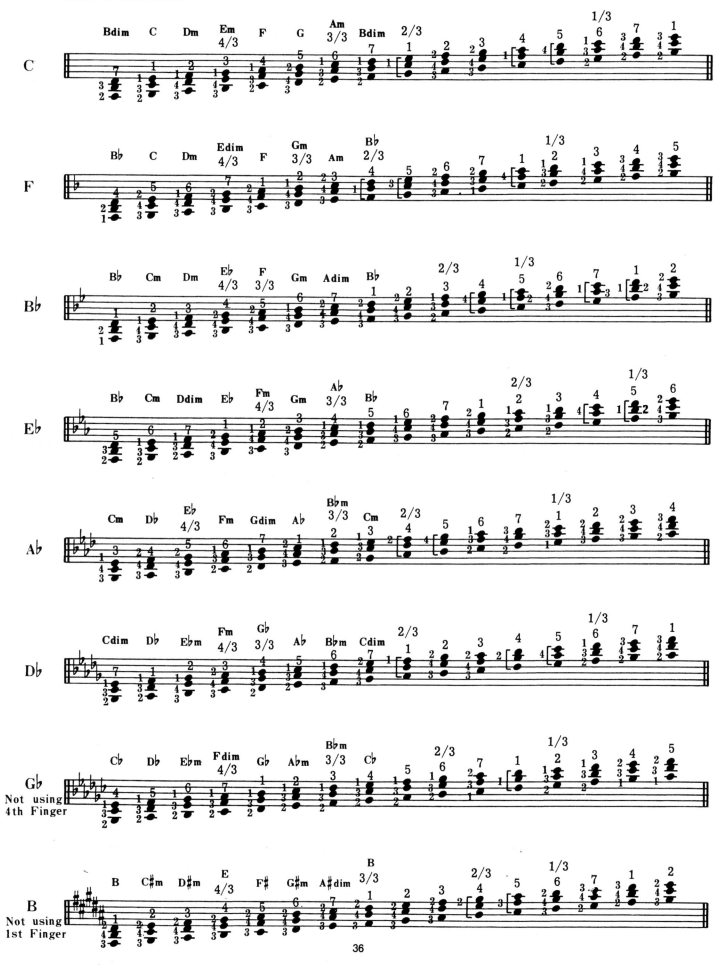

Scale in Second Inversion Triads

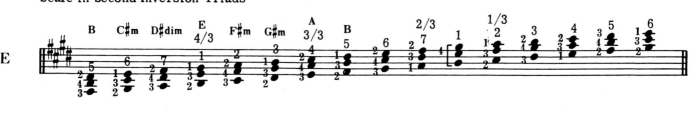

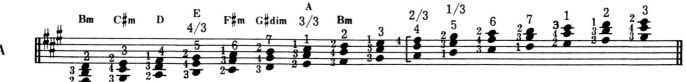

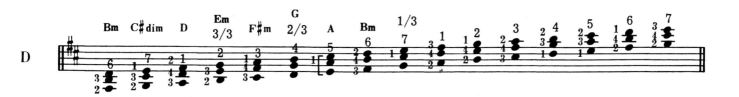

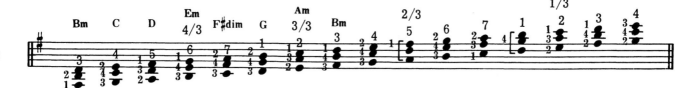

Scale in Second Inversion Triads - Cycle of fifths - 12 keys - full range-middle voice is tonic

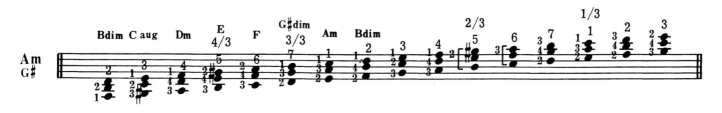

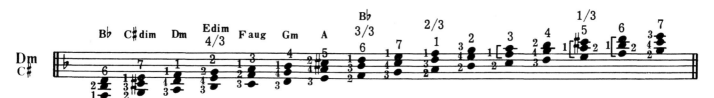

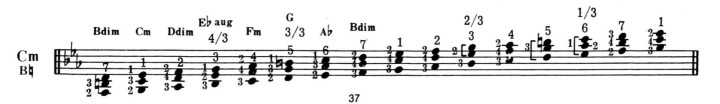

Scale in Second Inversion Triads

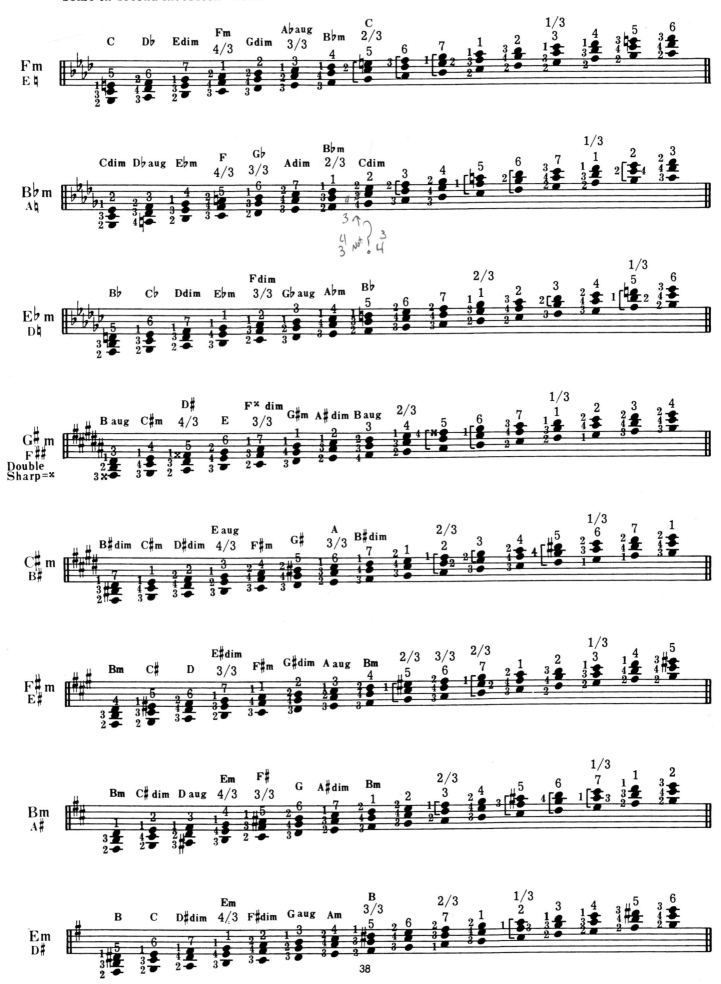

Scale in Second Inversion Triads - cycle of fifths - 12 keys - full range-middle voice is tonic-Descend in relative major keys

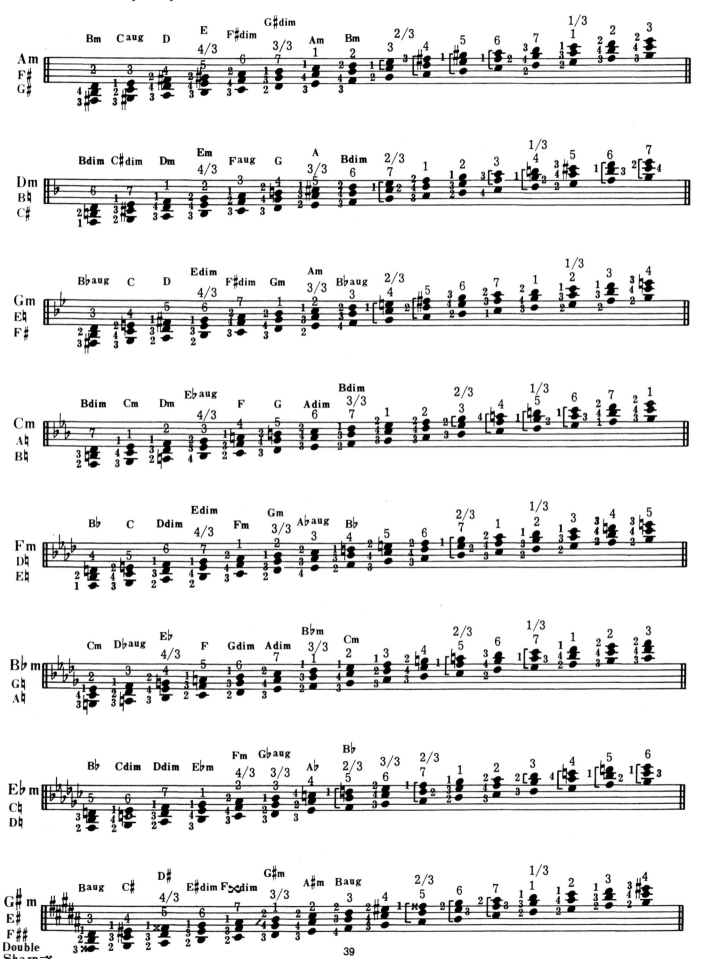

39

Scale in Second Inversion Triads -

4th finger is omitted - reverse by omitting the first finger - this is good practise-apply it to all of the scales - it is very necesarry for voice motion, as in the super & sub series

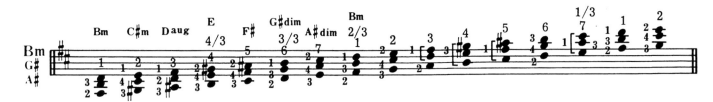

First finger is omitted

Scale in Root triads - cycle of fifths - 12 keys - full range-lower voice is the tonic

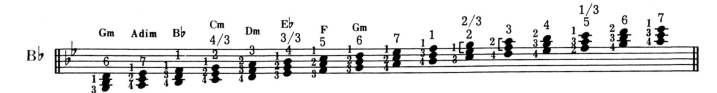

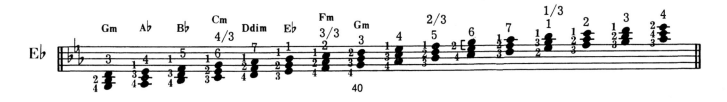

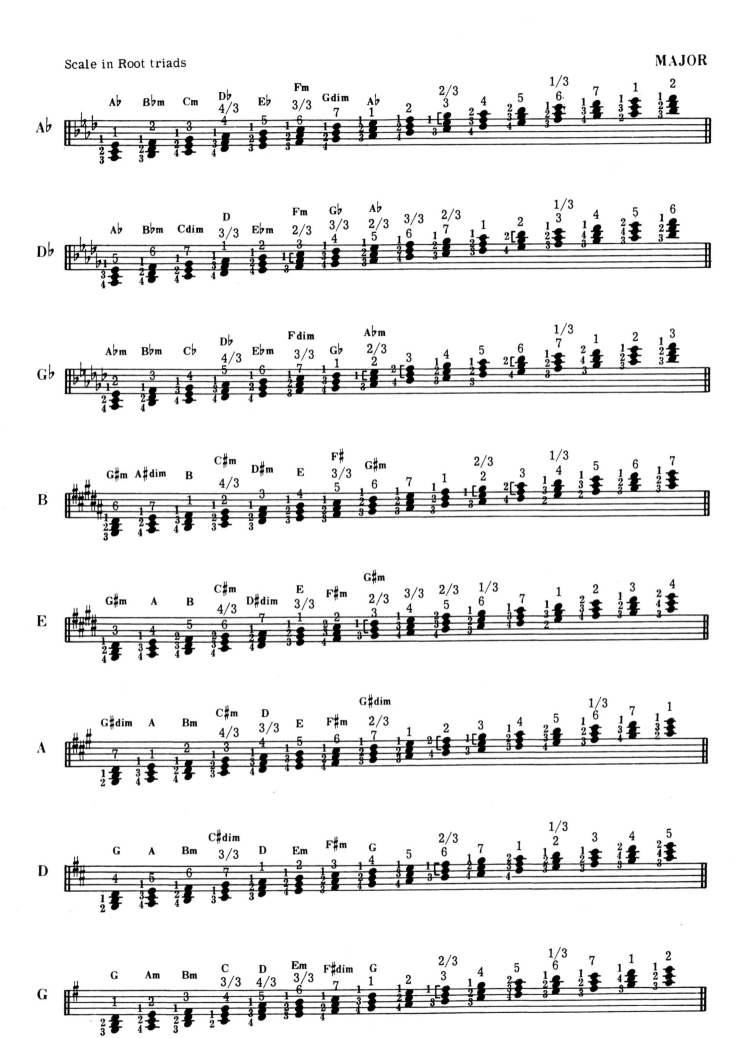

Scale in Root triads

MAJOR

Scale in Root triads - cycle of fifths - 12 keys - full range lower voice is the tonic

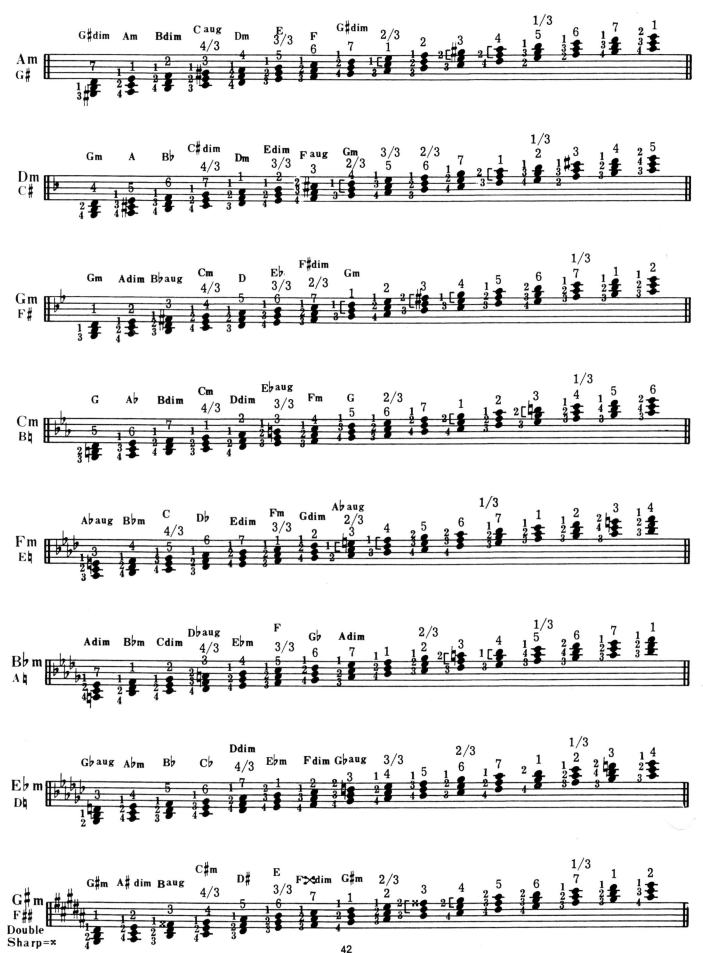

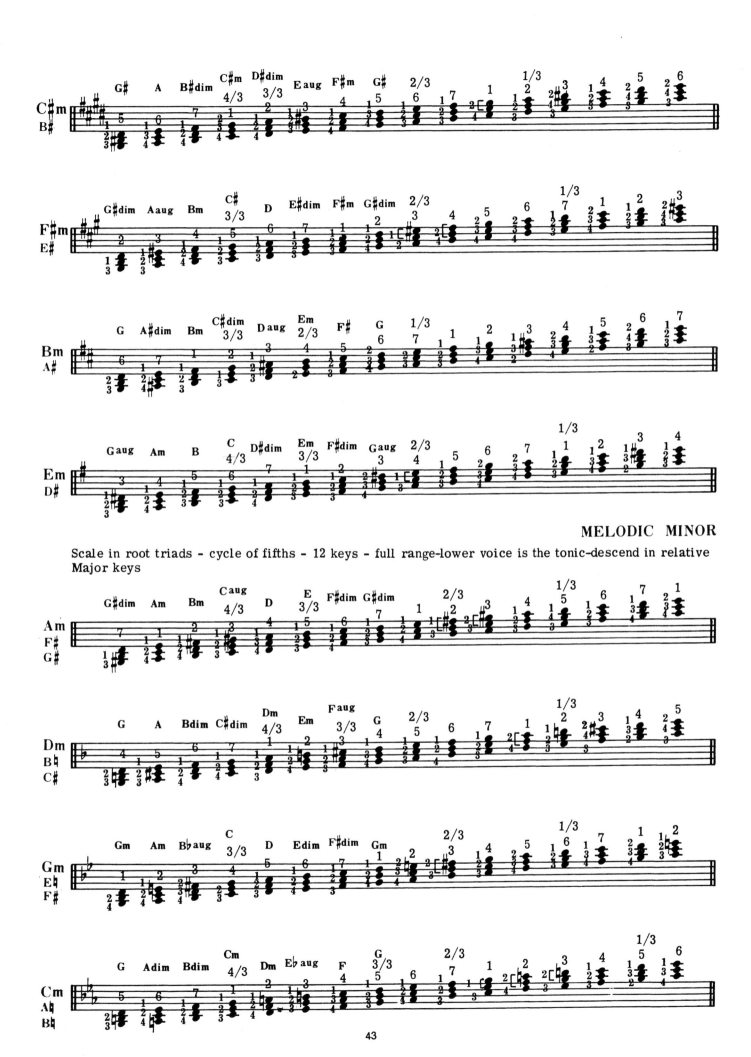

MELODIC MINOR

Scale in root triads - cycle of fifths - 12 keys - full range-lower voice is the tonic–descend in relative Major keys

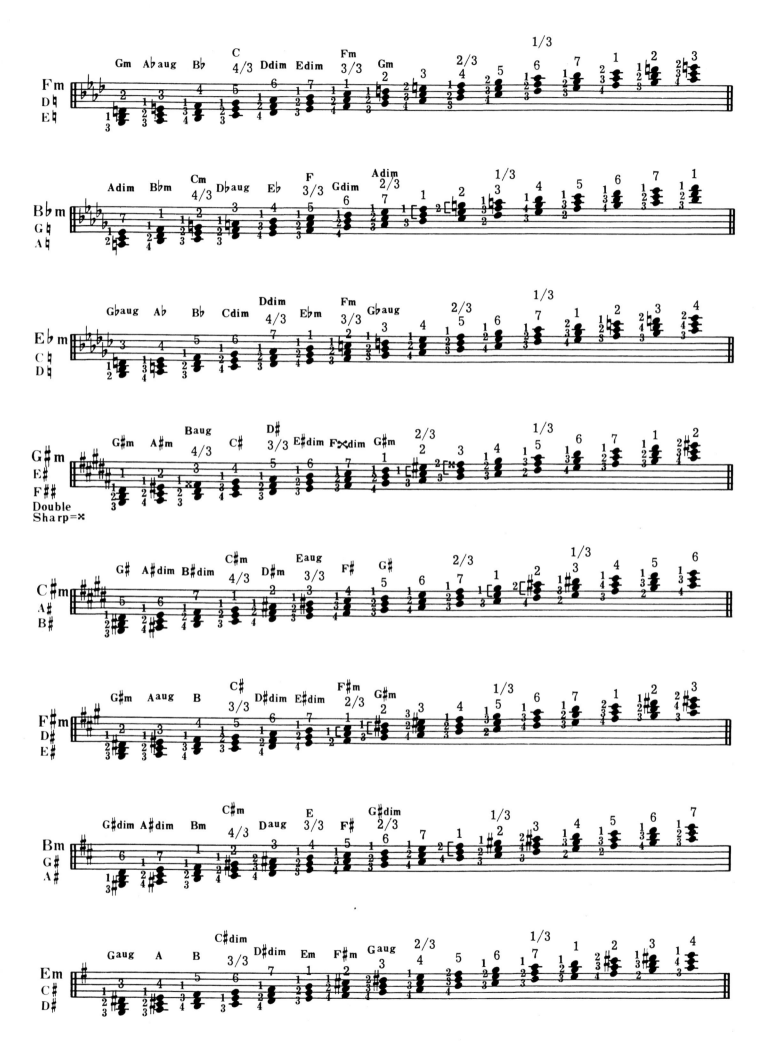

Scale in open 1st inversion triads - upper interval = 4ths - lower = 10ths-overall = 13ths-3rd down one octave -- 12 keys - full range

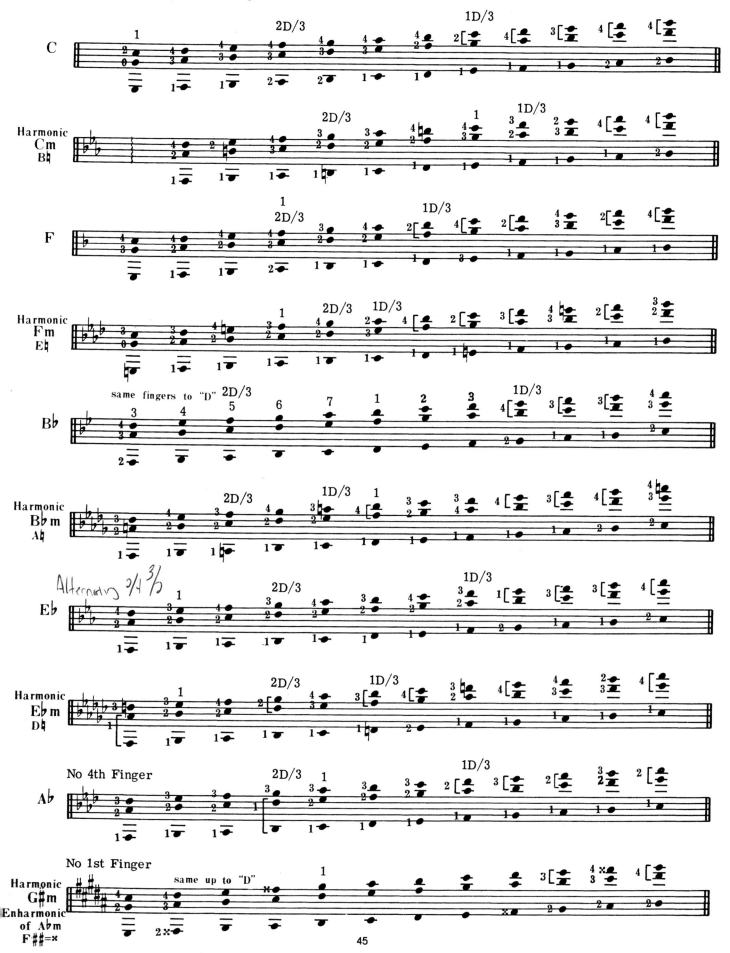

45

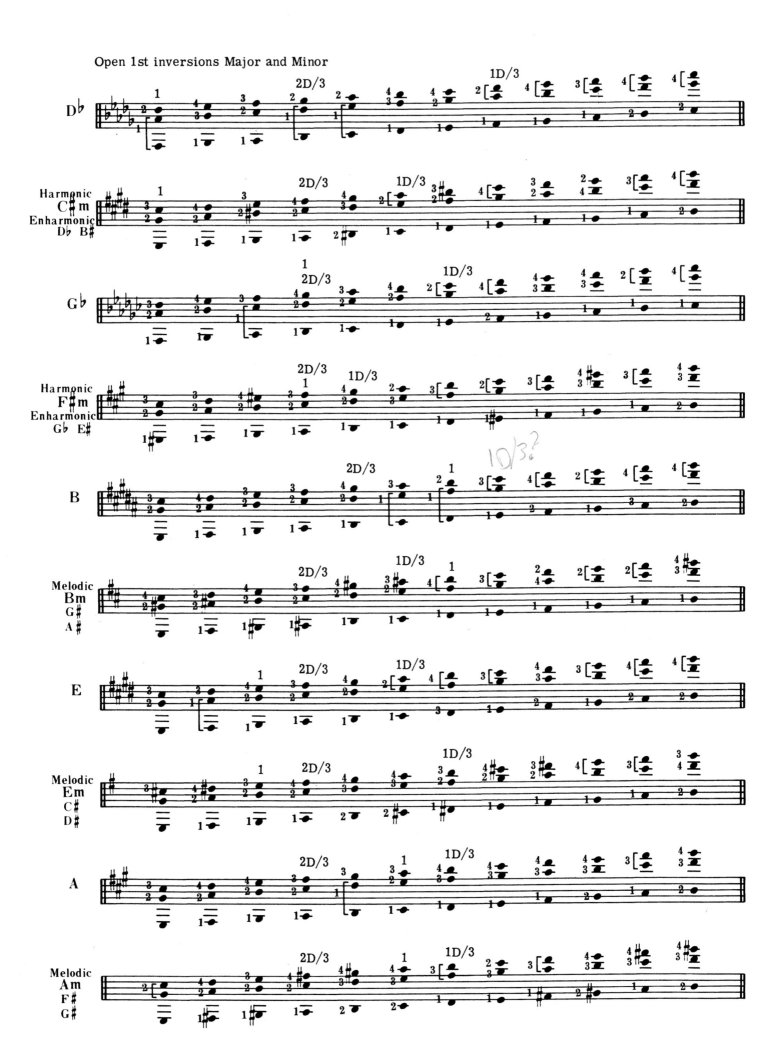

Open 1st inversions Major and Minor

Scale in open 1st inversion triads - Major and Minor - *Continued*

The examples below show a little bit of the vast potential of the past studies - they also explain the reasons for some of the different fingerings employed - each fingering has a purpose

G Scales were chosen only because of being last - place in all keys

Scale in open 2nd inversion triads - upper interval = 6ths - lower = 5ths - overall = 10ths

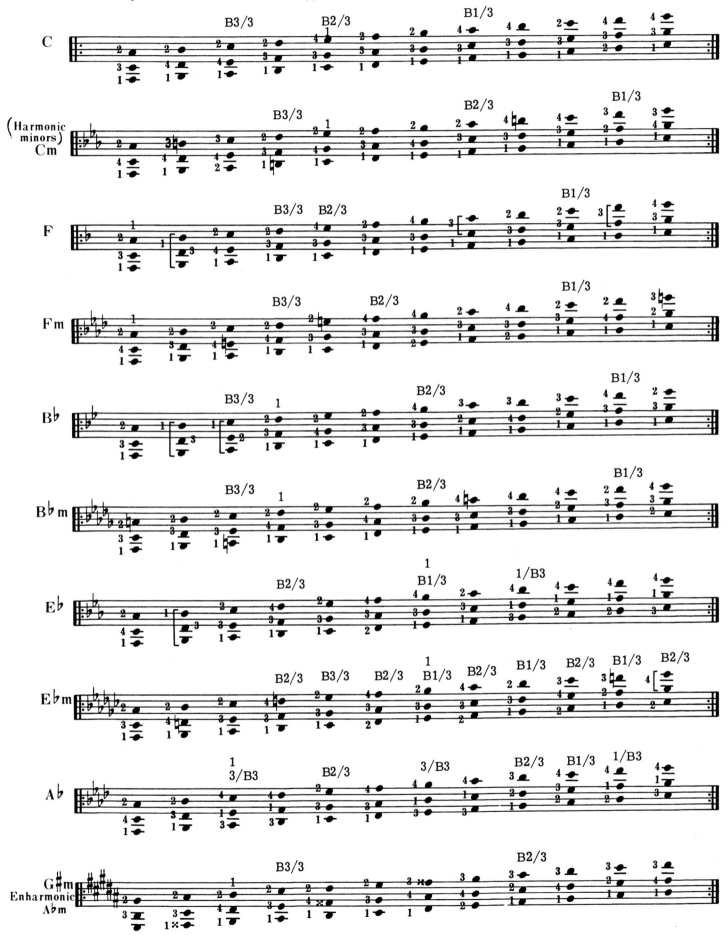

Scale in open 2nd inversion triads

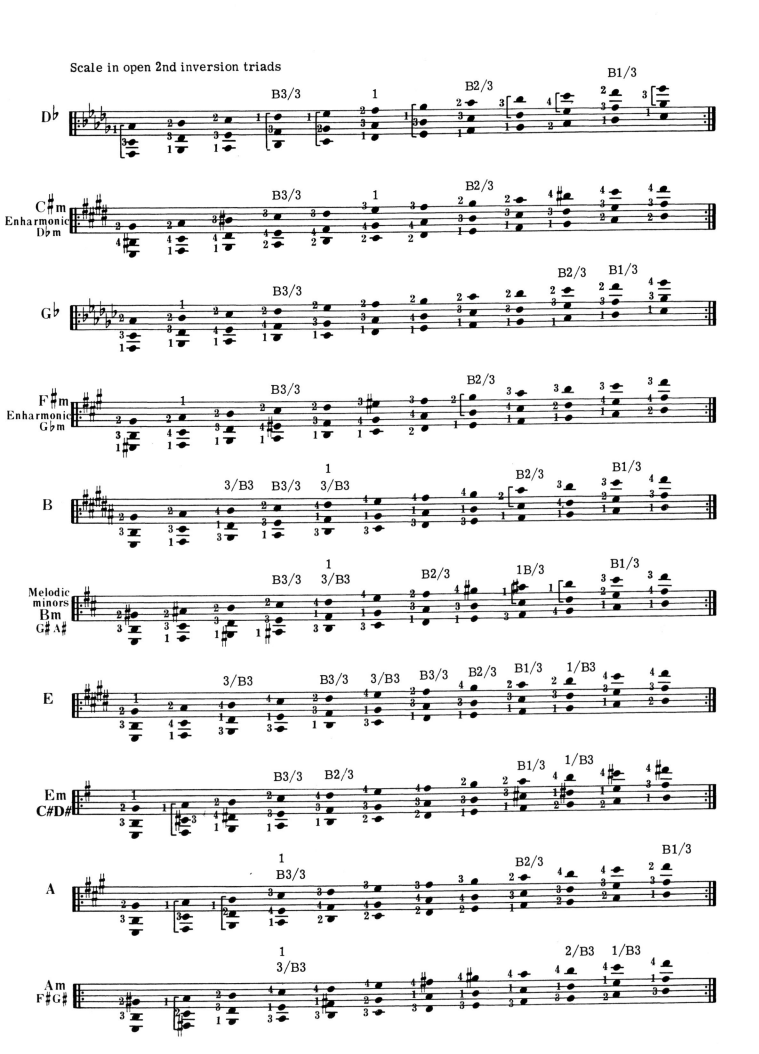

49

Scale in open 2nd inversion triads

D

Dm
B♮C♯

G

Gm
E♭F♯

> There are many other fingerings for the variation examples below - however, the string sets shown are in keeping with the above work–this notation can also be played on sets: 1/B3 - 2/B3-except for the 1st bar, as shown in second example - place in all keys

Example 1
Harmonic
Cm

Example 2
Cm

Scale in open root triads - tonic down one octave - 12 keys - full range
upper interval = 3rds - lower = 10ths - overall = 12ths

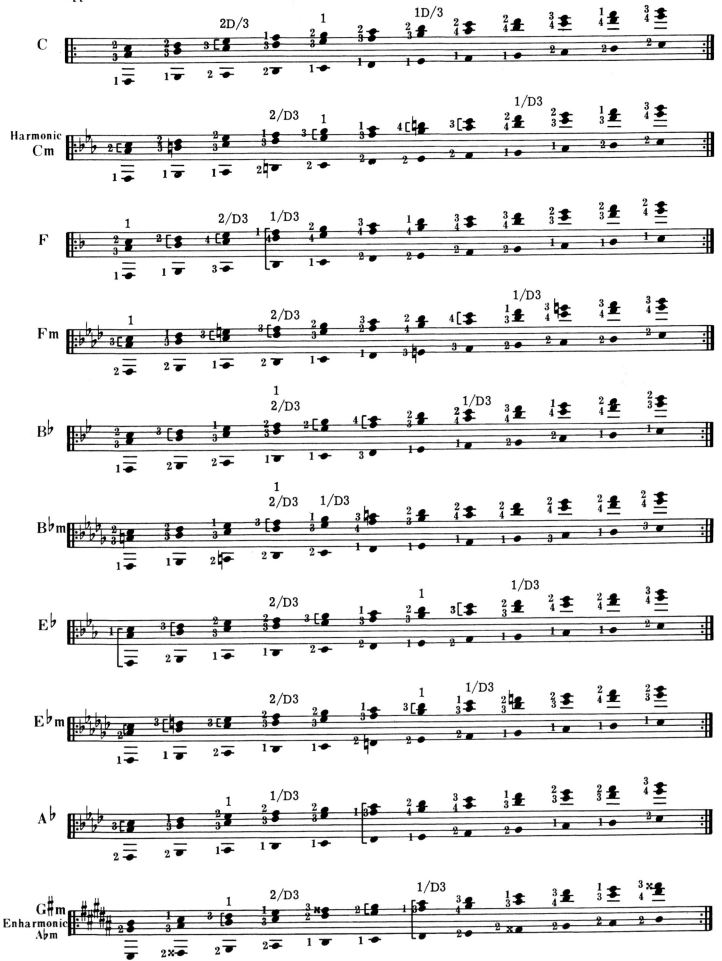

51

Scale in open root triads

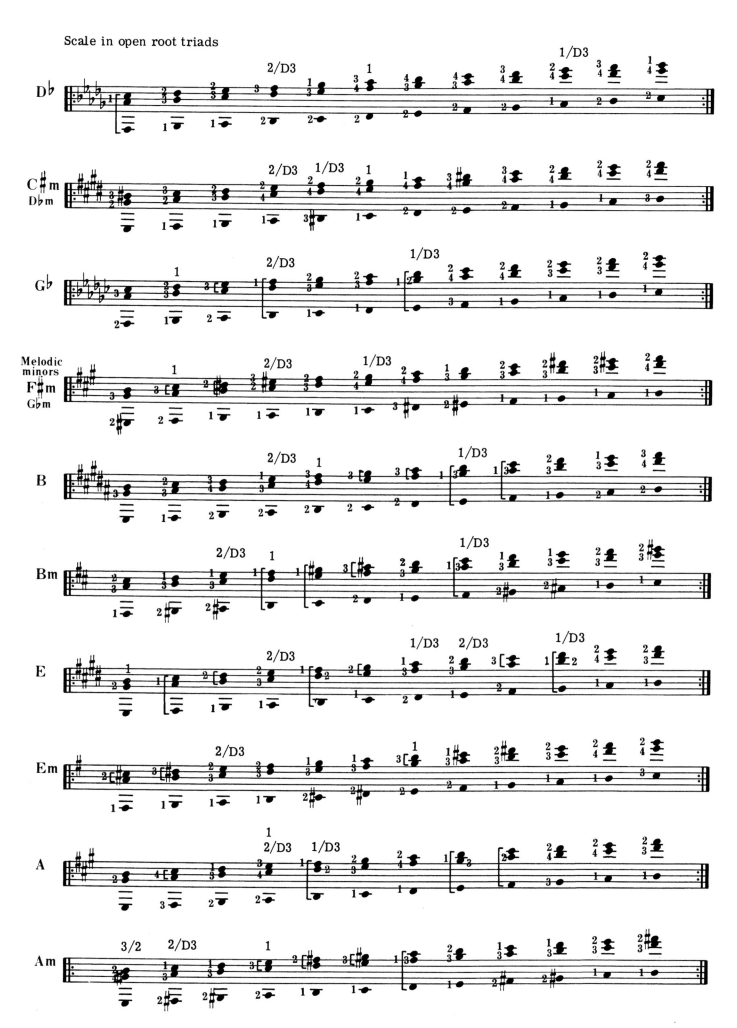

Scale in Open Root Triads

finger must be curved (arched) slightly so that the
tip of 1st finger sounds C♯ - 3rd joint sounds the G

This principle of sounding 2 notes on 2 frets with 1 finger will be
used in other studies

I refer to it as the 5th finger principle

MELODIC

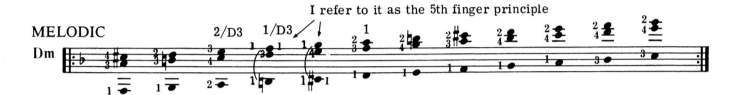

MELODIC

Place all variation examples in all keys - Major & Minor

These duplicates employ an added string - experiment with all types of fingering

Open root triad examples with upper voice motion in 1-3-2-4-3-5 etc. pattern - place in all
keys - employ other fingerings - change sets in other places etc. extend full range

Cm

Cm

Open root triad examples with middle and lower voice motion - apply the 1-3-2-4- etc.
Pattern-employ other fingerings - place in all keys

Cm

MAJOR

Triad arpeggios taken thru the cycle of fifths - 12 keys - full range-the lowest 3 inversions
are named, then they repeat - run each key up and down

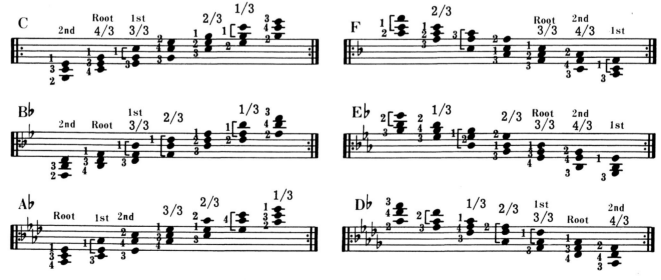

C   F

Bb   Eb

Ab   Db

Example "A" below is a fingering for crossing the fingerboard to continue on up-"B" is for continuing on down the finger board - become aware of these subtle differences

Variations - play in all keys - apply to all forms

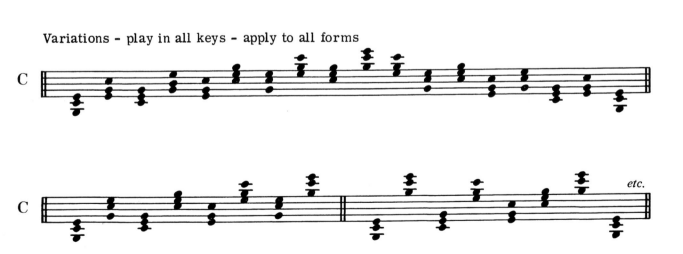

Triad Arpeggios - Cycle of fifths - 12 keys - full range

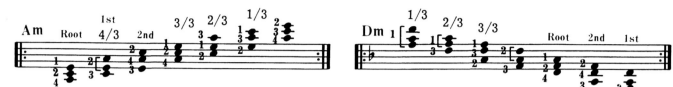

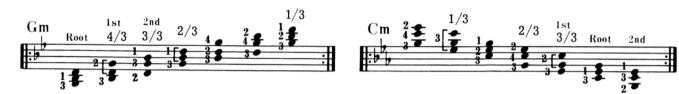

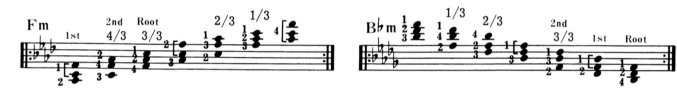

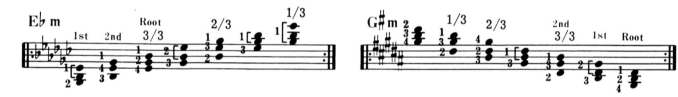

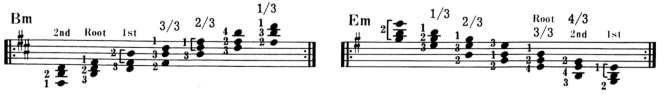

Apply the Major Variations - mix the fingering etc.

Triads - Contrary Motion = Crossing Lines in Triads - Scale of C -
1st Inversions—solid and hollow notes have same value—the purpose of the mixture is to keep the two triad lines separate—Employing a different set of strings for each triad is necessary for separation—the ability to divide the mind and concentrate on many things is very important—actually there are six voices involved in these studies—follow them—

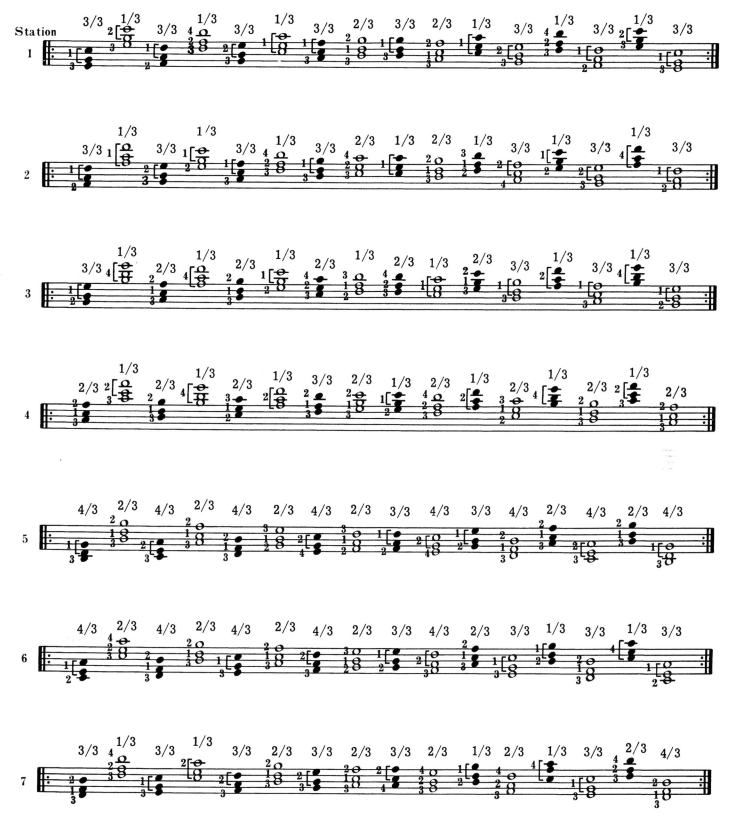

Apply this pattern to all inversions both major and minor - change the sets of strings.
Experiment - but each triad should be on a different set - alternating between two sets is ideal, but the fingerboard is not long enough to complete a whole scale - therefore a register change

Continued Next Page

must also be made (note - 5th-6th-7th stations down one octave - studies such as these help to develop agility, accuracy, mental discipline, triad relationships etc.

Select other key combinations - any keys - the examples below employ the keys of C and D-C and E♭

Select any two keys - three keys - four keys etc - Mix Major and Minors - 2nd inversions - roots etc. The harmonic results are secondary in this type of study but yet the information is valuable -gymnastic work is not always pleasing to the ear - but very necesarry

Triads - 1st Inversion - 2nd Inversion - Root position - upper voice describes diatonic scale-lower voices = the basic arpeggio of the key

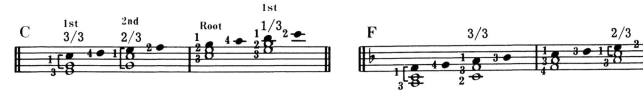

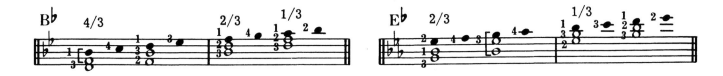

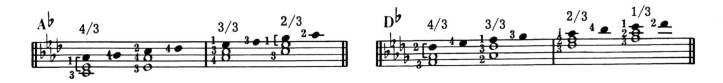

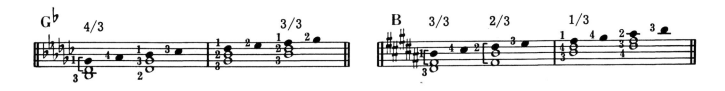

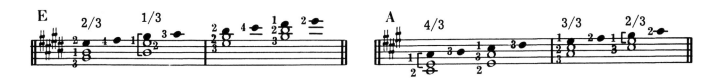

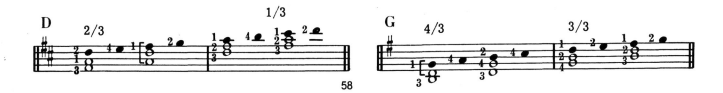

Triads - 1st Inversion - 2nd Inversion - Root position - middle voice up - lower voice down **MAJOR**

Triads - 1st - 2nd And Root - Melodic minor up, middle voice - harmonic minor down, lower voice - run each one separately in both directions-reverse them also=Harmonic middle voice-melodic lower voice etc.

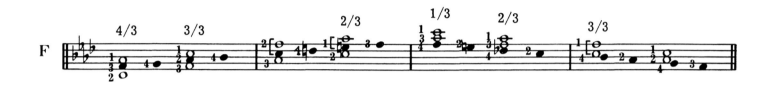

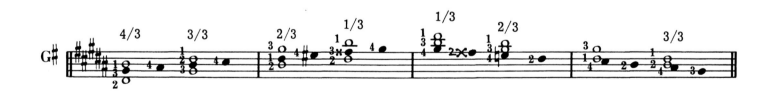

This is an **example** of changing registers because of range

These are substitute fingerings for the very long 2nd interval spread - however, try to play them as is

Extend all of these studies full range

Triads - 1st inversion - 2nd inversion - Root position - melodic up - harmonic down

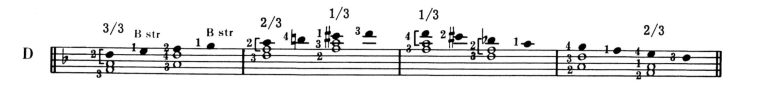

All the practical duplicates are shown below - look for them in middle and lower voice motion also

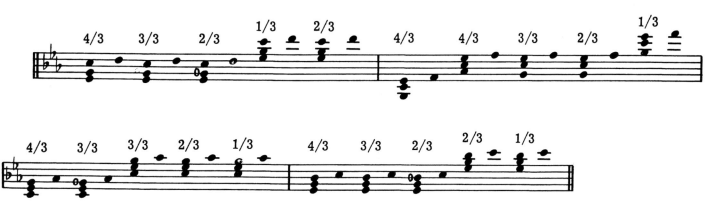

REDUCTIONS
6 TO 3—3 TO 6—MAJOR AND MINOR—

3rd Up to the 6th-
3rd Down to the 6th-
6th Up to the 3rd-
6th Down to the 3rd-

REDUCTIONS

SCALES WITHIN SCALES
THIRD TO SIXTH—SIXTH TO THIRD INTERVALS—

In the following studies visualize and memorize the varied mechanics and finger teams employed.

All harmonic mechanisms have distinctly recognizable form even though voices may be in motion.

Analyze these shapes; become familiar with the subtle differences between long angles—slight angles—parallels—squares etc.

Run the moving voice up and down repeatedly in each station (bar) while making sure to sustain the whole note.

The fingering, string sets, and crossovers are not always comfortable or logical—some are intentionally awkward and difficult for practice sake. Others are smooth and flowing—the instrumentalist must work with both types.

Practice all of these studies very slowly at first to avoid building up bad habits—mistakes are habit forming.

In many instances the third and fourth fingers are the main stays of the structures. With practice, a good long relaxed reach will result, but don't overdo at first.

STRING CHART
EXPLANATION OF THE STRING SET SYMBOLS:

A vertical or angled line thus— / —means "Set"—
The number in front of it is the set number—
The number after it indicates the number of strings employed—

EXAMPLE:
When the 1st-2nd-3rd-strings are employed the symbol is:
1/3—The first set of three—etc.
When the 1st-2nd-3rd-4th-strings are employed the symbol is:
1/4—The 1st set of four—etc.

THE BROKEN AND THE DIVIDED SETS:
Example:
When the 1st-2nd-4th-strings are employed (skipping the 3rd string) it is termed a broken set —the symbol is:
1/B3—The first set of broken three—etc.
When the order is reversed, (skipping the 2nd instead of the 3rd string) the word "broken" is used first, thus:
B1/3—The broken first set of three—etc.

When the 1st-2nd-4th-5th-strings are employed it is termed a divided set—the symbol is:
D1/4—The divided first set of four—etc.
When the 1st-3rd-5th-strings are employed the symbol is:
1/D3—The first set of divided three—and so on—
When the 1st-4th-strings are employed the symbol is:
A 1—
When the 2nd-5th-strings are employed the symbol is:
A 2—etc.
When the 1st-5th-strings are employed the symbol is:
B 1—etc.

NOTE
A symbol for the 1st-3rd-4th-6th-strings is not necessary because it would encompass all of the strings, therefore, the very notation dictates where and on what strings the notes are located.

3 to 6 up—Repeat the fingering until changed—resolution chord at end of each measure need not be sounded—it is there for orientation—1st inversion—the fourth set of three is marked in the fourth measure because that is the first cross over point to the third set of three. In other words, stay on the 4th set until changed.

Open strings are used in the lower register only where absolutely necessary

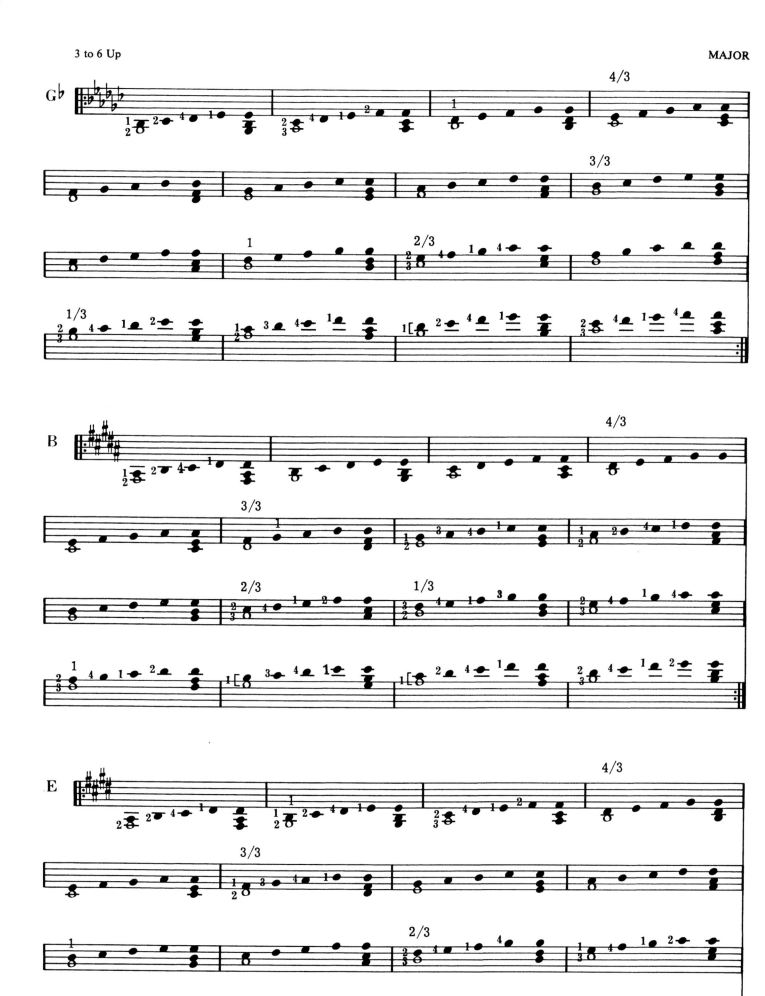

Notice that the 1st finger is ready to take the place of the open strings in the 1st bar of the "A" scale - this is a necessary mechanism because it can be raised a half tone without change-this mechanism will appear often - check back

Example below shows basic use of the mechanics - Experiment with the idea, be selective

6 to 3 Up

C

F

6 to 3 Up

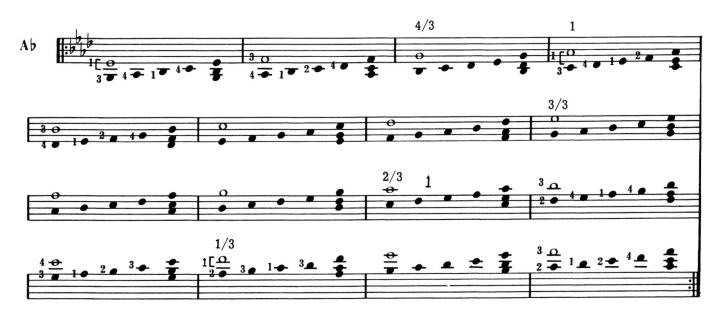

G

C

F

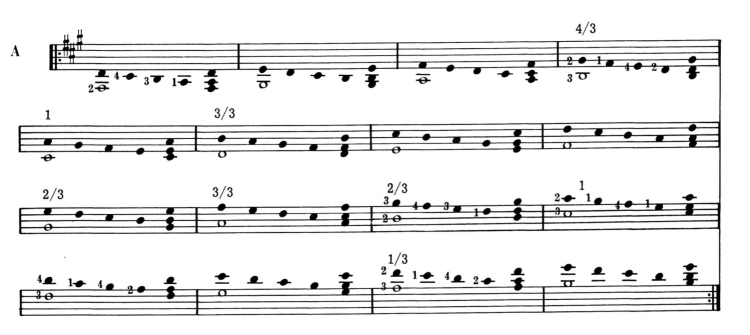

3 to 6 Up

HARMONIC MINOR

3 to 6 Up

HARMONIC MINOR

3 to 6 Up

Em
D#

3 to 6 Down

Am
G#

Dm
C#

3 to 6 Down

3 to 6 Down

6 to 3 Up

6 to 3 Up

6 to 3 Down

6 to 3 Down

3 to 6 Up

3 to 6 Up

3 to 6 Down

3 to 6 Down

MELODIC MINOR

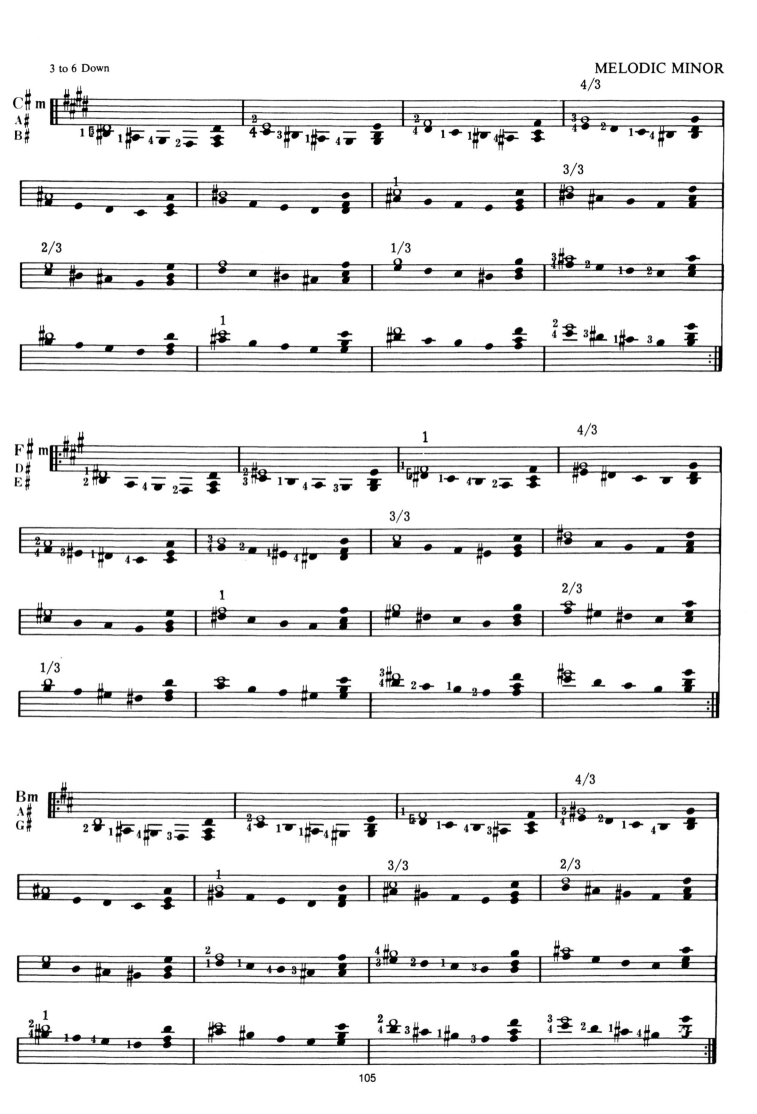

6 to 3 Up

MELODIC MINOR

6 to 3 Up

MELODIC MINOR

6 To 3 Down

MELODIC MINOR

110

MELODIC MINOR

6 to 3 Down

6 to 3 Down

6 To 3 - 3 To 6 Variation examples - play all 1st stations - 2nd stations etc.
Then 1st stations & 3rd stations - compound the stations both **Major** & **Minor** - mix the forms

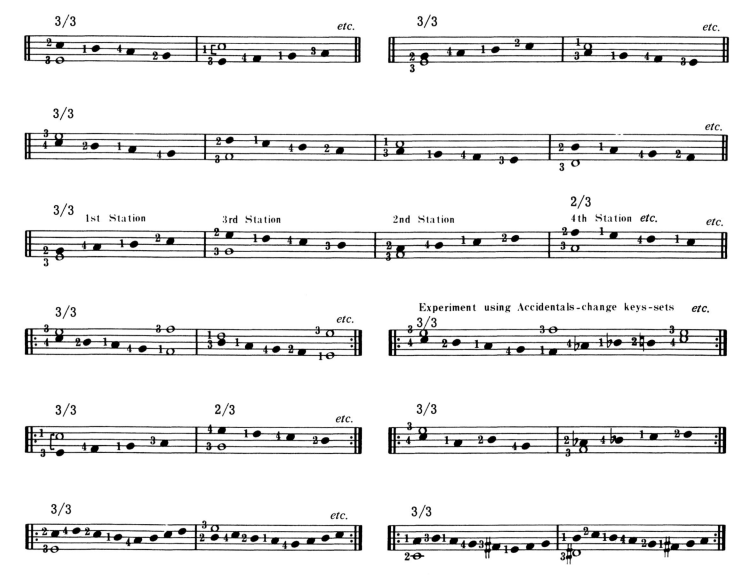

6ths with upper line motion = 1-5-3-1—5-1-3-5-
Sixths opening up to tenths—
Major and minor—12 keys—full range—
The visual fingerboard—

Experience has shown that this scale form provides an interesting and very important link in the chain of harmonic mechanisms. To begin with, there is reference to two of the basic triads in each station (bar) as is indicated in the model stations. A first inversion triad is inferred with the middle note deleted in the first half of each station, and a root position triad is present in arpeggio form in the middle to last half of each station. The stations also contain major and minor tenths that occur on the first and second beats of the measures, depending on the upper line inversion.

The left hand mechanisms required are few but demanding. Occasionally double stops are used, but there are no small or grand barres employed for many reasons; the main one being: the barre system is not suitable for this notation because it is too harplike in nature. In this type of study the tones in each station must not be allowed to ring over each other, except when indicated by the ties. In other words, a quarter note must not sound like a half note unless it is tied over to another quarter note. A (walking on the fingers) mechanism is much more suitable, in which the fingers are arched like little hammers that can provide the so-important individual finger control that is so necessary. Plus, great velocity can be achieved. The barre has a tendency to produce a residual chordlike sound because the notes cannot be stopped when necessary, except at very slow tempos where they die out naturally or can be damped with a finger.

When working with sixths it is very important to identify the related first or second inversion triad. In all of these studies, identify the opening sixth with the basic triad, then the upper line arpeggio with the root position triad. Also, be aware of the major and minor tenths involved. Because the notation is the same in both directions, the major form is shown ascending in one key and descending in the next key of the descending circle of fifths. However, each key should be practiced up and down.

SIXTHS WITH UPPER LINE MOTION

In the melodic form of these studies the ascending station numbers cannot match the descending numbers notationally because the scale descends in the relative major key. Note that station number one in the ascension becomes station number six in the relative major descension, and so it is with all of the other descending stations.

The upper line interval relationship remains constant in the major and both of the minor forms.

RIGHT HAND FOR 6ths WITH UPPER LINE MOTION
Thumb Sounds the "E" Whole note

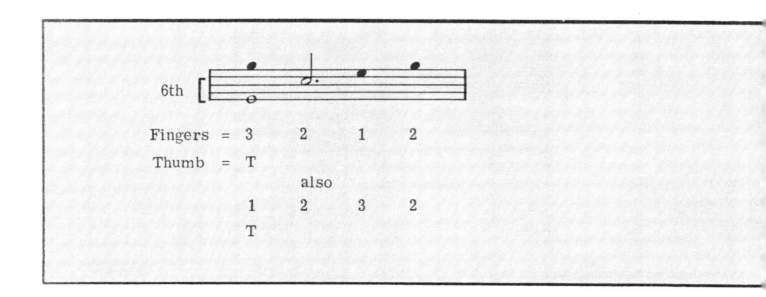

6th						Marking below is traditional			
Fingers =	1	2	3	2	=	I	M	A	M
Thumb =	T					P			
		also							
	1	2	3	2					
	T								

6th				
Fingers =	3	2	1	2
Thumb =	T			
		also		
	1	2	3	2
	T			

Apply these fingerings to the following studies

GENERAL REMARKS
ABOUT FINGER AND STRING SET MARKING

When there are finger markings in one bar and none in the next bar or bars, it usually means that the fingering remains the same or that it is so obvious it need not be indicated. In many of these studies fingering will appear in the first bar only. That is done to show the type of finger mechanism to be employed. In other words, the fingers to be used may vary from bar to bar, but the "type" of mechanics does not change.

It is almost impossible to indicate all of the fingering choices in these studies. However, enough of the various mechanisms have been employed to cover most all harmonic situations, and in many cases with alternatives.

Always sustain the half and whole notes for their full value.

STRING CHART
EXPLANATION OF THE STRING SET SYMBOLS:

A vertical or angled line thus- / -means "Set"—
The number in front of it is the set number—
The number after it indicates the number of strings employed—
Example:
When the 1st-2nd-3rd-strings are employed the symbol is:
1/3—The first set of three–etc.
When the 1st-2nd-3rd-4th-strings are employed the symbol is:
1/4—The 1st set of four–etc.

THE BROKEN AND THE DIVIDED SETS:

Example:
When the 1st-2nd-4th-strings are employed (skipping the 3rd string) it is termed a broken set—the symbol is:
1/B3—The first set of broken three–etc.
When the order is reversed, (skipping the 2nd instead of the 3rd string) the word "broken" is used first, thus:
B1/3—The broken first set of three–etc.

When the 1st-2nd-4th-5th-strings are employed it is termed a divided set—the symbol is:
D1/4—The divided first set of four–etc.
When the 1st-3rd-5th-strings are employed the symbol is:
1/D3—The first set of divided three—and so on—
When the 1st-4th-strings are employed the symbol is:
A 1—
When the 2nd-5th-strings are employed the symbol is:
A 2—etc.
When the 1st-5th-strings are employed the symbol is:
B 1—etc.

NOTE
A symbol for the 1st-3rd-4th-6th-strings is not necessary because it would encompass all of the strings, therefore, the very notation dictates where and on what strings the notes are located.

STRING SET CHART
SYMBOLS:—STRINGS EMPLOYED—

1/2—1st-2nd-
2/2—2nd-3rd-
3/2—3rd-4th-
4/2—4th-5th-
5/2—5th-6th-

1/3—1st-2nd-3rd-
2/3—2nd-3rd-4th-
3/3—3rd-4th-5th-
4/3—4th-5th-6th-

1/4—1st-2nd-3rd-4th-
2/4—2nd-3rd-4th-5th-
3/4—3rd-4th-5th-6th-

1/5—1st-2nd-3rd-4th-5th-
2/5—2nd-3rd-4th-5th-6th-

THE BROKEN AND DIVIDED SETS:

1/B2—1st-3rd-
2/B2—2nd-4th-
3/B2—3rd-5th-
4/B2—4th-6th-

1/B3—1st-2nd-4th-
2/B3—2nd-3rd-5th-
3/B3—3rd-4th-6th-

B1/3—1st-3rd-4th-
B2/3—2nd-4th-5th-
B3/3—3rd-5th-6th-

1/B4—1st-2nd-3rd-5th-
2/B4—2nd-3rd-4th-6th-

B1/4—1st-3rd-4th-5th-
B2/4—2nd-4th-5th-6th-
1D/3—1st-2nd-5th-
2D/3—2nd-3rd-6th-

1/D3—1st-3rd-5th-
2/D3—2nd-4th-6th-

D1/3—1st-4th-5th-
D2/3—2nd-5th-6th-

D1/4—1st-2nd-4th-5th-
D2/4—2nd-3rd-5th-6th-

A1—1st-4th-
A2—2nd-5th-
A3—3rd-6th-

B1—1st-5th-
B2—2nd-6th-

01—1st-6th-

6ths With Upper Line Motion - based on basic triad scale - 10ths are formed on 2nd beat-bracketed
triad identifies each station - relate to the triads in all the keys - numbers above and below staff show
station (step of the scale - upper line intervals = 1-5-3-1-5-1-3-5

When pattern is inverted 10ths are formed on the 1st and 4th beat–6ths with upper line motion=1-5-3-1-5-1-3-5

6ths with Upper Line Motion

Variations - Do in all keys Major and Minors

In the above variation the lowest note is sounded on the 1st beat - 2nd beat - 3rd beat - then 4th beat

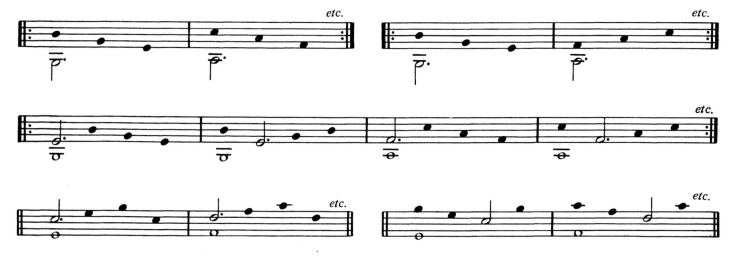

Employ Previous Variation Formats - Full range - All keys

6ths with Upper Line Motion

Circle 5

From here on in this study, markings are omitted - the required mechanisms should be established by this time

6ths with Upper Line Motion

6ths with Upper Line Motion

6ths with upper line motion

EMPLOY PREVIOUS VARIATION FORMATS-ALL KEYS-FULL RANGE

Circle 5 —6ths with upper line motion = 1-5-3-1-5-1-3-5—melodic minor—12 keys—full range
The melodic minor scale descends in the relative major key

Descension in the 1st two keys is a reverse pattern - continue the pattern thru the remaining keys-mix them for variety

From here on in this study, just the ascension will be shown - descend in relative Major keys

Descend in B♭ Major

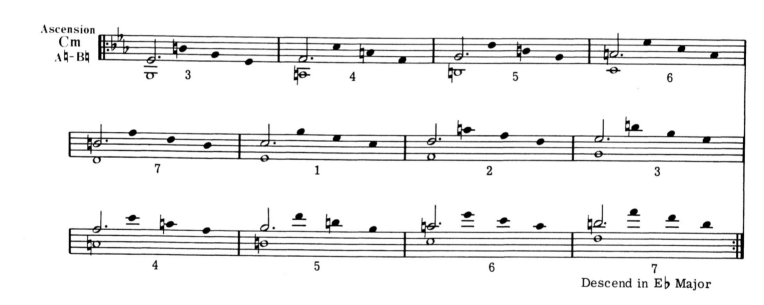

Descend in E♭ Major

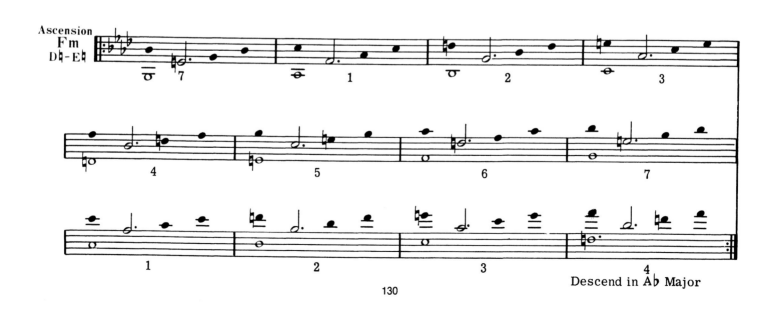

Descend in A♭ Major

6ths with Upper Line Motion

Descend in D♭ Major

Descend in G♭ Major

Descend in B Major

6ths with Upper Line Motion

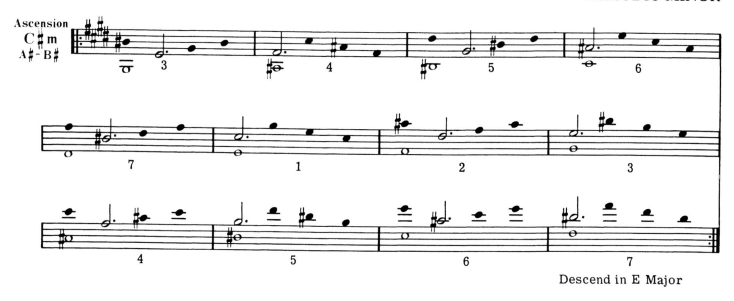

Descend in E Major

Descend in A Major

Descend in D Major

6ths with upper line motion

These are Fm 3rd station examples (both harmonic and melodic minors)

Do not place fingers in position in advance - left and right hand attack must be together for best results in articulated situations - velocity demands it

Employ previous variation formats - all keys - full range

SIXTHS WITH UPPER LINE

The following study is the same pattern as the others in this chapter with this difference:
The overall spread of notes is one octave instead of a tenth

Many different fingerings and string sets are employed—be aware of the subtle differences.

This is a condensed form to save space. However, each pattern should be worked with in scale form separately—one by one, in all keys, major and minor. The whole and half notes must be sustained full value; keep the pressure applied firmly, while the quarter notes are in motion. The left hand must be trained to apply and hold pressure with any one of the fingers while the others articulate with relaxed control, power, and agility.

MAJOR

6 To 8 - In various combinations with a mixture of fingerings, therefore string markings above the staff are necessary - do these in both minors, also all keys

Variation - Combined forms Apply the above mixture also

1 Octave Spread
Eighth

1 Octave and a 3rd
Tenth

THE VISUAL FINGERBOARD

THE SHAPES OF FINGERBOARD SOUNDS—THE EARS SEE
THE SOUNDS OF FINGERBOARD SHAPES—THE EYES HEAR

If the first four strings were barred silently at the fifth fret by someone else while you're looking, familiarity should tell you what it sounds like—the chord should be heard mentally.

If that same chord were sounded while your back was turned—the chord should be visualized.

Every chord, mechanism, notation, has a shape.

THE VISUAL FINGERBOARD

PHYSICAL SHAPES

There are all sorts of shapes and patterns on the fingerboard. All chords and articulated mechanisms have their special shapes. Recognizing these shapes is very necessary for the overall understanding of the fingerboard and tuning.

For this concept the fingerboard must be visualized from above. Of course this has been done for years (ukulele chords) but in the following examples the shapes are moved from one set of strings to another, which results in notational changes, then the notational change is moved back to the other sets.

Become familiar with the subtle physical and notational changes that take place when harmonic structures are shifted back and forth from set to set to set.

This is not in any way meant to be a method for playing; it is purely informational. It develops better, clearer understanding of the geometry of the instrument.

PHYSICAL SHAPES - every mechanism has an overall shape no matter how complicated it may be - it is of great importance to be able to recognize all of the parallels - triangles of various shapes - rectangles, el's etc.   Below are a few basic examples of how shapes change slightly when transfered from one set to another

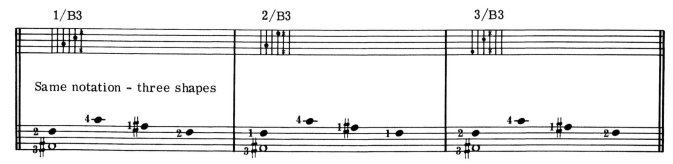

A and B are same shape but different notation - B and C are same notation but different shape - C and D are same shape but different notation etc.   It is a form of mutation

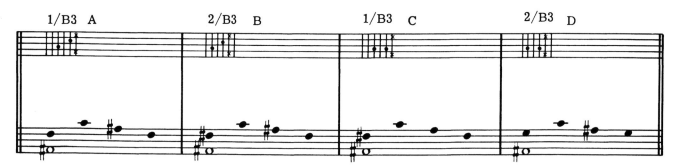

The idea is to transfer them back and forth - transfer the shape, then transfer the resulting notation back to the other sets - there are many more than shown here - it is almost endless-select your own notations - experiment

The passage below requires but two shapes by transfer

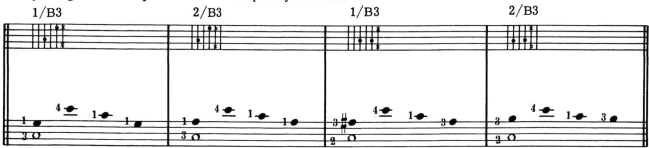

3 shapes to play a 6 step passage by transfer

The visual aspect of the fingerboard is very important - know what mechanisms look like in the learning stage - after while they become visable in the minds eye.

This principle applies to any notation or Voicing that involves the B and G string because of the Major third in the tuning - If the tuning was all fourths, this difference would not exist - It is this difference that allows the great variety of notational and fingering choices - what is imposible in one location is possible in another

Physical Shapes - Mirrored reflections - opposites - parallels etc
The Visual Aspect of the Fingerboard

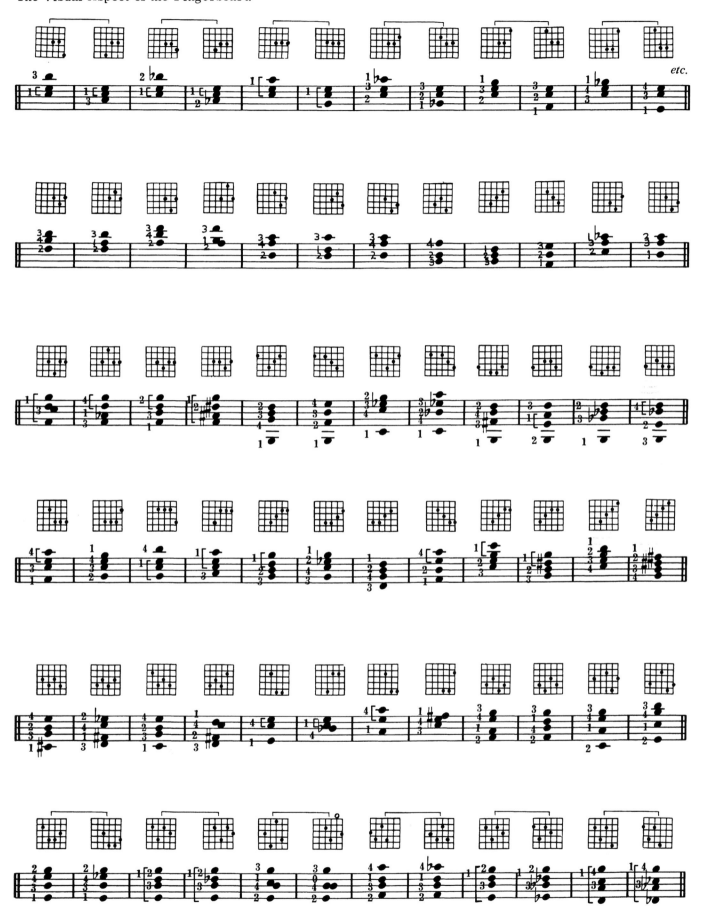

"CHROMATIC TRIADS"

The three triads used chromatically with a pedal bass—
Tenths to thirds—thirds to tenths—chromatically—
Chromatic scales in:
2nds-
3rds-
4ths-
5ths-
6ths-
8ths-
10ths-
12ths-
13ths-
15ths-
Raised and lowered intervals chromatically—

ALL THROUGH MY BOOKS THE EMPHASIS WILL BE ON "CHROMATICS"—
CHROMATICS, CHROMATICS, AND MORE CHROMATICS——

STRING CHART
EXPLANATION OF THE STRING SET SYMBOLS:

A vertical or angled line thus— / —means "Set"—
The number in front of it is the set number—
The number after it indicates the number of strings employed—

EXAMPLE:
When the 1st-2nd-3rd-strings are employed the symbol is:
1/3—The first set of three—etc.
When the 1st-2nd-3rd-4th-strings are employed the symbol is:
1/4—The 1st set of four—etc.

THE BROKEN AND THE DIVIDED SETS:
Example:
When the 1st-2nd-4th-strings are employed (skipping the 3rd string) it is termed a broken set —the symbol is:
1/B3—The first set of broken three—etc.
When the order is reversed, (skipping the 2nd instead of the 3rd string) the word "broken" is used first, thus:
B1/3—The broken first set of three—etc.

When the 1st-2nd-4th-5th-strings are employed it is termed a divided set—the symbol is:
D1/4—The divided first set of four—etc.
When the 1st-3rd-5th-strings are employed the symbol is:
1/D3—The first set of divided three—and so on—
When the 1st-4th-strings are employed the symbol is:
A 1—
When the 2nd-5th-strings are employed the symbol is:
A 2—etc.
When the 1st-5th-strings are employed the symbol is:
B 1—etc.

NOTE
A symbol for the 1st-3rd-4th-6th-strings is not necessary because it would encompass all of the strings, therefore, the very notation dictates where and on what strings the notes are located.

STRING SET CHART
SYMBOLS:—STRINGS EMPLOYED—

1/2 . . . . 1st-2nd-
2/2 . . . . 2nd-3rd-
3/2 . . . . 3rd-4th-
4/2 . . . . 4th-5th-
5/2 . . . . 5th-6th-

1/3 . . . . 1st-2nd-3rd-
2/3 . . . . 2nd-3rd-4th-
3/3 . . . . 3rd-4th-5th-
4/3 . . . . 4th-5th-6th-

1/4 . . . . 1st-2nd-3rd-4th-
2/4 . . . . 2nd-3rd-4th-5th-
3/4 . . . . 3rd-4th-5th-6th-

1/5 . . . . 1st-2nd-3rd-4th-5th-
2/5 . . . . 2nd-3rd-4th-5th-6th-

THE BROKEN AND DIVIDED SETS:

1/B2 . . . . 1st-3rd-
2/B2 . . . . 2nd-4th-
3/B2 . . . . 3rd-5th-
4/B2 . . . . 4th-6th-

1/B3 . . . . 1st-2nd-4th-
2/B3 . . . . 2nd-3rd-5th-
3/B3 . . . . 3rd-4th-6th-

B1/3 . . . . 1st-3rd-4th-
B2/3 . . . . 2nd-4th-5th-
B3/3 . . . . 3rd-5th-6th-

1/B4 . . . . 1st-2nd-3rd-5th-
2/B4 . . . . 2nd-3rd-4th-6th-

B1/4 . . . . 1st-3rd-4th-5th-
B2/4 . . . . 2nd-4th-5th-6th-

1D/3 . . . . 1st-2nd-5th-
2D/3 . . . . 2nd-3rd-6th-

1/D3 . . . . 1st-3rd-5th-
2/D3 . . . . 2nd-4th-6th-
D1/3 . . . . 1st-4th-5th-
D2/3 . . . . 2nd-5th-6th-
D1/4 . . . . 1st-2nd-4th-5th-
D2/4 . . . . 2nd-3rd-5th-6th-

A1 . . . . 1st-4th-
A2 . . . . 2nd-5th-
A3 . . . . 3rd-6th-

B1 . . . . 1st-5th-
B2 . . . . 2nd-6th-

01 . . . . 1st-6th-

LONG REACHES

Some of the reaches are quite extended in these studies. However, the notations must be shown for the information and continuity of thought they contain; the knowledge is very necessary.

The art of accomplishing long reaches is based on relaxed power control—not a large hand.

Reach must be developed gradually by patiently working with material that contains extended spreads. It must be practiced on the fingerboard under actual playing conditions—not forcing fingers apart with wedges etc.

Practicing extended spreads is very necessary, but avoid over doing. Prolonged practice of this nature may cause temporary discomfort. If this happens, work on something else for a while—then continue.

If some of the spreads are really too long, there are many fingering alternatives plus string set duplicates shown to choose from.

The goal is to achieve the maximum reach potential for the size of the hand.

Naturally there is a limit—the fingers can't become longer but the tendons between the fingers gradually stretch, loosen, and become more relaxed, and this increases the overall reach.

Forcing the fingers by tensing tightens the tendons and actually shortens the reach.

The hand can be trained to apply a gentle, relaxed, type of controlled power, but it takes time and work.

CHROMATIC TRIADS WITH PEDAL BASS "G"—

All the bass and triad relationships of the three basic triads are covered in the following group of studies—

All of the duplicates are shown—

Chromatic Triads with pedal bass "G" full range

1st Inversion

The G♮7♭3♭5 above is also an E diminished 9th—in other words the symbol for a chord depends on its use—its place in a progression etc. The symbols for the 2nd inversion and root are the same as the first inversion when starting on "G" - just the voicing changes

2nd Inversion

Root Position

Chromatic 1st inversion triads with pedal bass "G"

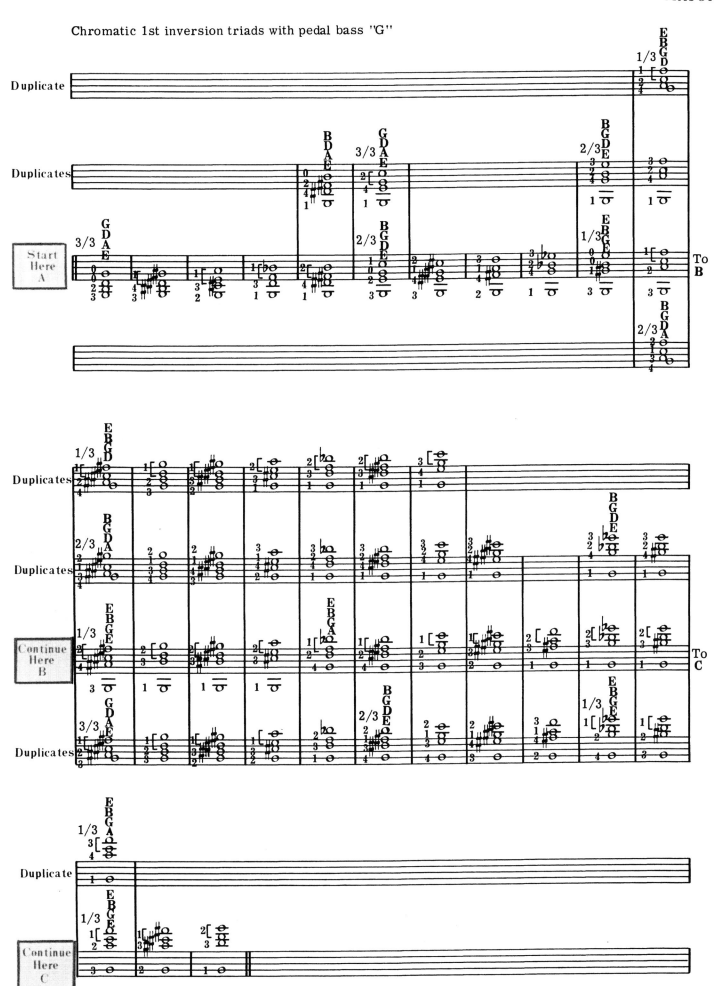

Chromatic 2nd inversion triads with pedal bass "G"

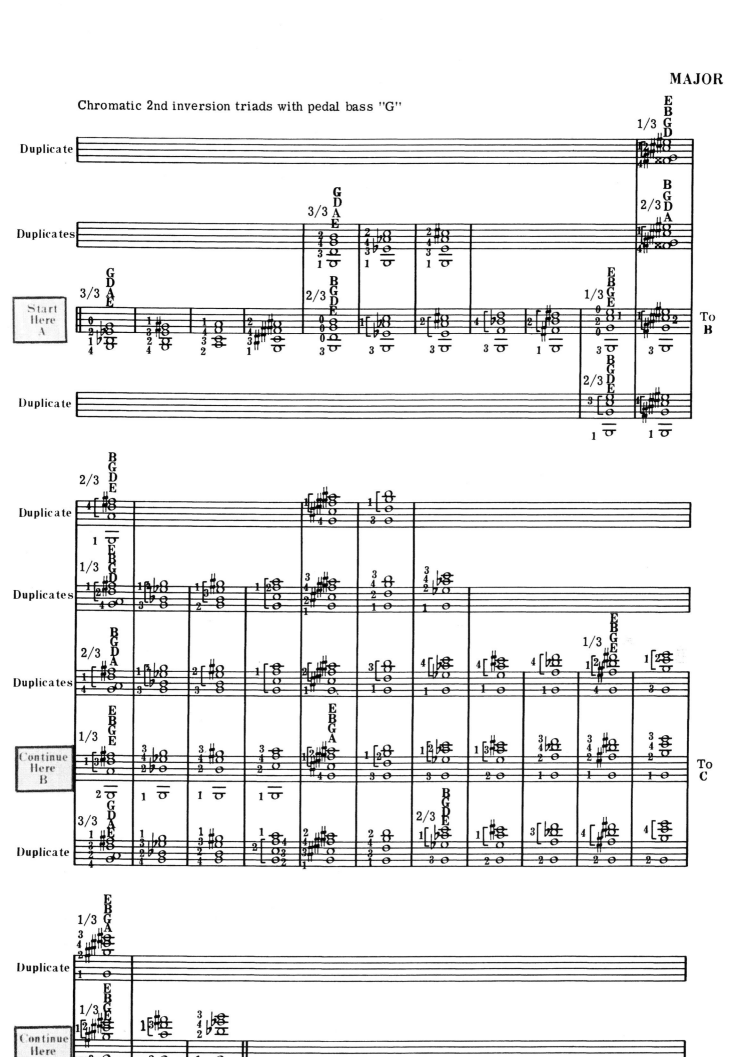

Chromatic triads - root position with pedal bass "G"

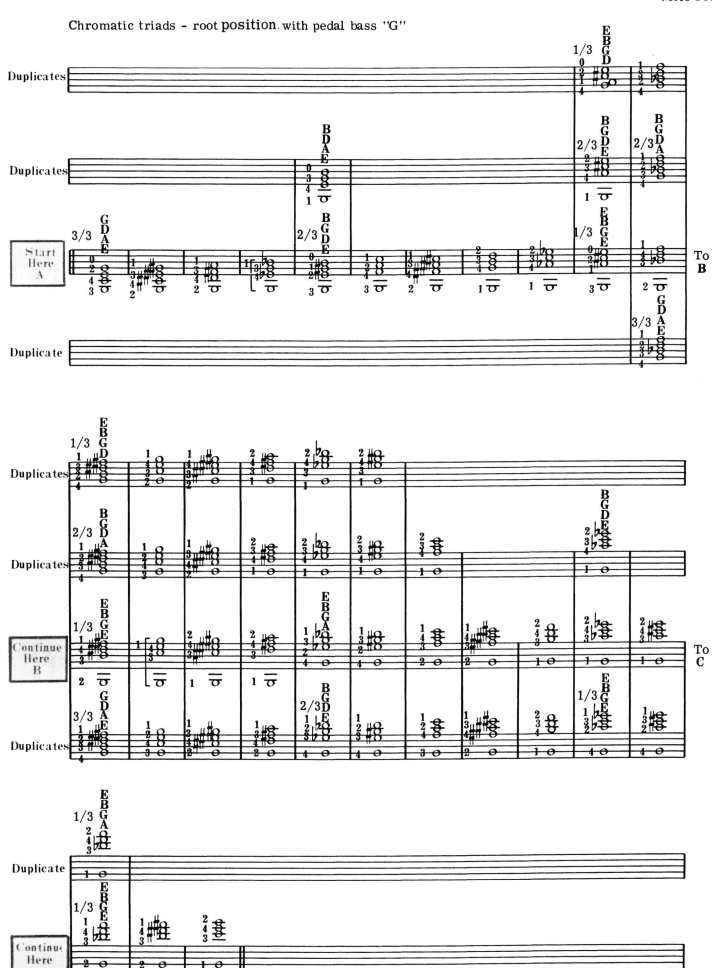

Chromatic triads with pedal bass "G" - full range

1st Inversion

2nd Inversion

Root Position

MINOR

Chromatic 1st inversion triads with pedal bass "G"

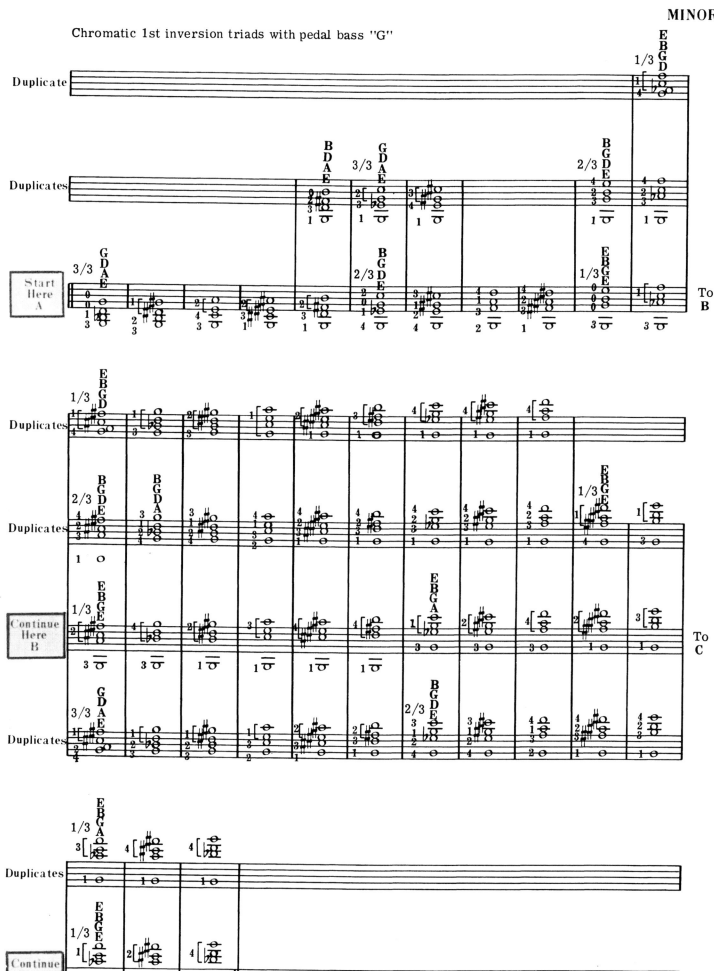

146

Chromatic 2nd inversion triads with pedal bass "G"

MINOR

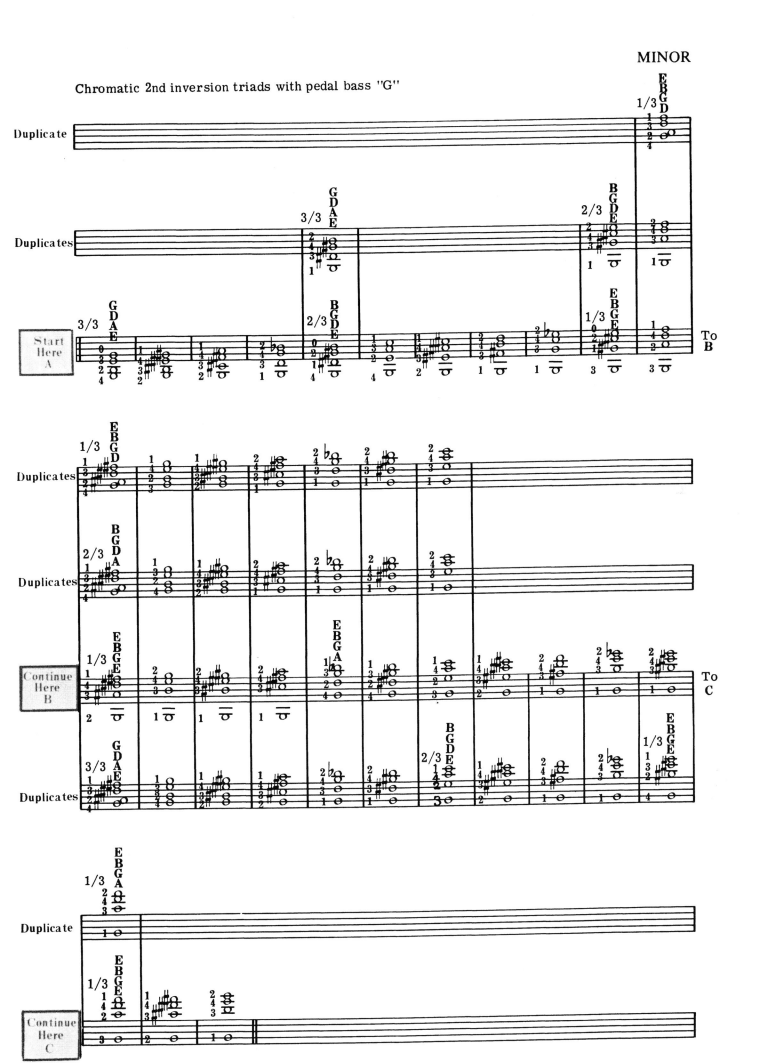

147

Chromatic Root Position triads with pedal bass "G"

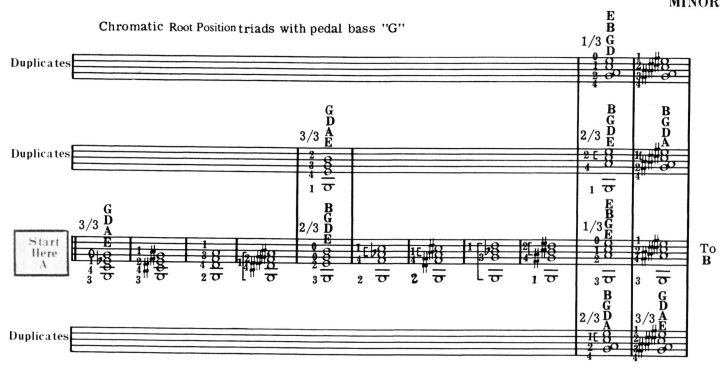

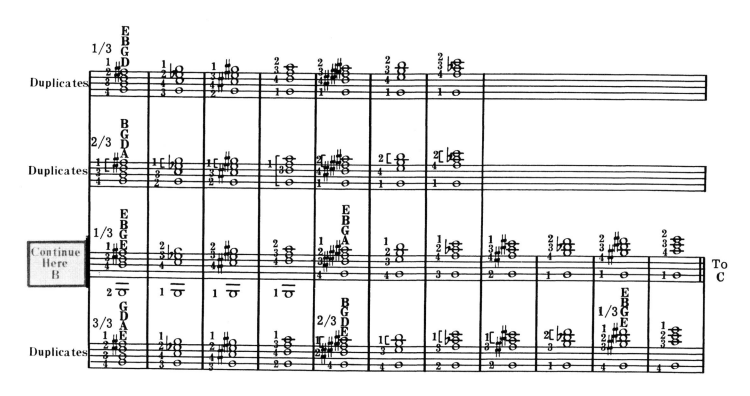

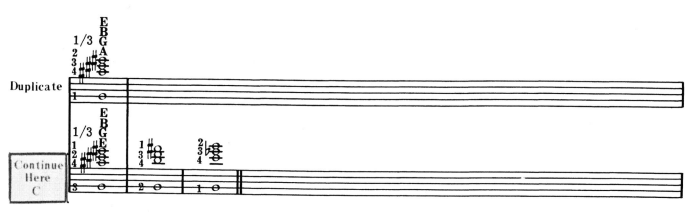

10th to 3rd down   Chromatically   Major & Minor showing some of the many fingerings. By using
3 to 10 up   these chromatic exercises in all their various forms, positions, and combinations, all
scales Maj., Min., Dim., Aug. may be constructed. Practice using descending
fingering both directions, then ascending fingering both directions.

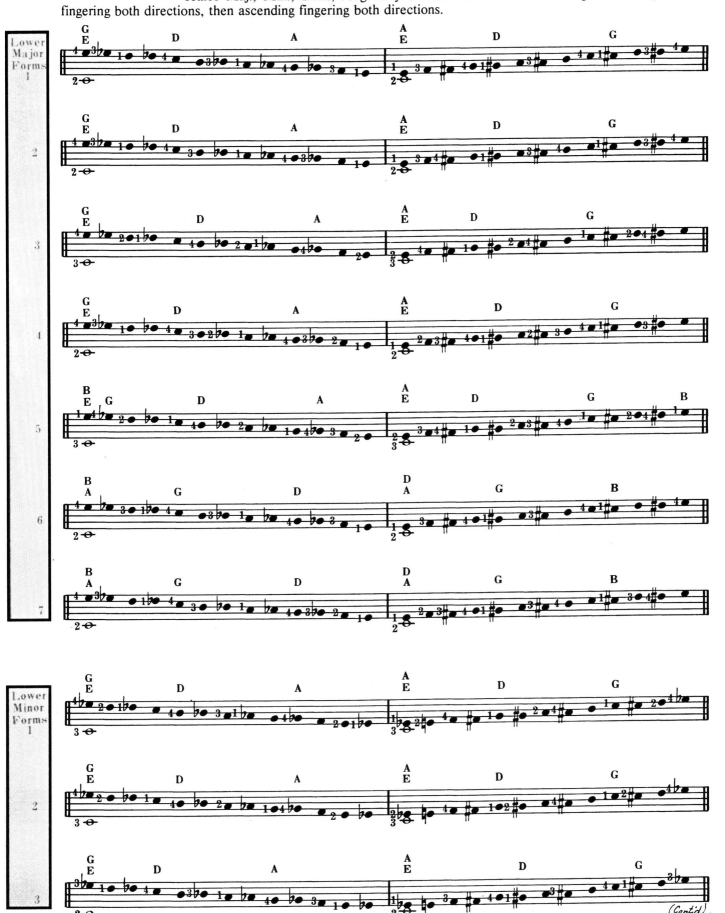

Construct your own exercises by using portions of these forms, and all the other exercises in these
books. use 1 note, 2 notes, 4 notes etc. Selected from the beginning, the middle or any place in the
groups. Practise of this nature helps to increase reach and flexibility. If muscular discomfort is
noticed, stop, rest the hand. Some discomfort is normal.

10 To 3 To 10 Chromatically   Major & Minor
Down & Up

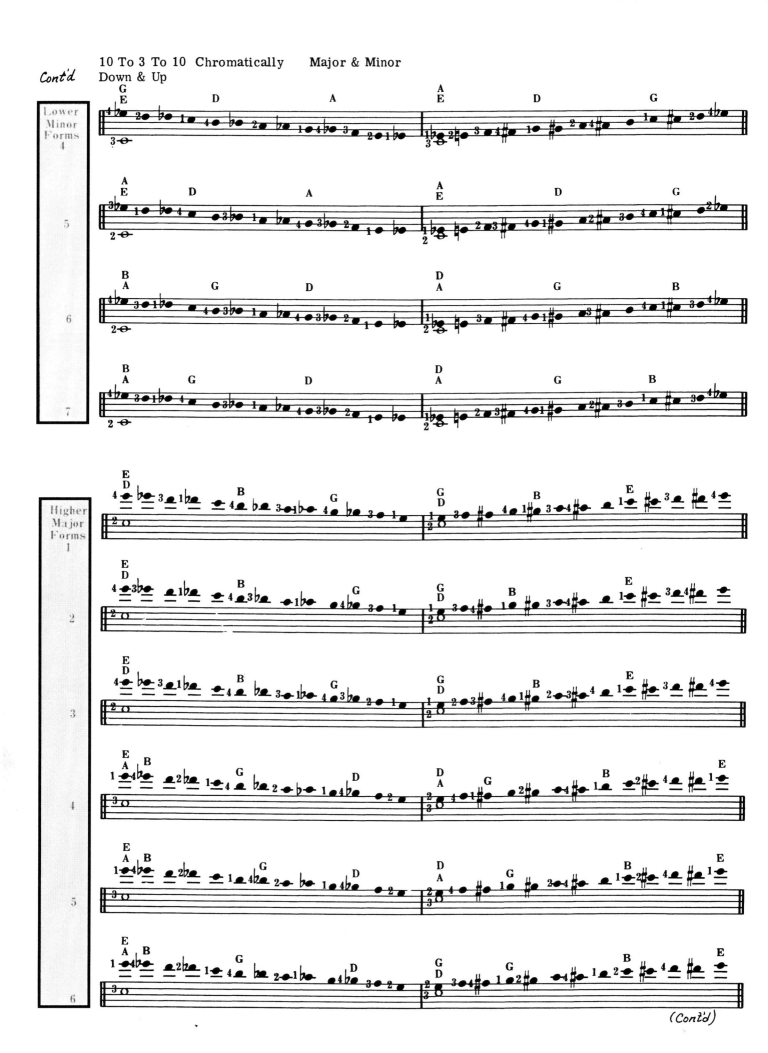

Lower Minor Forms 4

Lower Minor Forms 5

Lower Minor Forms 6

Lower Minor Forms 7

Higher Major Forms 1

Higher Major Forms 2

Higher Major Forms 3

Higher Major Forms 4

Higher Major Forms 5

Higher Major Forms 6

(Cont'd)

10 To 3 To 10 chromatically — Major & Minor
Down & Up — Major & Minor Thirds & Tenths can make up any scale desired

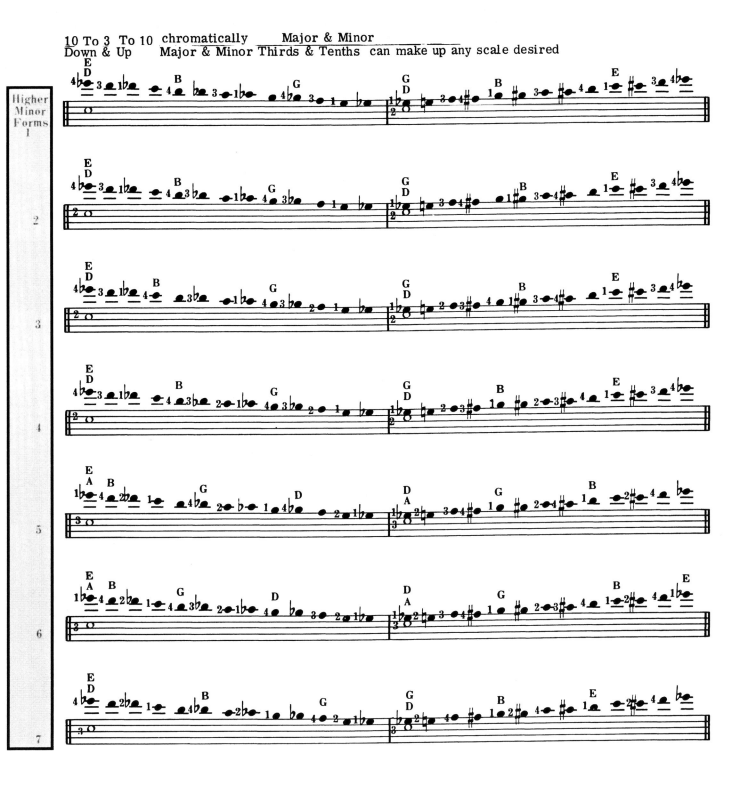

EXAMPLES: These are but a very small fraction of the vast possibilities. Vary the notation and fingering. Experiment.

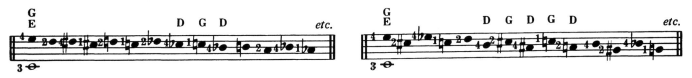

Also employ the higher forms.

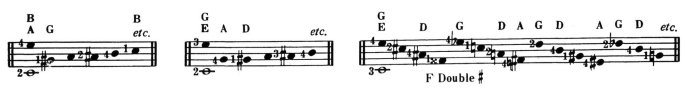

3 To 10 Down Chromatically Major & Minor (Inverted)
10 To 3 Up

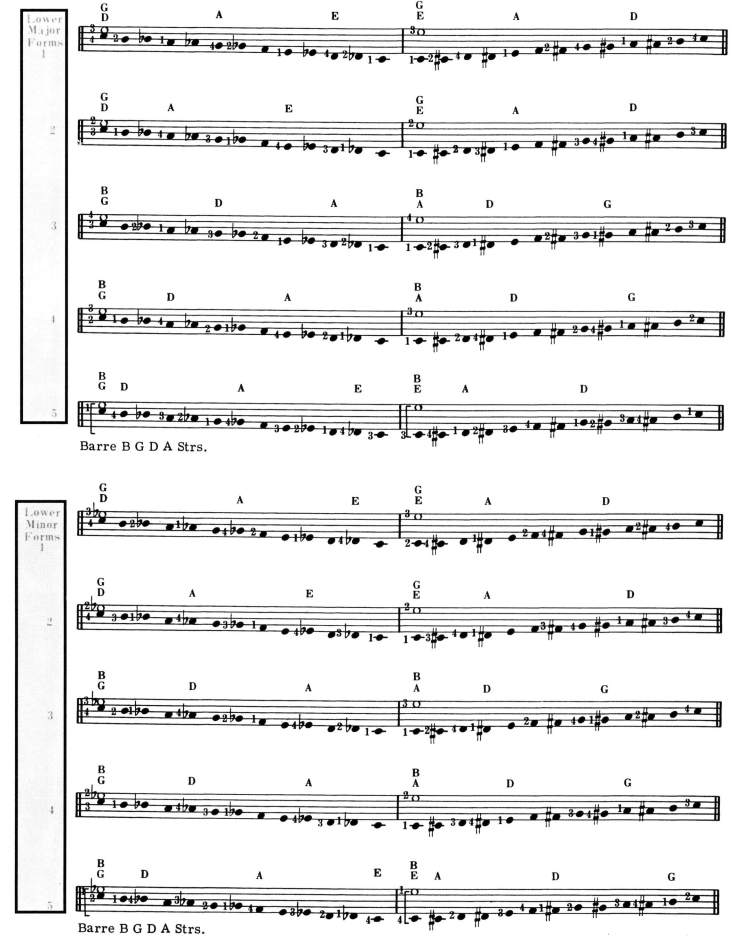

Barre B G D A Strs.

Barre B G D A Strs.

Always Treat each measure as a separate exercise-sustain the whole note for the full measure

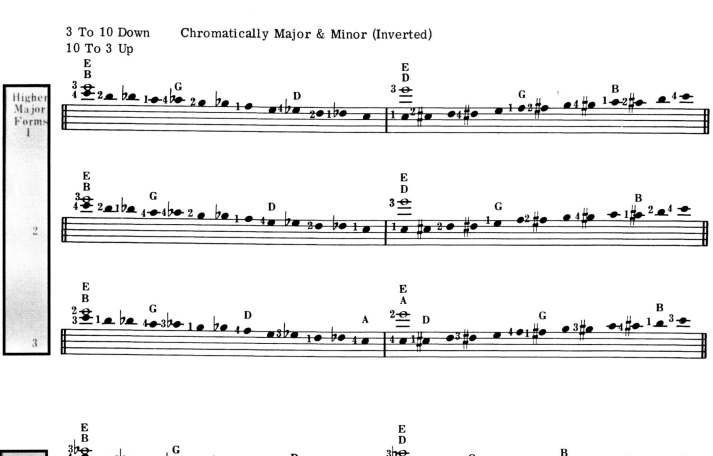

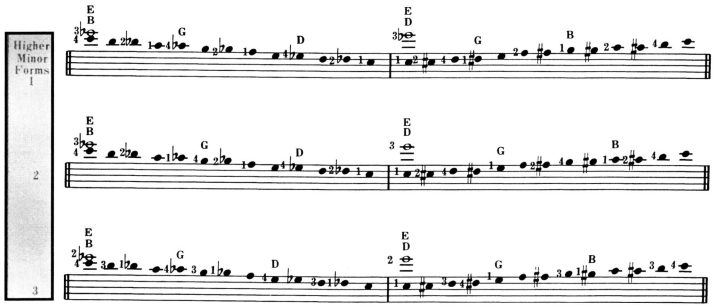

EXAMPLES:

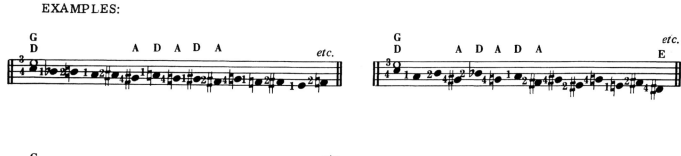

Chromatic Octave With lower note sustained using varied left hand fingering. A line of chromatic
8 To 1 - Down - 1 To 8 Up   tones ascending or descending an octave can describe any interval in any
key to build any scale.

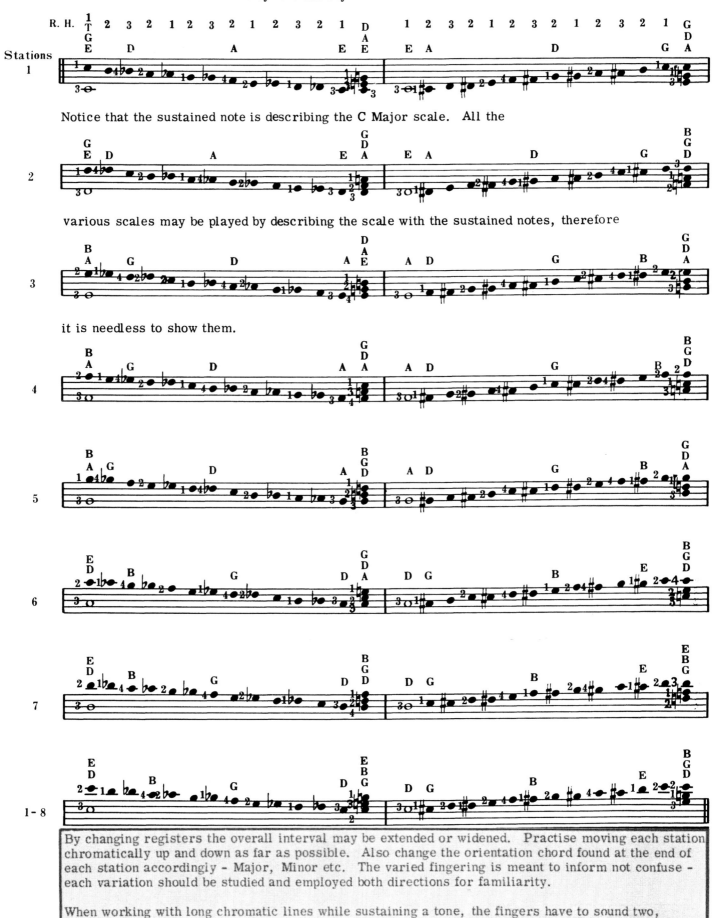

Notice that the sustained note is describing the C Major scale. All the

various scales may be played by describing the scale with the sustained notes, therefore

it is needless to show them.

By changing registers the overall interval may be extended or widened. Practise moving each station
chromatically up and down as far as possible. Also change the orientation chord found at the end of
each station accordingly - Major, Minor etc. The varied fingering is meant to inform not confuse -
each variation should be studied and employed both directions for familiarity.

When working with long chromatic lines while sustaining a tone, the fingers have to sound two,
sometimes three half steps in succession with the same finger, smoothly.

Chromatic Octave With upper note sustained - (Inverted)
1 To 8 - Down 8 To 1 - Up

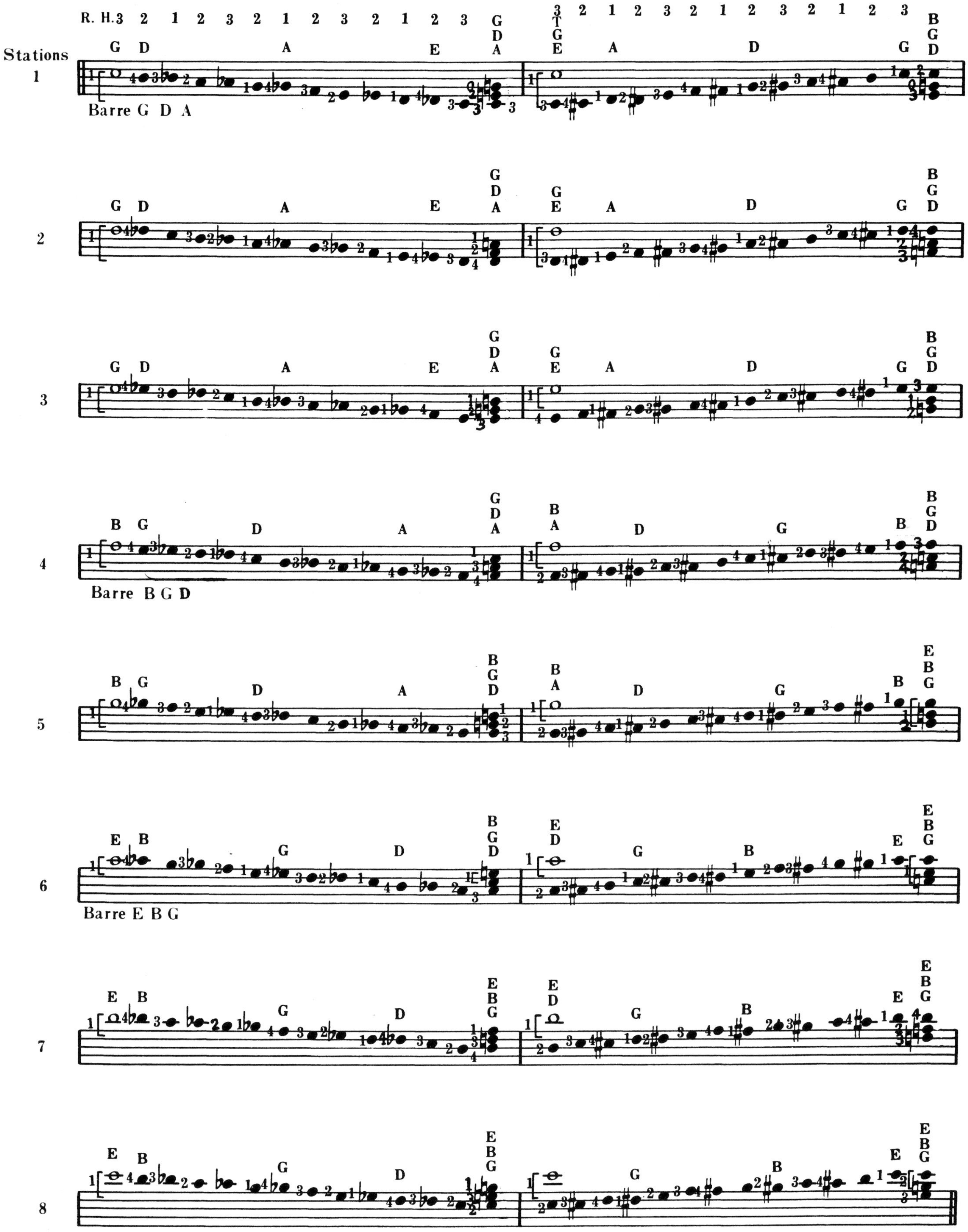

155

Chromatic Scales in 2nds - 3rds, 4ths, 5ths, 6ths, 8ths - many varied and mixed fingings are employed in these exercises - also string combinations - note them carefully.

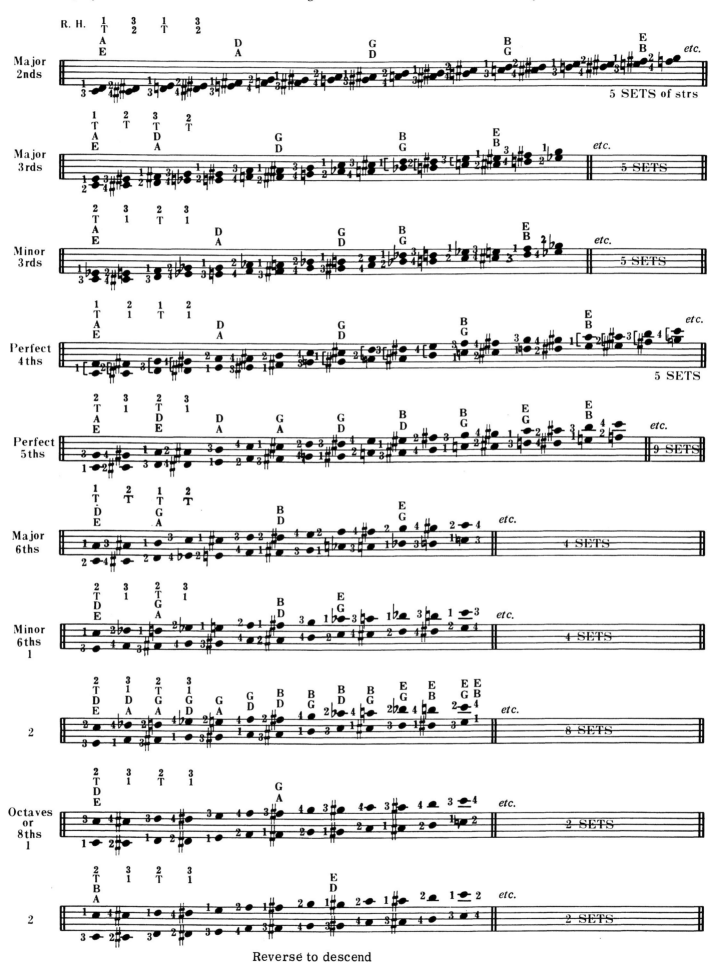

Reverse to descend

Chromatic scales in 8ths, 10ths, 13ths, 15ths

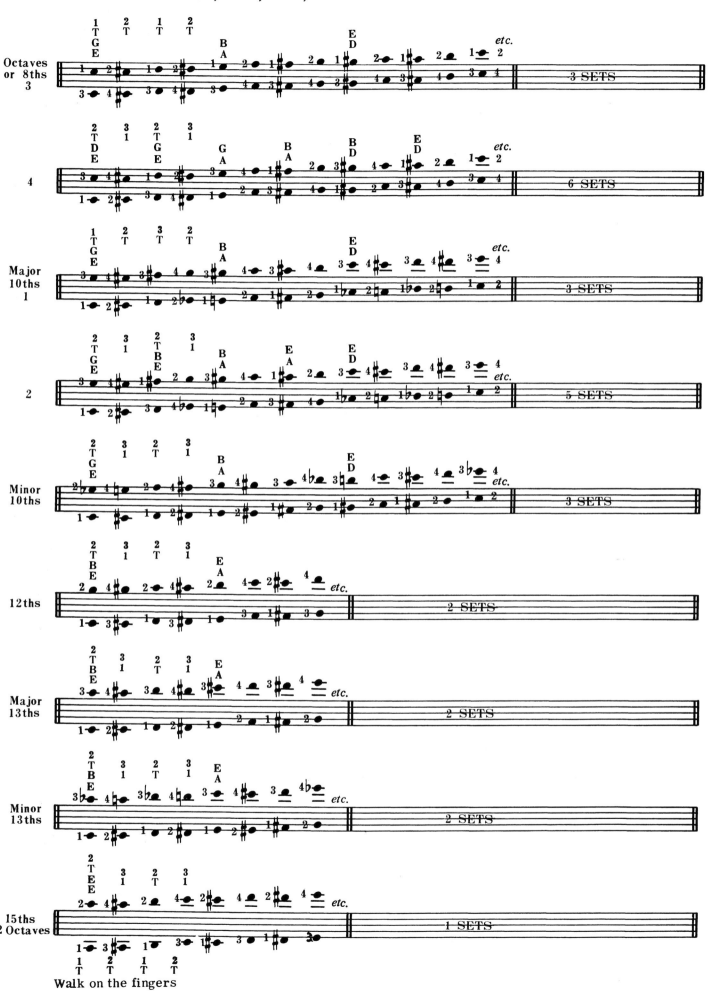

Walk on the fingers

Chromatics

All the intervals up to two octaves except the minor 2nd are represented in combined form below. Each measure is a separate exercise and should be studied carefully. In practice move each one up and down as far as possible on the same strings. Later when they are playable, combine them to make the continuous long forms shown earlier. Notice that raised and lowered intervals are included in these exercises.

These exercises are shown ascending - reverse them to descend

Space does not permit showing all of the possible fingerings. Explore the possibilities, keeping articulation in mind always. See examples of mixed fingering below.

158

Chromatics - Chromatic Upper Voice coupled with diatonic thirds
Apply to all keys full range

The Minor Modes Can't Parallel the Major because of the Minor third interval-it is shortened by one semitone

MAJOR and MINOR

TRIAD VOICES SUPER AND SUB - Contrary multi voice motion - Chromatic upper voice
Super & Sub notes Sharp & Flat

"SUPER AND SUB SERIES"

Each note in the three basic triads are placed in the position of being one diatonic step above and below normal—

Major and minor—12 keys—full range—

SUPER AND SUB SERIES

EXPLANATION

When the three basic triad inversions (first, second, and root) are placed in scale form the three voices (tonic, third, and fifth) all follow the same scale except that they obviously start on different steps of the scale.

Each triad on each step of any scale will contain the tonic, third, and fifth regardless of the inversion used or the step of the scale, with the exception of the diminished/seventh steps which naturally don't contain a perfect fifth. On these steps the fifth is shortened a semitone but is referred to as a fifth interval.

THE MEANING OF THE TERMS "SUPER" AND "SUB":

When any one of the voices in a triad is raised one step of the scale it is placed in super position.

When it is lowered one step of the scale it is placed in sub position.

> For instance:
> When the "C" (tonic) in a "C" triad is raised one step to "D" it is termed the super tonic—when it is lowered to "B" it is termed the sub tonic. When the "D" (tonic) in a "D" minor triad is raised one step to "E" it is termed the super tonic also—When it is lowered one step to "C" it is termed the sub tonic, and so on up the "C" scale. Apply this reasoning also to the other voices in the triads thusly:
>
> When the "E" (third) in the "C" triad is raised one step to "F" it is placed in super position—when it is lowered one step to "D" it is placed in sub position. When the "G" (fifth) is raised one step to "A" it is placed in super position—when it is lowered one step to "F" it is placed in sub position, and of course this reasoning applies to second inversions and the root triads as well.

Another basic example: "C" super is "D"—"D" super is "E"—"E" super is "F"—etc. "C" sub is "B"—"B" sub is "A"—"A" sub is "G"—etc. And of course the principle applies to all keys and all scales, arpeggios, progressions, etc.

—RESULT—

When the voice motion in a triad (regardless of direction,) moves one step above normal, or, returns from above normal to normal position, it is termed "super" motion—

When the voice motion moves one step below normal, or, returns from below normal to normal position, it is termed "sub" motion.

In this super and sub series all the voices in the first, second, and root position triads take turns in "super" and "sub" motion.

Interesting changes take place when the super and sub notes are introduced to triad work, such as:

A first inversion triad with the middle voice super automatically becomes a member of the second inversion family—
A first inversion with the upper voice sub becomes a member of the root position triads—
A second inversion triad with the lower voice super becomes a root position triad—
A root position triad with the lower voice sub becomes a second inversion triad, and so on—

> Study the subtle differences carefully for these are very important to the understanding of the very close relationships they all enjoy.
>
> Space does not permit showing all of the many different scales employing this format, however, the mechanics shown apply to all of them.
>
> The following scales will not be shown because:
>
> The natural minor scale is the same as the major scale sixth step to sixth step—the mixed minor scale is a mixture of the melodic scale ascending and the harmonic scale descending, or vice versa.

When working with the super and sub principle it is necessary to keep the named inversion in each study in mind at all times because "it" is the "origin"; it is the original voicing that is going to produce others. Therefore, it becomes the "boss"—it is the dominating factor regardless of the other inversions produced. The resulting voicings become bi-products of the inversion named in the heading of each study. Think of the original inversion as the center of activity with its voices being able to go "super" or "sub" at any time—in other words, even though duplicate inversions appear, they must be viewed differently because any one of the three inversions can produce the other two—the original inversion is the "cause," the resulting voicing the "effect". One is produced by voice motion, the other is not. Examples below:

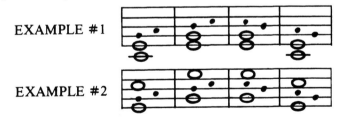

EXAMPLE #1

EXAMPLE #2

When working with root triads, example #1 is termed: root triads with upper voice motion "super"—
When working with first inversion triads, example #1 is termed: first inversion triads with upper voice motion "sub"—

When working with second inversion triads, example #2 is termed: second inversion triads with middle voice motion "sub"—
When working with first inversion triads, example #2 is termed: first inversion triads with middle voice motion "super"—etc.

The direction of voice motion does not alter the terminology.

Analysis: they are different in concept only.

SUPER AND SUB CONCEPT - All chords are centers - When voices in a chord are moved one
step up or down in any scale the resulting change becomes another center.
Below: The C Major scale stations showing all voices super and sub from their primary centers

Centers

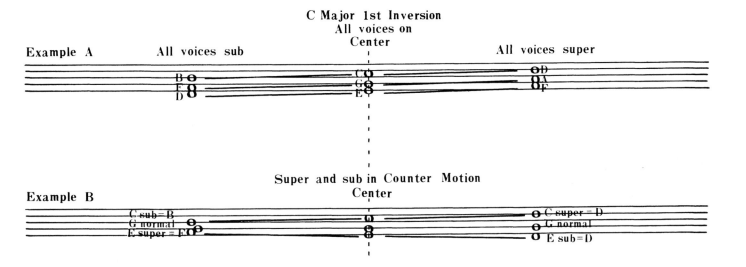

C Major 1st Inversion
All voices on
Center

Example A   All voices sub   All voices super

Super and sub in Counter Motion
Center

Example B

Even tho the triads shown in example "A" are the exact same notation as steps 7, 1, and 2, found
in the "C" Major scale in first inversions there is a concept difference:

The center triad is the original - triads number 7 and 2 are products of the super and sub process.

There is a distinction without a difference which is very similar to the enharmonic difference in notes
by the use of accidentals.

In the key of G# the tonic can't be called A♭ - G# can't be called the tonic of the key of A♭ - and
so on - they must be thought of differently and yet they are the same notes.

The super and sub principle can be applied to any chord voicing whether open or closed.

Naturally, any voicing in any key can be the center at any time - in other words, all the steps of
all the scales, arpeggios progressions, are centers.

The first inversion, first step of the C scale was chosen just as an example.

Example "B" shows the use of counter motion - experiment with various combinations of all kinds

SUPER AND SUB EXAMPLES

THESE PRINCPLES APPLY TO ALL KEYS

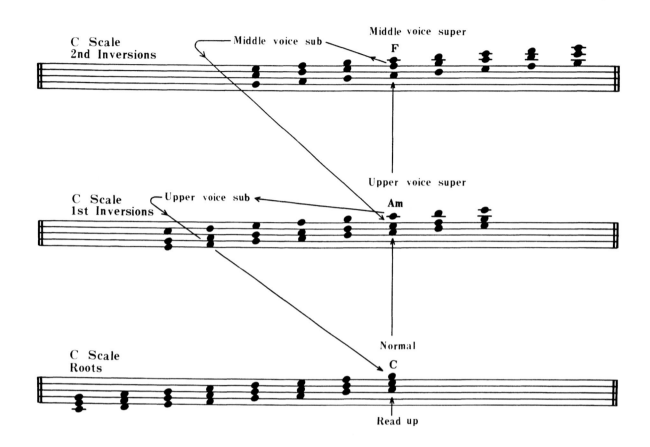

A 1st inversion triad with the upper voice sub becomes a root triad

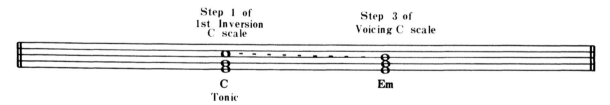

These Examples are all respective inversions of the C Major Scale

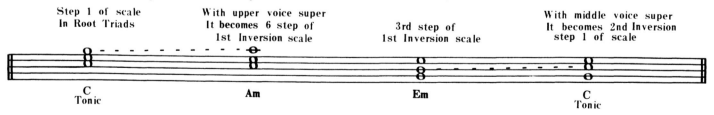

SUPER AND SUB SERIES

(REPETITION IN FINGERING)

It is very necessary in the early learning stage to show these studies in all keys, because, if shown in just one key to be transposed to all of the others, there is too much room for error. Wrong notes are very harmful particularly in the learning stage.

Every wrong note plants the germ of a bad habit because the ear retains the sound of the mistake, and therefore it becomes subconsciously influential; there is a very strong chance that the mistake will be repeated, and that is why any new study should be gone over very slowly and correctly.

The fingerings shown are good both directions. However, the choice of combinations when ascending or descending may be changed for the sake of ease to suit individual hands—experiment with them.

Hands are all different; what may feel comfortable to one pair may not feel as comfortable to others.

To the novice almost everything is awkward—even well-trained and well disciplined hands have certain fingering preferences. However, by working with difficult studies many of these preferences can be eliminated.

Voice motion is shown one direction in many of these studies for the sake of clarity, but should be reversed of course.

Repetition in fingering is necessary in all studies that are shown just descending or ascending, because they must be read in reverse to return. It is also necessary in order to become completely familiar with the many different teams and combinations of fingers available.

The mechanics employed can be condensed, broadened, elongated, distorted in all directions—they should become instinctive and ready.

STRING CHART
EXPLANATION OF THE STRING SET SYMBOLS:

A vertical or angled line thus— / —means "Set"—
The number in front of it is the set number—
The number after it indicates the number of strings employed—

EXAMPLE:
When the 1st-2nd-3rd-strings are employed the symbol is:
1/3—The first set of three—etc.
When the 1st-2nd-3rd-4th-strings are employed the symbol is:
1/4—The 1st set of four—etc.

THE BROKEN AND THE DIVIDED SETS:
Example:
When the 1st-2nd-4th-strings are employed (skipping the 3rd string) it is termed a broken set —the symbol is:
1/B3—The first set of broken three—etc.
When the order is reversed, (skipping the 2nd instead of the 3rd string) the word "broken" is used first, thus:
B1/3—The broken first set of three—etc.

When the 1st-2nd-4th-5th-strings are employed it is termed a divided set—the symbol is:
D1/4—The divided first set of four—etc.
When the 1st-3rd-5th-strings are employed the symbol is:
1/D3—The first set of divided three—and so on—
When the 1st-4th-strings are employed the symbol is:
A 1—
When the 2nd-5th-strings are employed the symbol is:
A 2—etc.
When the 1st-5th-strings are employed the symbol is:
B 1—etc.

NOTE
A symbol for the 1st-3rd-4th-6th-strings is not necessary because it would encompass all of the strings, therefore, the very notation dictates where and on what strings the notes are located.

STRING SET CHART
SYMBOLS:—STRINGS EMPLOYED—

1/2 . . . . 1st-2nd-
2/2 . . . . 2nd-3rd-
3/2 . . . . 3rd-4th-
4/2 . . . . 4th-5th-
5/2 . . . . 5th-6th-

1/3 . . . . 1st-2nd-3rd-
2/3 . . . . 2nd-3rd-4th-
3/3 . . . . 3rd-4th-5th-
4/3 . . . . 4th-5th-6th-

1/4 . . . . 1st-2nd-3rd-4th-
2/4 . . . . 2nd-3rd-4th-5th-
3/4 . . . . 3rd-4th-5th-6th-

1/5 . . . . 1st-2nd-3rd-4th-5th-
2/5 . . . . 2nd-3rd-4th-5th-6th-

THE BROKEN AND DIVIDED SETS:

1/B2 . . . . 1st-3rd-
2/B2 . . . . 2nd-4th-
3/B2 . . . . 3rd-5th-
4/B2 . . . . 4th-6th-

1/B3 . . . . 1st-2nd-4th-
2/B3 . . . . 2nd-3rd-5th-
3/B3 . . . . 3rd-4th-6th-

B1/3 . . . . 1st-3rd-4th-
B2/3 . . . . 2nd-4th-5th-
B3/3 . . . . 3rd-5th-6th-

1/B4 . . . . 1st-2nd-3rd-5th-
2/B4 . . . . 2nd-3rd-4th-6th-

B1/4 . . . . 1st-3rd-4th-5th-
B2/4 . . . . 2nd-4th-5th-6th-

1D/3 . . . . 1st-2nd-5th-
2D/3 . . . . 2nd-3rd-6th-

1/D3 . . . . 1st-3rd-5th-
2/D3 . . . . 2nd-4th-6th-
D1/3 . . . . 1st-4th-5th-
D2/3 . . . . 2nd-5th-6th-
D1/4 . . . . 1st-2nd-4th-5th-
D2/4 . . . . 2nd-3rd-5th-6th-

A1 . . . . 1st-4th-
A2 . . . . 2nd-5th-
A3 . . . . 3rd-6th-

B1 . . . . 1st-5th-
B2 . . . . 2nd-6th-

01 . . . . 1st-6th-

1st Inversion
Upper Voice Super

TRIAD VOICES SUPER
1st Inversion
Upper Voice Super

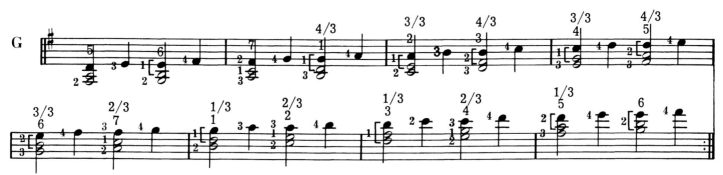

Alternating string sets as shown above and else where in these studies is necessary practise for building hand shift accuracy plus the ability to change sets either up or down any time or place within range

Variations to be applied to all triad scale exercises - upper - middle - lower voices super & sub reversed articulation

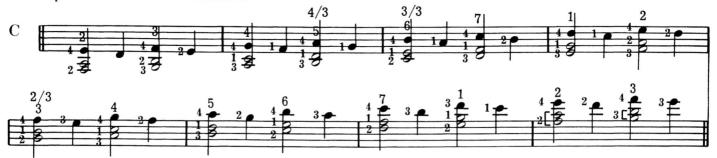

Alternate articulation patterns

Up three steps – back one step etc.

Reverse and double reverse patterns – practise in all keys – full range

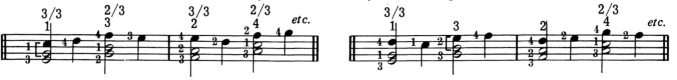

Vary the string set change overs in all of these studies – Vary the finger marking order for smoothness of continuity (short hand shifts) then long shifts etc.

Triad Voices Super - 12 Keys - Full Range
1st Inversion
Middle Voice Super   Same as 2nd inversion middle voice sub

MAJOR

169

TRIAD VOICES SUPER
1st Inversion
Middle Voice Super

Triad Voices Super
1st Inversion
Middle Voice Super

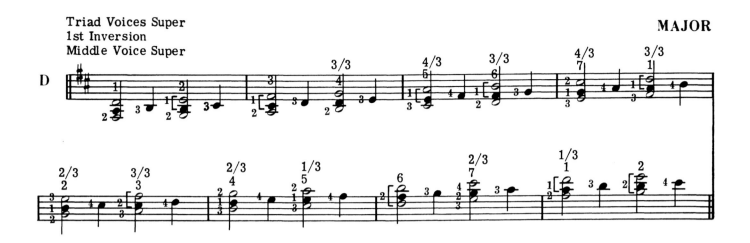

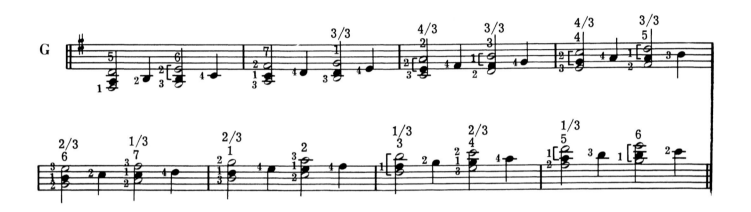

Variations - the reason for using 3 fingers to sound triads such as bar 1 is obvious in the Examples below

TRIAD VOICES SUPER - 12 keys - full range
1st Inversion
Lower Voice Super

C

F

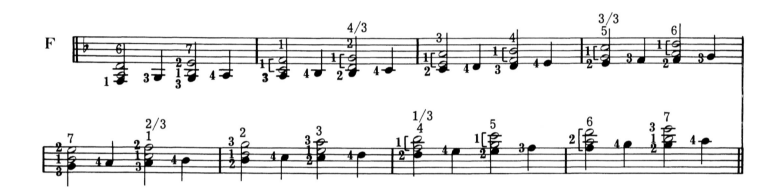

Bb

Eb

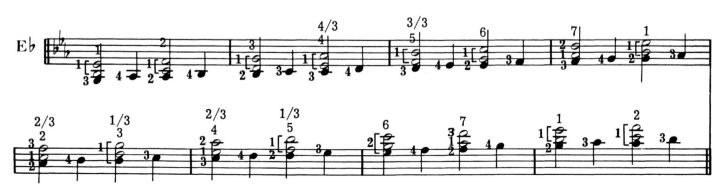

TRIAD VOICES SUPER
1st Inversion
Lower Voice Super

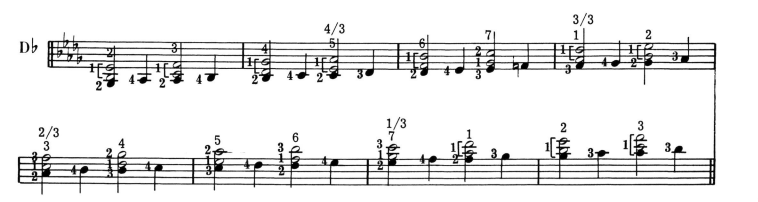

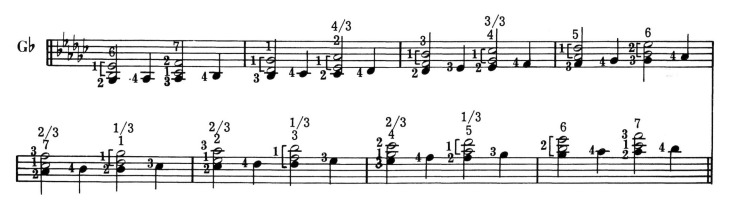

TRIAD VOICES SUPER
1st Inversion
Lower Voice Super

Apply all previous variations and formats

SUPER AND SUB SERIES

(FIRST INVERSION UPPER VOICE SUB DUPLICATION)
(EXAMPLES IN KEY OF "C")

First inversion triads with the upper voice motion sub are the exact same notation as root triads with the upper voice motion super—but of course the tonic first step triad will appear on a different numbered scale step as the examples show:

FIG. ONE   RESOLUTION = FIRST INVERSION, STEP ONE OF C SCALE

In figure one, the opening statement is the same as the *third* step of the root triad scale—
The resolution is the *first* step of the scale in first inversions—

FIG. TWO   RESOLUTION = FIRST INVERSION, STEP SIX OF C SCALE

In Fig. two, the opening statement is the same as the *first* step of the root scale—
The resolution is the *sixth* step of the first inversion scale—

This notational pattern of the scale will not be shown later on in the root position triad scales "super" because the duplication is unnecessary—this also applies to the harmonic and melodic minor scales in root triads with the upper voice super.

TRIAD VOICES SUB - 12 keys - full range
1st Inversion
Upper Voice Sub

As was mentioned earlier, notice how 1st inversion triads with the upper voice sub produce
Root triads on the 1st and 3rd beats of each measure

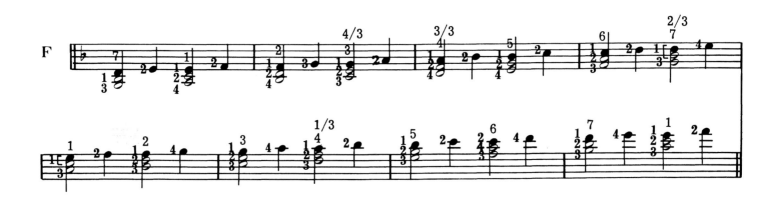

TRIAD VOICES SUB
1st Inversion
Upper Voice Sub

MAJOR

177

TRIAD VOICES SUB
1st Inversion
Upper Voice Sub

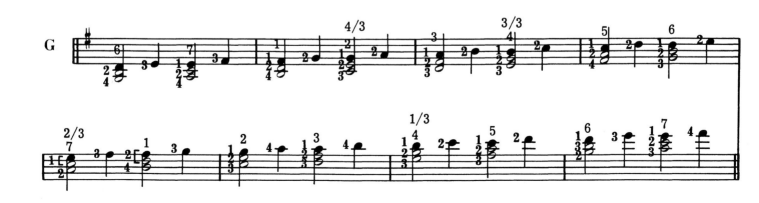

TRIAD VOICES SUB
1st Inversion
Middle Voice Sub

TRIAD VOICES SUB
1st Inversion
Middle Voice Sub

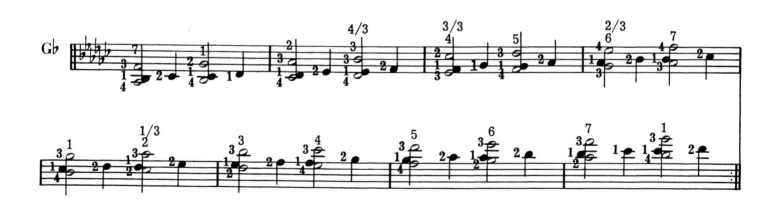

TRIAD VOICES SUB
1st Inversion
Middle Voice Sub

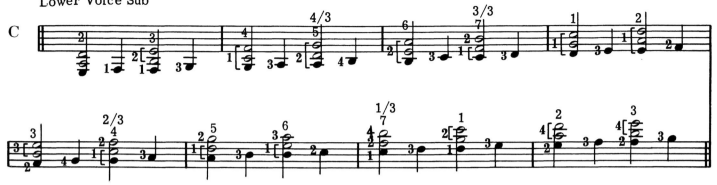

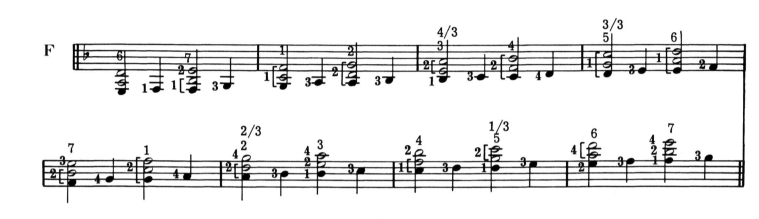

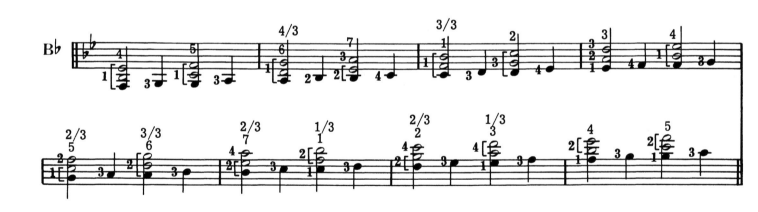

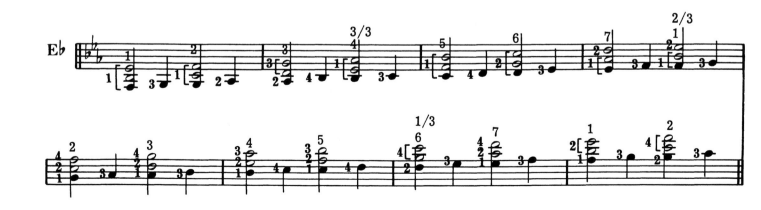

TRIAD VOICES SUB
1st Inversion
Lower Voice Sub

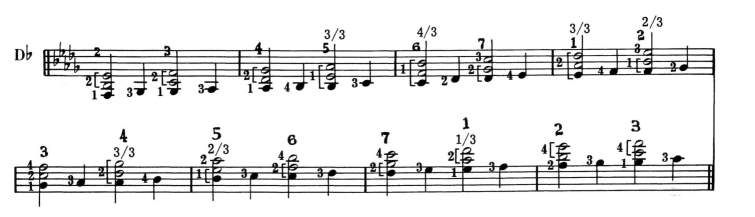

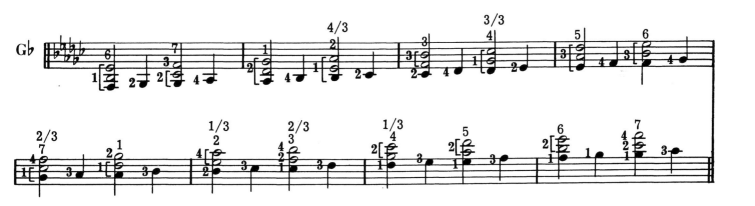

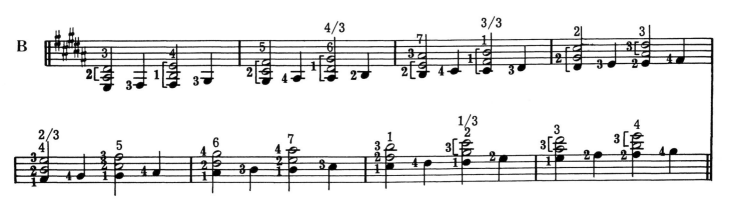

TRIAD VOICES SUB
1st Inversion
Lower Voice Sub

MAJOR

EXAMPLE AT RIGHT SHOWS REASON FOR USING
CROSS FINGERING AT TIMES - EMPLOY IT ELSEWHERE

THE FOUR STRING SPREAD FOR ARTICULATED TRIADS

TRIADS
SUPER   **UPPER VOICE ONLY**

SUPER

The following examples explain the mechanics of this type of articulation which is a very necessary part of the harmonic system. The two notes in the moving upper line of each step move from the tonic to the next diatonic step of the scale notationwise as usual, except that they are now sounded on two strings instead of the usual one, which makes a four string overall spread. In other words, the single step melodic interval is sounded on two strings—one note per string.

The timing of the articulating fingers must be very precise because the two notes in the moving line must not be heard ringing together; they must be very closely linked but not ring over each other. When properly executed just a trio of tones is heard, never four, unless a hold-over effect is desired.

The mechanics involved are as follows:

1st Finger
2nd Finger
3rd Finger

     The first joint of the second finger plays the double stop in flattened position (just the first joint flat, not the whole finger), and at the precise moment must be arched into hammer position while making certain that the middle note "A" on the D string is sustained—the note must be held full value. As the second finger becomes arched, the first finger, which must be held ready, sounds the note "E" on the B string. The action of raising the flattened first joint of the second finger to arched position and lowering the first finger must be simultaneous and smooth as though they were mechanically linked together and therefore unable to be either up or down at the same time.
     The mechanical linkage thought line between articulating fingers applies to all four-string spread-articulated triads regardless of the finger attitudes—arched, double stops etc.

The letter above the second note denotes the extra string used—X's denote the voice motion.

TRIAD VOICES SUPER - Examples of Articulated Triads Employing 4 Strings
1st Inversion - this type of articulation will appear often in the Minor studies, upper voice super.

Examples

A smoothness is gained by a mixture of both the 4 string articulation and the 3 string fingering in various places as this example shows

Sixth step of the **A** Major scale - this key was chosen because of comfortable range for both types of articulation

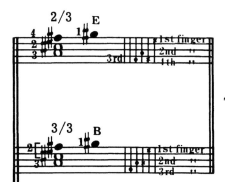

The articulating fingers must work as a precision team

Practice pattern for each step - repeat the articulated line over and over while sustaining the whole notes full value - employ both fingerings

Practice the articulation reversed as shown below

Mixture - 1 octave of the C Major scale

TRIAD VOICES SUPER
1st Inversion
Upper Voice Super

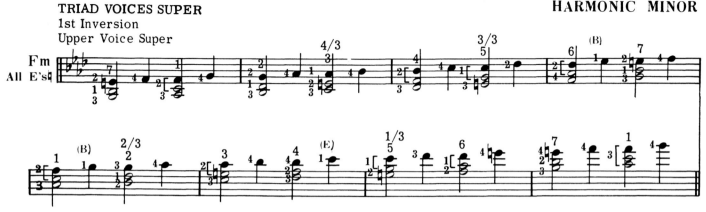

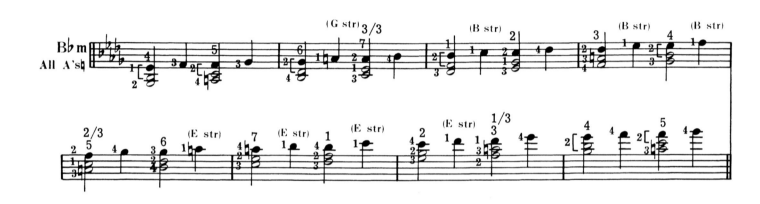

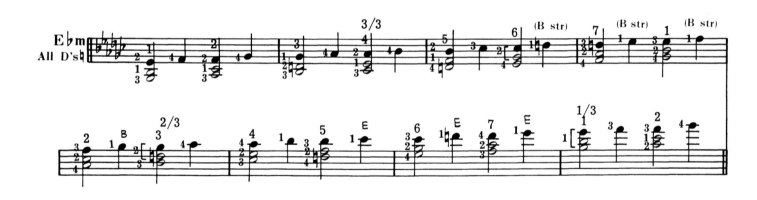

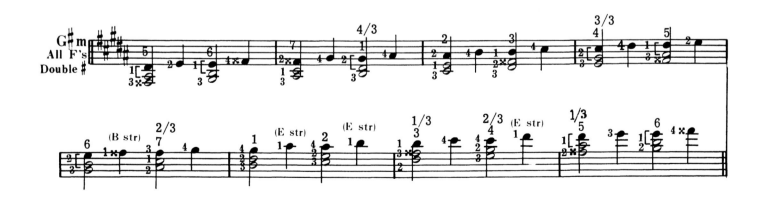

TRIAD VOICES SUPER
1st Inversion
Upper Voice Super

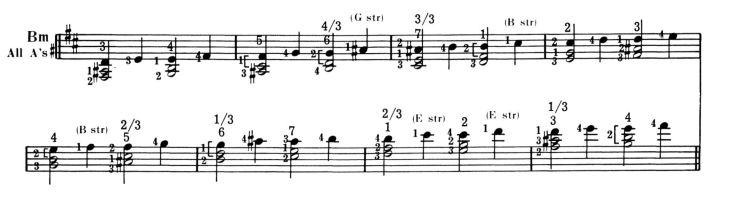

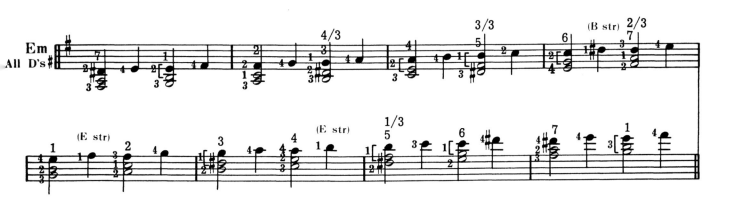

TRIAD VOICES SUPER
1st Inversion
Middle Voice Super   same as 2nd inversion middle voice sub

TRIAD VOICES SUPER
1st Inversion
Middle Voice Super

Triad Voices Super
1st Inversion
Middle Voice Super

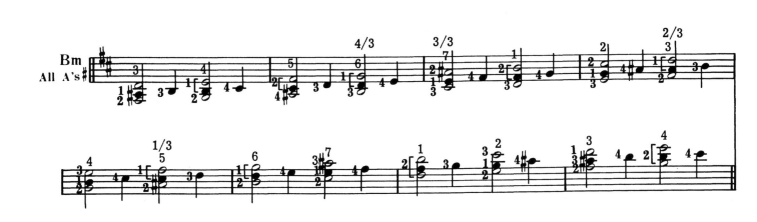

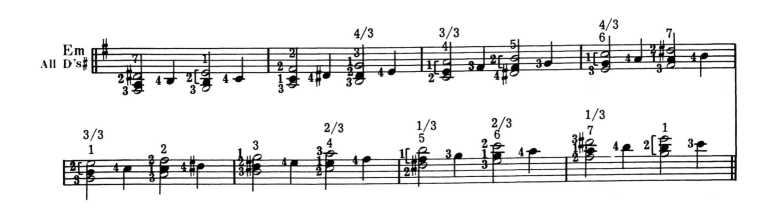

TRIAD VOICES SUPER
1st Inversion
Lower Voice Super

TRIAD VOICES SUPER
1st Inversion
Lower Voice Super

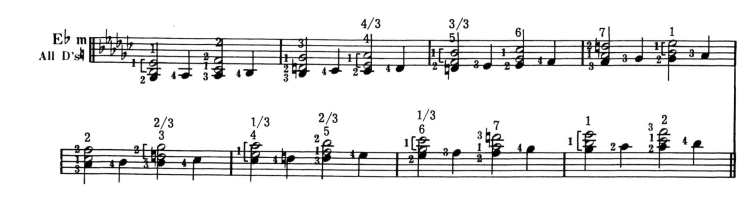

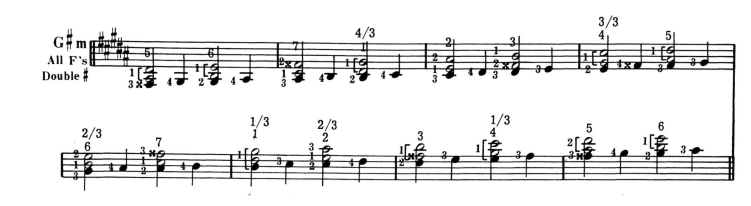

TRIAD VOICES SUPER
1st Inversion
Lower Voice Super

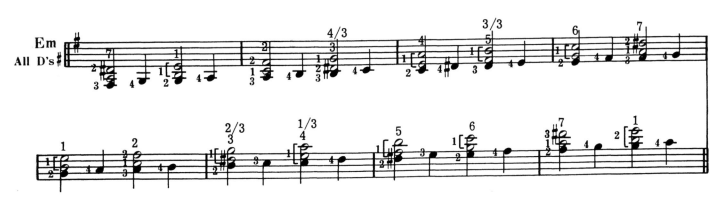

Apply all Previous Formats

The following notation is identical to root triads with the upper voice motion super, therefore, only the middle and lower voice motion super will be shown later on in the root triad section—

TRIAD VOICES SUB - 12 keys - full range   HARMONIC MINOR
1st Inversion
Upper Voice Sub

TRIAD VOICES SUBER - 12 keys - full range
1st Inversion
Upper Voice Super

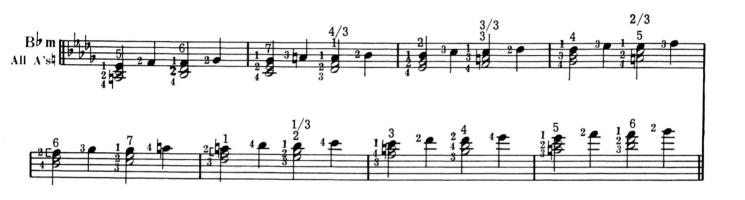

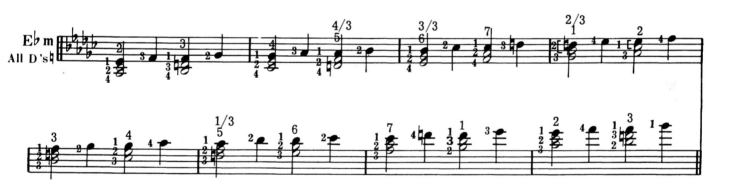

TRIAD VOICES SUB
1st Inversion
Upper Voice Sub

TRIAD VOICES SUB
1st Inversion
Middle Voice Sub

TRIAD VOICES SUB
1st Inversion
Middle Voice Sub

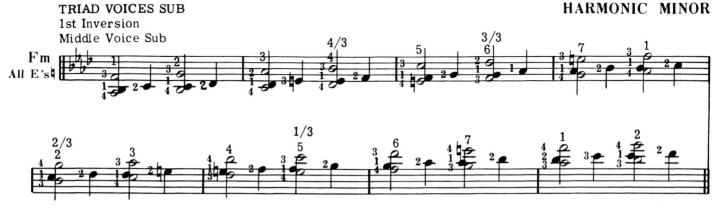

TRIAD VOICES SUB
1st Inversion
Middle Voice Sub

TRIAD VOICES SUB
1st Inversion
Lower Voice Sub

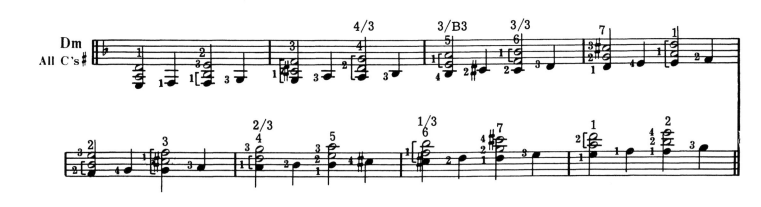

TRIAD VOICES SUB
1st Inversion
Lower Voice Sub

TRIAD VOICES SUB
1st Inversion
Lower Voice Sub

Apply All Previous Formats

204

TRIAD VOICES SUPER
1st Inversion- A letter above a note indicates a string not in the set marking
Upper Voice Super

TRIAD VOICES SUPER
1st Inversion-
Upper Voice Super

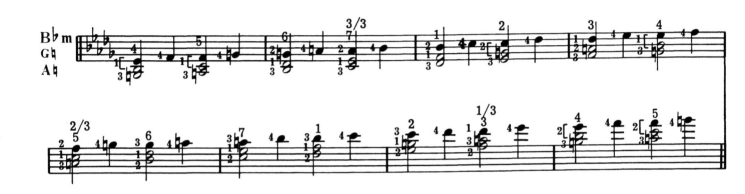

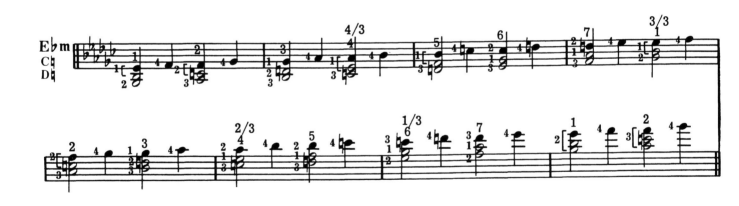

TRIAD VOICES SUPER
1st Inversion
Upper Voice Super

TRIAD VOICES SUPER
1st Inversion
Middle Voice Super   Same as 2nd inversion middle voice sub

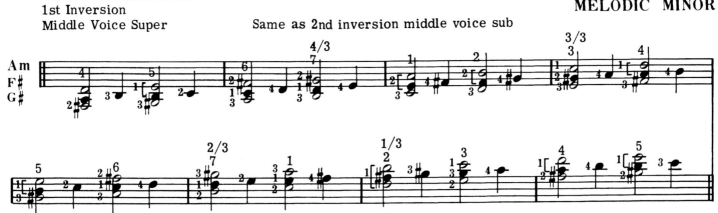

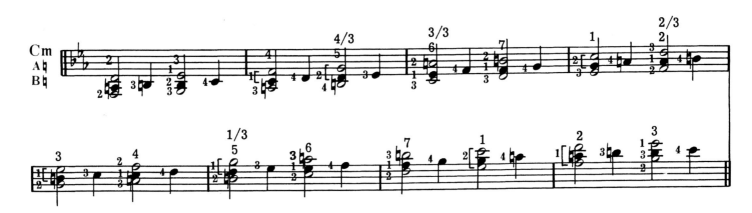

TRIAD VOICES SUPER
1st Inversion
Middle Voice Super

TRIAD VOICES SUPER
1st Inversion
Lower Voice Super

TRIAD VOICES SUPER
1st Inversion
Lower Voice Super

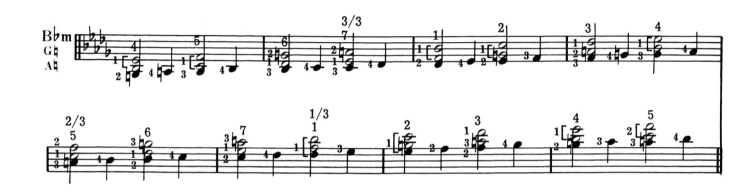

TRIAD VOICES SUPER
1st Inversion
Lower Voice Super

Apply all Previous Formats

TRIAD VOICES SUB
1st Inversion
Upper Voice Sub

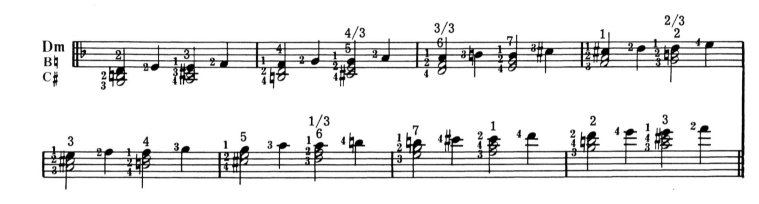

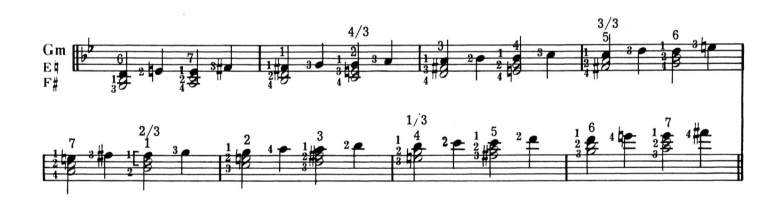

TRIAD VOICES SUB
1st Inversion
Upper Voice Sub

TRIAD VOICES SUB
1st Inversion
Upper Voice Sub

TRIAD VOICES SUB
1st Inversion

Middle Voice Sub

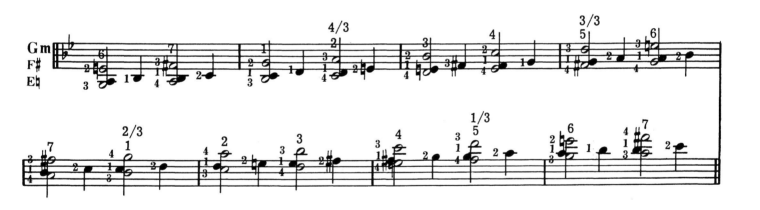

TRIAD VOICES SUB
1st Inversion

Middle Voice Sub

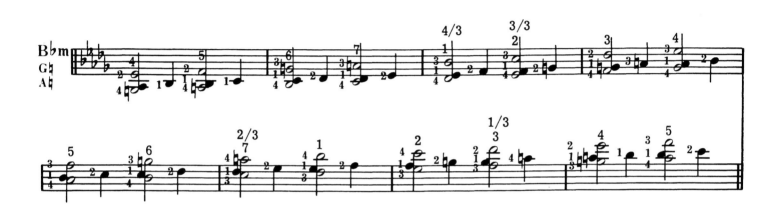

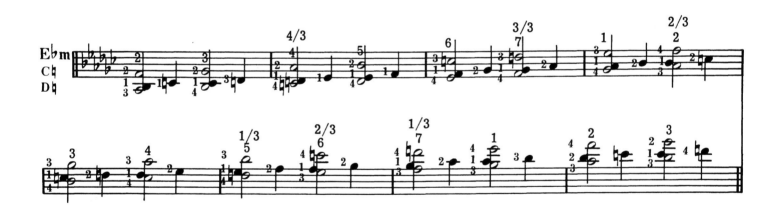

TRIAD VOICES SUB
1st Inversion

Middle Voice Sub

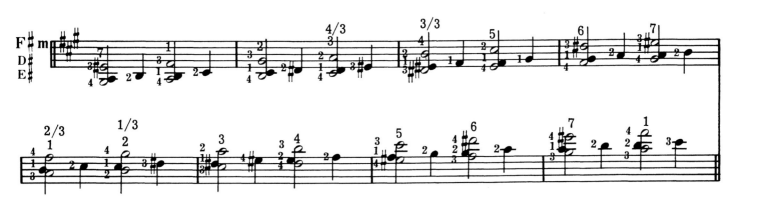

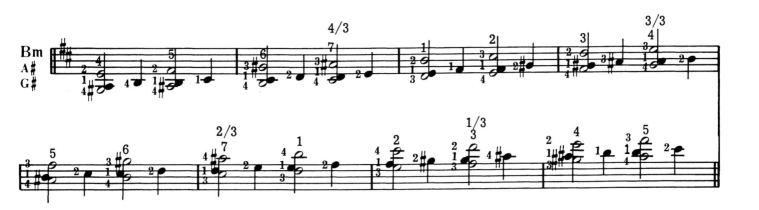

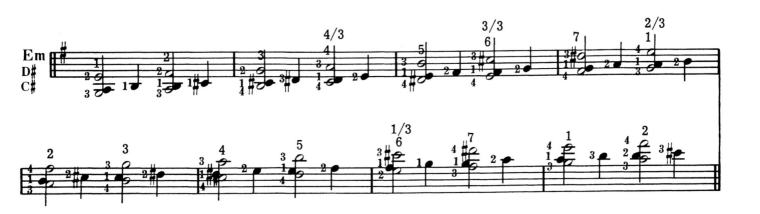

TRIAD VOICES SUB
1st Inversion
Lower Voice Sub

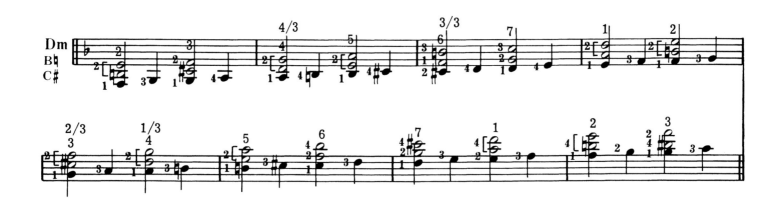

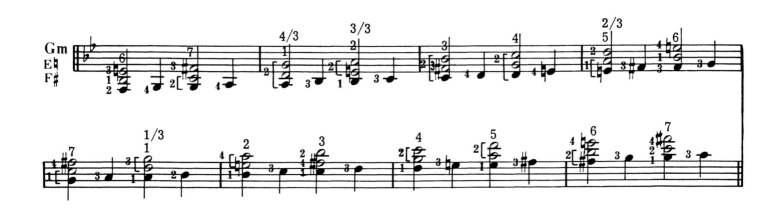

TRIAD VOICES SUB
1st Inversion
Lower Voice Sub

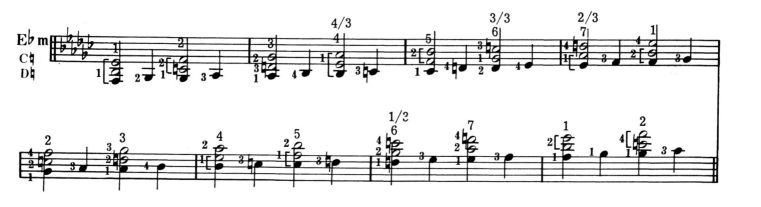

TRIAD VOICES SUB
1st Inversion
Lower Voice Sub

Apply all previous formats

SUPER AND SUB SERIES
SECOND INVERSION TRIADS

To conserve space the following studies will have an upper, middle, lower voice change every four keys of the cycle of fifths instead of the usual twelve. However, the fingering for all of the keys will be represented in this way:

There is no difference in finger mechanics between the keys of: F sharp/G flat and the Key of "G" natural—"F" natural; C sharp/D flat and the Key of "D" natural—"C" natural etc., etc., except that most of the time there is a one step difference in the range of the scale on each end.

When a step is lost on the low end because of running out of fingerboard a step is always added on the high end, and vice versa.

Analyze the different types of mechanics employed and apply them to other harmonic situations and notations.

TRIAD VOICES SUPER - 4 keys each voice = 12 keys - full range
2nd Inversion - from here on in this series note stems are deleted

Upper Voice Super

C

F

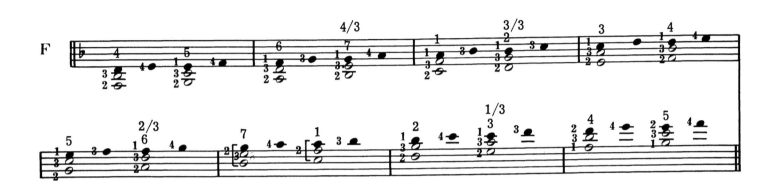

B♭

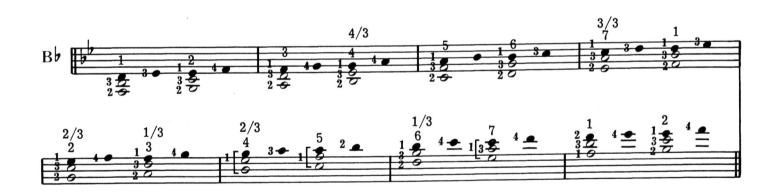

E♭

TRIAD VOICES SUPER
2nd Inversion

Middle Voice Super

Ab

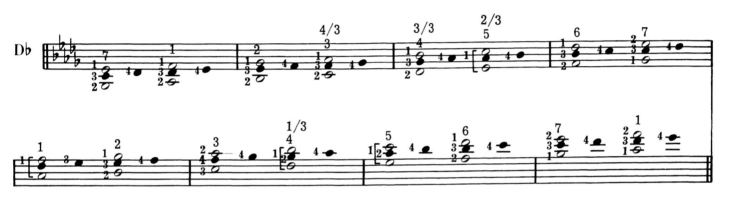

Db

Gb

B

TRIAD VOICES SUPER
2nd Inversion
Lower Voice Super -same notation as root/lower voice sub-

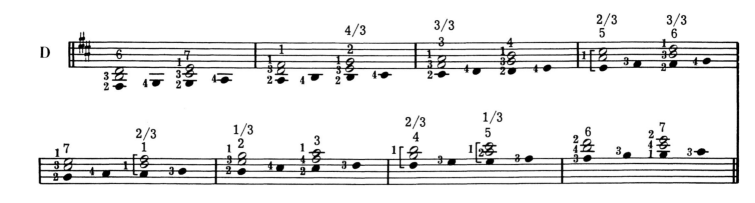

The 2nd inversion lower voice super is the same notation as root triads lower voice sub, but the tonic step is in a different place-take the above G scale as an example: When applying it as a root scale the 3rd step is the tonic chord=D-B-G-therefore, 3 becomes 1-this applies to all keys Major or Minor

TRIAD VOICES SUB - 4 keys each - full range
2nd Inversion
Upper Voice Sub

Middle voice sub - the next four keys are duplicates - refer back to 1st inversions "middle voice super" for the keys of A♭-D♭-G♭-B- but remember to think 2nd inversion middle voice sub - keep them separate in thought

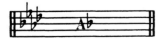
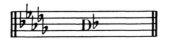
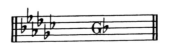
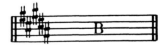

TRIAD VOICES SUB
2nd Inversion
Lower Voice Sub

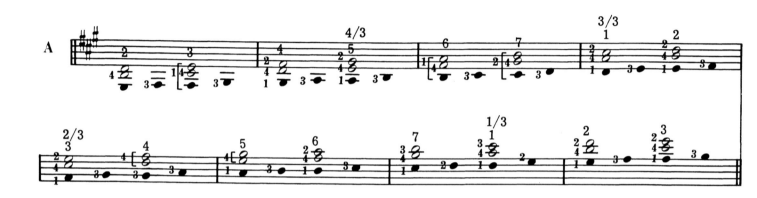

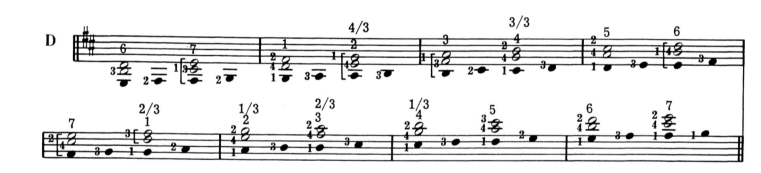

Apply all previous formats

TRIAD VOICES SUPER - 4 keys each - full range
2nd Inversion
Upper Voice Super

Middle Voice Super

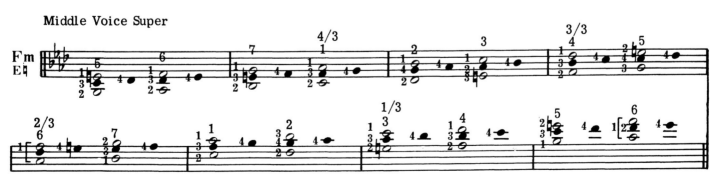

TRIAD VOICES SUPER
2nd Inversion
Middle Voice Super

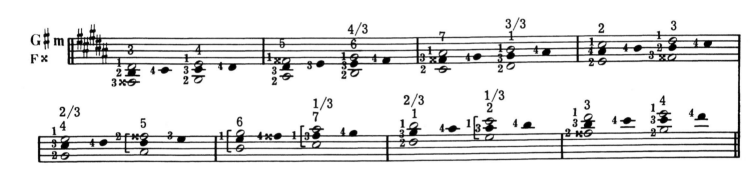

Lower Voice Super - same notation as root lower voice sub -

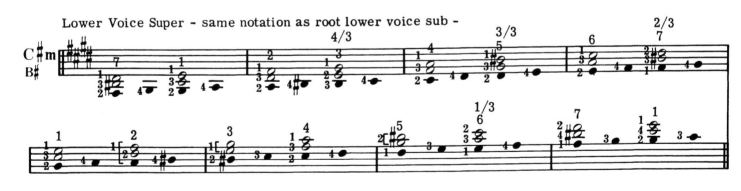

TRIAD VOICES SUPER
2nd Inversion
Lower Voice Super - same as root sub -

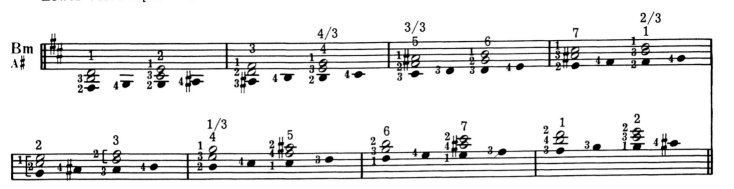

Apply all previous formats

2nd Inversion
Upper Voice Sub

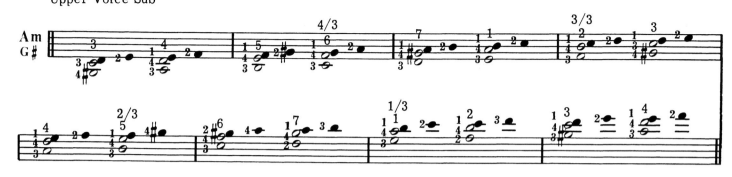

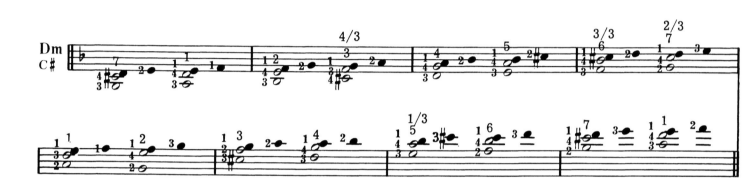

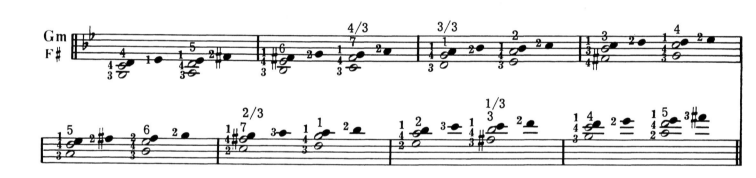

Middle Voice Sub - same notation as 1st inversion super - refer back for next 4 keys

2nd Inversion
Lower Voice Sub

TRIAD VOICES SUPER - 4 keys each = 12 keys - full range
2nd Inversion - descend in relative Major
Upper Voice Super

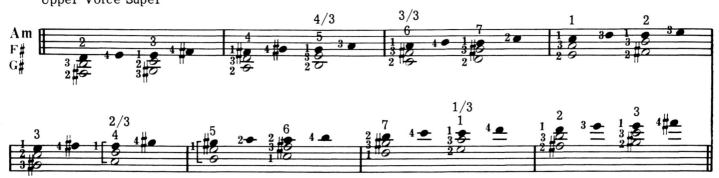

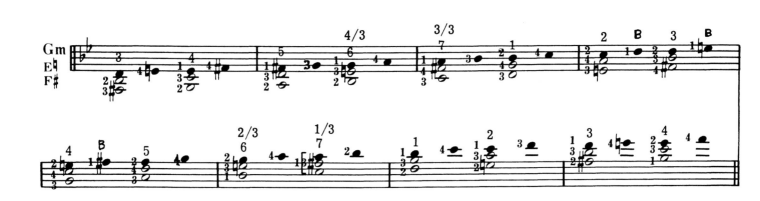

TRIAD VOICES SUPER
2nd Inversion
Middle Voice Super

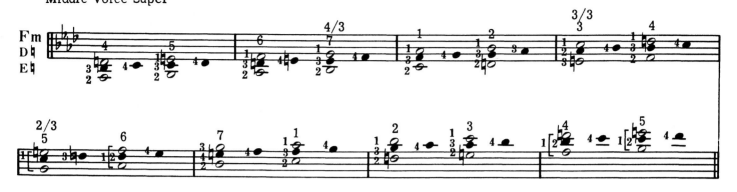

TRIAD VOICES SUPER - 4 keys each
2nd Inversion
Middle Voice Super

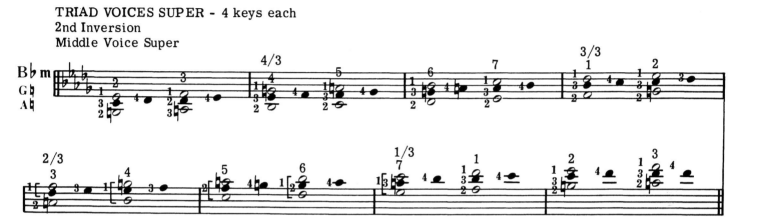

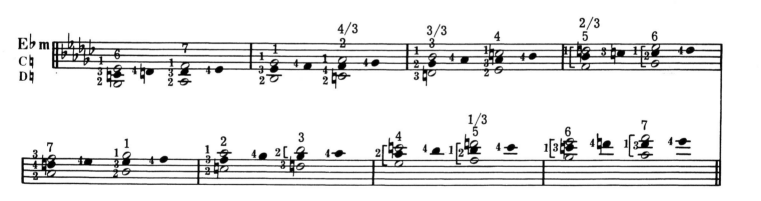

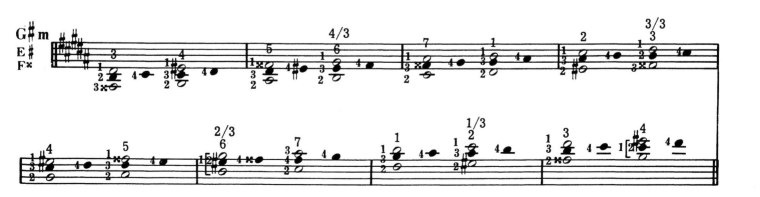

TRIAD VOICES SUPER - 4 keys each
2nd Inversion
Lower Voice Super

Reverse the voice motion

2nd Inversion
Upper Voice Sub

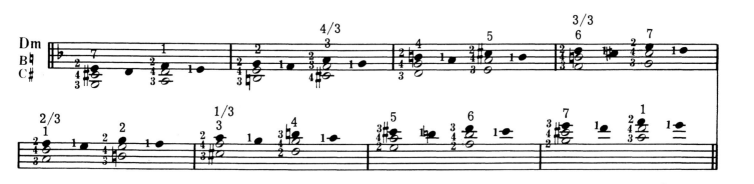

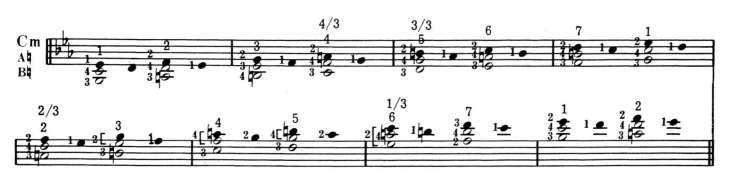

Middle Voice Sub – same notation as 1st inversion middle voice super – refer back for the next 4 keys

TRIAD VOICES SUPER AND SUB
2nd Inversion
Lower Voice Sub

Variation - Exercises such as this develop independent finger control - study carefully

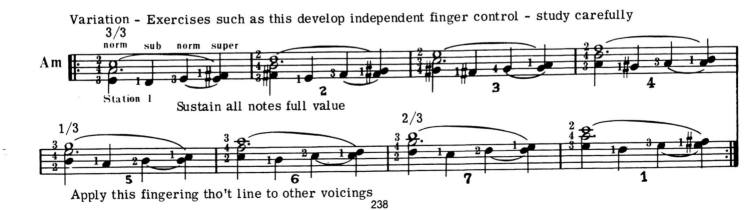

Sustain all notes full value

Apply this fingering tho't line to other voicings

238

SUPER AND SUB SERIES
ABOUT ROOT POSITION TRIADS

When the upper or lower voices in any of the triads move away from the other two voices as in: upper voice sub, or lower voice super, extended finger spreads result.

In root triads most of the reaches are quite great. However, these voicings must be included no matter how impractical they may appear, because by design they belong to the family of basic triads. In other words, the voice motion cannot be ignored just because the reaches become extended. The same treatment for all the triads is necessary in order to keep the continuity of the concept—what is done to one must be done to the others.

The super and sub series would not be complete unless the first, second, and root triads received the very same treatment.

The voice motion must be presented, understood, and evaluated in original form whether easily playable or not.

There are alternative fingerings for these very long spreads which are compromises.

The difference between an original notation and a compromise fingering is noticeable harmonically when the tones are sustained, but when the moving voice is detached and sounded separately there is no notation difference. The original form as written is the ideal objective of course. However, the compromise notations and fingerings adhere in essence to the musical form closely enough to be highly usable, but don't require the extra long reaches.

The mechanics of the following compromise fingering examples should be applied to all of the scales in all keys—all triads—all stations—

SUPER AND SUB SERIES
ROOT TRIADS

The root position triads super and sub are shown in the Key of "C" only because by this time the format of the concept should be established enough for transposition to all of the other keys.

Remember to always transpose slowly, correctly. Also, when transposing these studies adhere to the cycle of fifths to keep the continuity.

Because of notational duplication some of the forms in the following studies will just be referred to.

Practice all scale forms, major and minor, first station to first staion, second station to second station, third station to third station, etc. Both directions, up, and down.

To do this, some register changes have to be made because of running out of fingerboard.

This pattern helps to build mental agility while building physical dexterity. The ability to be able to pick up a phrase or a progression (etc.) an octave higher or lower is a golden asset.

239

Triad Voices super and sub - Root triads-the examples below are all C minor root triads

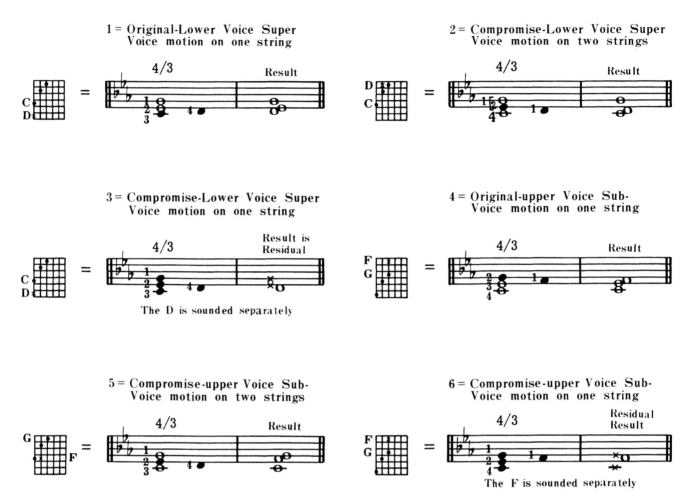

1 = Original-Lower Voice Super
Voice motion on one string

2 = Compromise-Lower Voice Super
Voice motion on two strings

3 = Compromise-Lower Voice Super
Voice motion on one string

The D is sounded separately

4 = Original-upper Voice Sub-
Voice motion on one string

5 = Compromise-upper Voice Sub-
Voice motion on two strings

6 = Compromise-upper Voice Sub-
Voice motion on one string

The F is sounded separately

Apply these mechanisms to the 1st and second inversions also

These examples show the first three scale steps and relate directly to the examples above by number

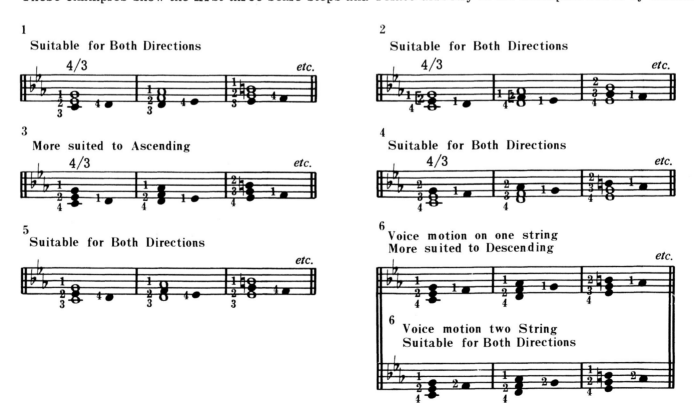

1
Suitable for Both Directions

2
Suitable for Both Directions

3
More suited to Ascending

4
Suitable for Both Directions

5
Suitable for Both Directions

6
Voice motion on one string
More suited to Descending

6
Voice motion two String
Suitable for Both Directions

TRIAD VOICES SUPER AND SUB
Root Positions - Root triads super and sub are shown in one key only, but must be placed in all keys
Upper Voice Super - Major & Harmonic Minor

Root Upper Voice Super is same as 1st inversion upper voice sub - refer back for Major & Minor

Middle Voice Super

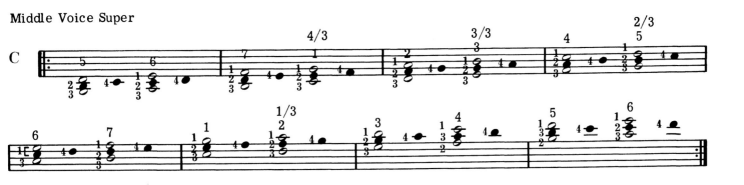

Lower Voice Super

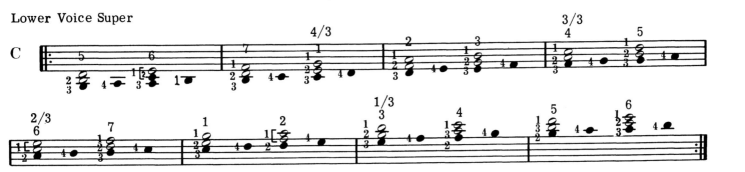

Middle Voice Super - Harmonic Minor - Upper voice super is same as 1st inversion sub - refer back

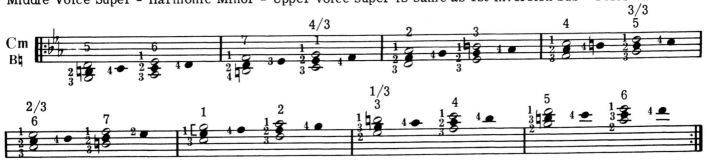

Lower Voice Super

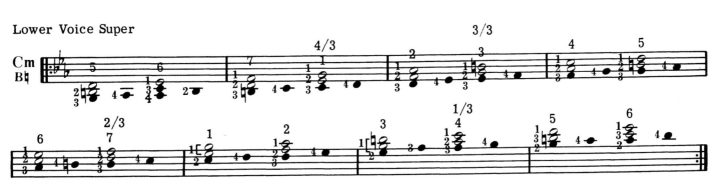

TRIAD VOICES SUPER AND SUB
Root Positions
Upper Voice Sub - Major & Harmonic Minor

Middle Voice Sub

Root Lower Voice sub is the same as 2nd inversion lower voice super - Refer back for Major

Upper Voice Sub - Harmonic Minor

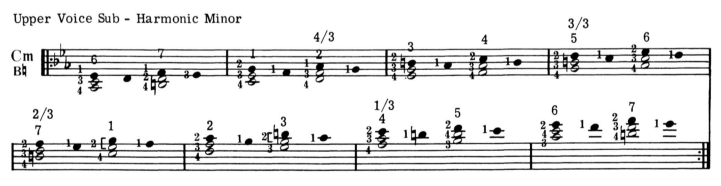

Middle Voice Sub

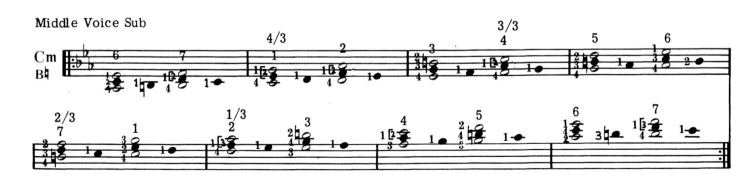

Root Positions Upper Voice Super

Same as 1st inversion sub - refer back

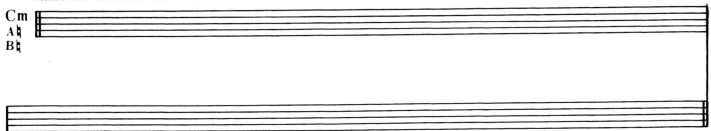

Middle Voice Super

Lower Voice Super

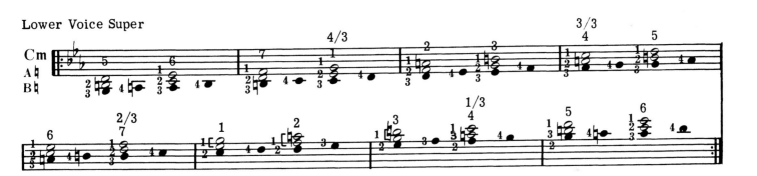

Upper Voice Sub

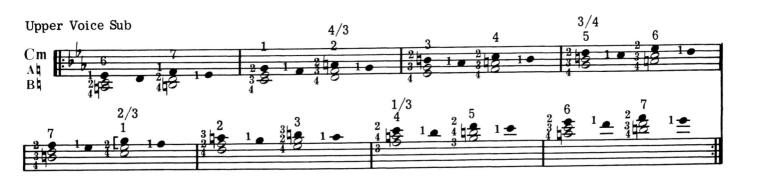

Middle Voice Sub

Lower Voice Sub is same as 2nd inversion lower voice super - refer back

Super & Sub Series - Triads - Open Voicing = 3rd down 1 octave -   Key of C
1st Inversions   Extend These Scales
Upper Voice Super

C

Cm

Middle

C

Cm

Lower

C

Cm
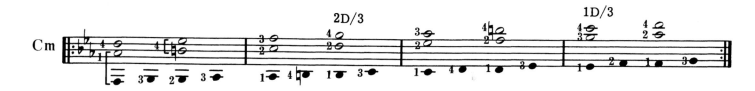

Upper Voice Sub

C

Cm

Super & Sub Series - Triads - Open Voicing
1st Inversion
Middle Voice Sub

MAJOR and MINOR

C

Cm

Many times individual fingers are used where double stops and small barres could be employed;
when voice motion continues, double stops wont work - practise both ways-mix fingerings and
sets - change cross over points etc.

lower voice sub

C

Cm

5th Down 1 Octave Upper Voice Super

C

Cm

Middle

C

Cm

Lower

C

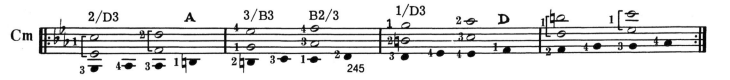

Cm

245

Super & Sub Series - Triads - Open Voicing = 5th Down 1 Octave MAJOR and MINOR
1st Inversion
Upper Voice Sub

Middle

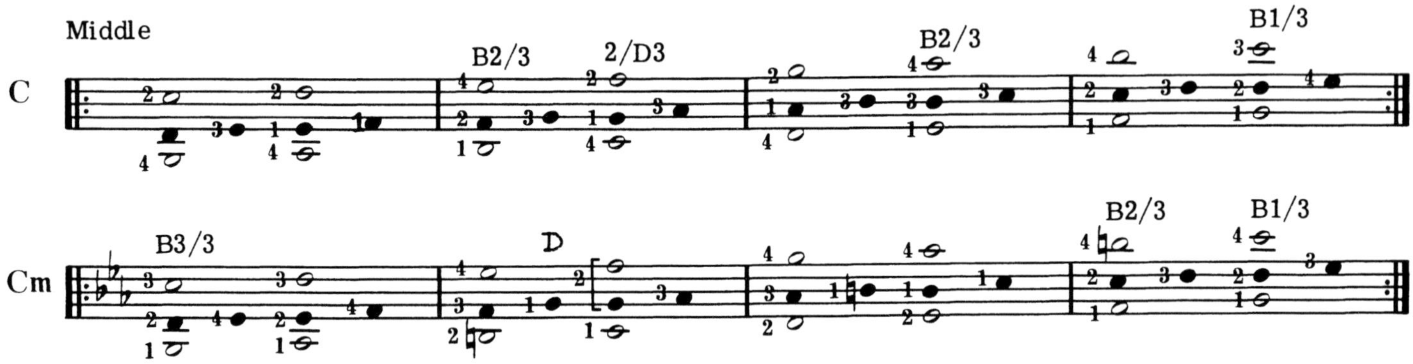

Lower

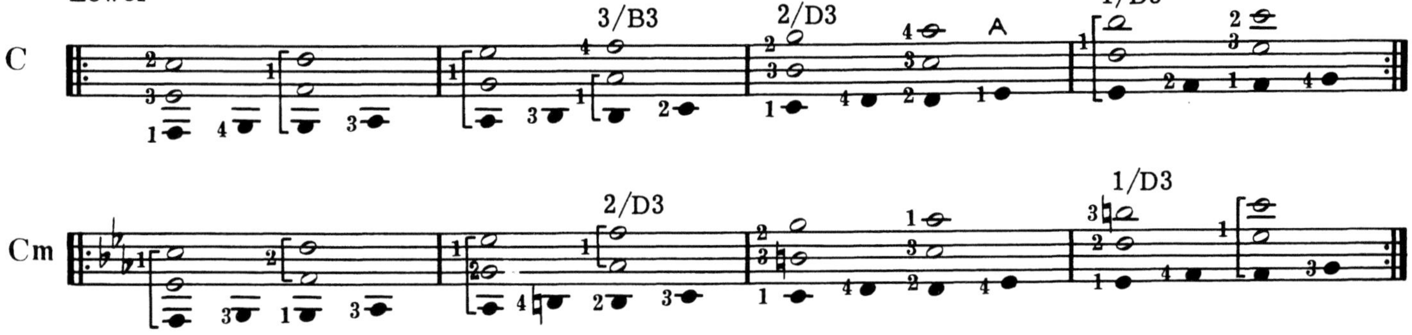

2nd Inversion Upper Voice Super - Tonic Down 1 Octave

Middle

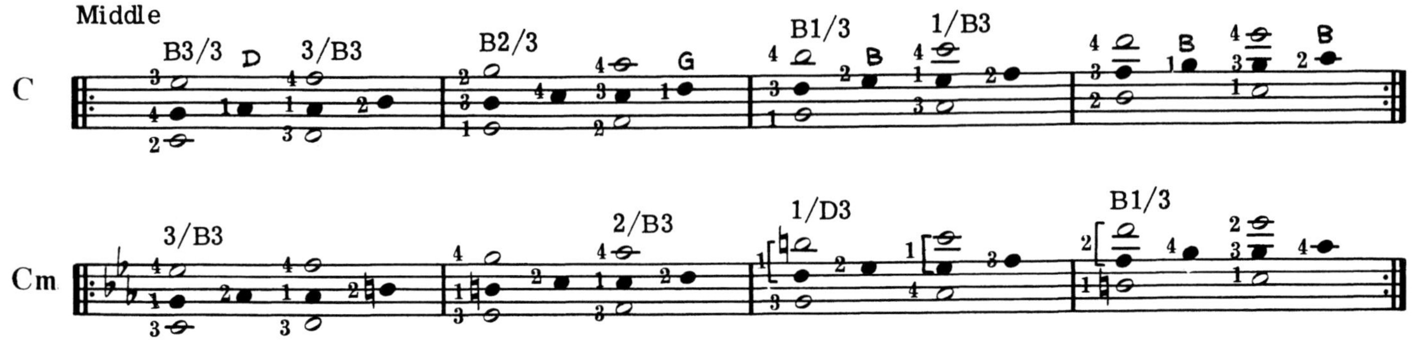

Super & Sub Series
2nd Inversion
Lower Super

Open Voicing

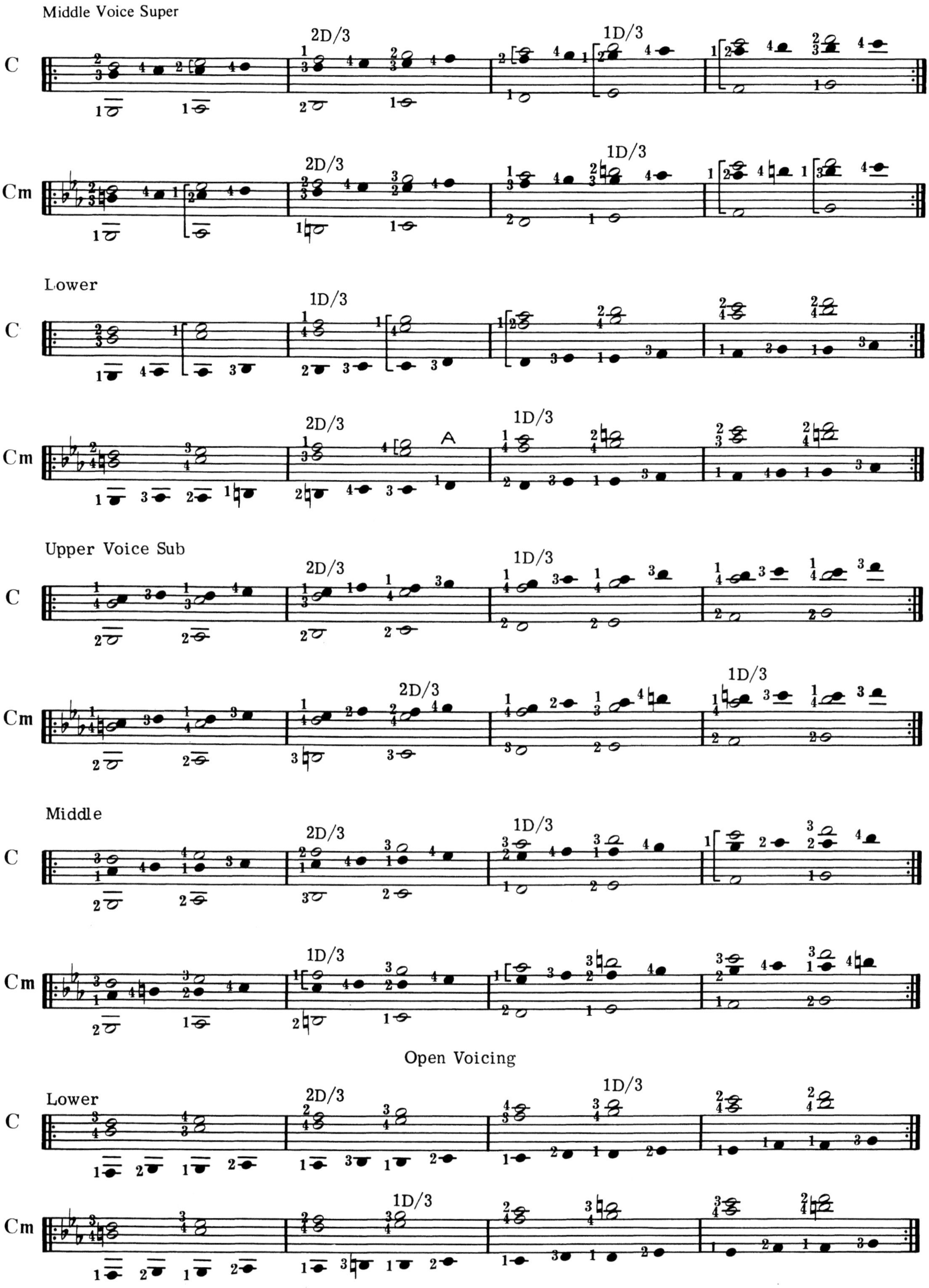
Middle Voice Super
C
2D/3
1D/3
Cm
2D/3
1D/3
Lower
C
1D/3
Cm
2D/3
A
1D/3
Upper Voice Sub
C
2D/3
1D/3
Cm
2D/3
1D/3
Middle
C
2D/3
1D/3
Cm
1D/3
Open Voicing
Lower
C
2D/3
1D/3
Cm
1D/3

In all of these studies, it's very necessary to note the subtle differences in shapes and notation when changing from one set to another - some shapes and fingerings will be identical, but the notation is not.

SUPER AND SUB SERIES
MULTI-VOICE MOTION

Two voices in motion while sustaining a third, requires a few long reaches. If at first some of the reaches are too great, it is permissible to treat the half note as though it were a quarter note—to let go of the half note after sounding the triad. However, endeavor to sustain the half note full value.

Hearing and understanding the voice motion even though it is slightly disconnected is just as important as being able to physically sound all of the notes as written, because the harmonic knowledge is necessary.

From the creative aspect, abundant technique is useless, unless it is coupled with harmonic knowledge and a sound understanding of voice motion.

The ability to recognize, analyze, and assimilate melodic and harmonic voice motion is very necessary to the art of improvisation.

249

Super and Sub series examples of multi - voice motion - Major and Minor

Both Upper Voices in Super Motion

1st Inversions
C

Cm

Upper and Lower Voices in Super Motion

C

Cm

Both Upper Voices in Super Motion

2nd Inversions
C

Cm

Upper and Lower Voices in Super Motion

C

Cm

Super and Sub series examples of multi - voice motion - Major and Minor

Both Upper Voices in Super Motion

Place all of these examples in all keys

Middle and Lower Voices in Super Motion

Middle and Lower Voices in Sub Motion

Upper and Lower Voices in Super Motion

Upper and Middle Voices in Super Counter Motion

251

Super and Sub series examples of multi - voice motion - Major and Minor

Counter and Parallel Motion

C

Cm

Both Lower Voices in Sub Motion

1st
Inversion
C

Cm

Upper Voice Motion Sub - Middle Voice Motion Super

C

Cm

Super and Sub Series - closed to open voicing in progressive steps - 2 bars equal one station key of C Major - there are many other fingerings and string combinations - experiment with them

Place in all keys - Major and both Minors - sustain the middle voice - reverse the direction of voice motion = open to closed

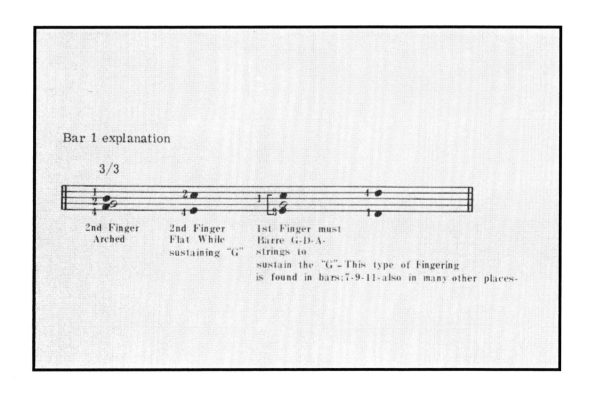

Bar 1 explanation

3/3

2nd Finger Arched

2nd Finger Flat While sustaining "G"

1st Finger must Barre G-D-A- strings to sustain the "G"-This type of fingering is found in bars:7-9-11-also in many other places-

Super and Sub series
key of C Minor - all B's natural

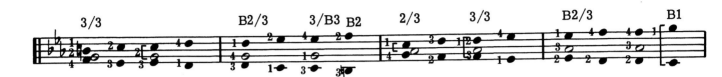

See Major Instructions

The examples below are two steps from both scales, first Major then Minor employing Various fingering mechanisms repeatedly - apply this format to all of the steps - be aware of the similies

Repeating steps of any study over and over is very good for finger control

Super and Sub series

- Examples of left hand finger team articulation -
The deleted middle voice of the 1st inversion triad that begins each station is marked with a cross = +
In example 1, the entire one octave scale is played on string sets shown in bar 1

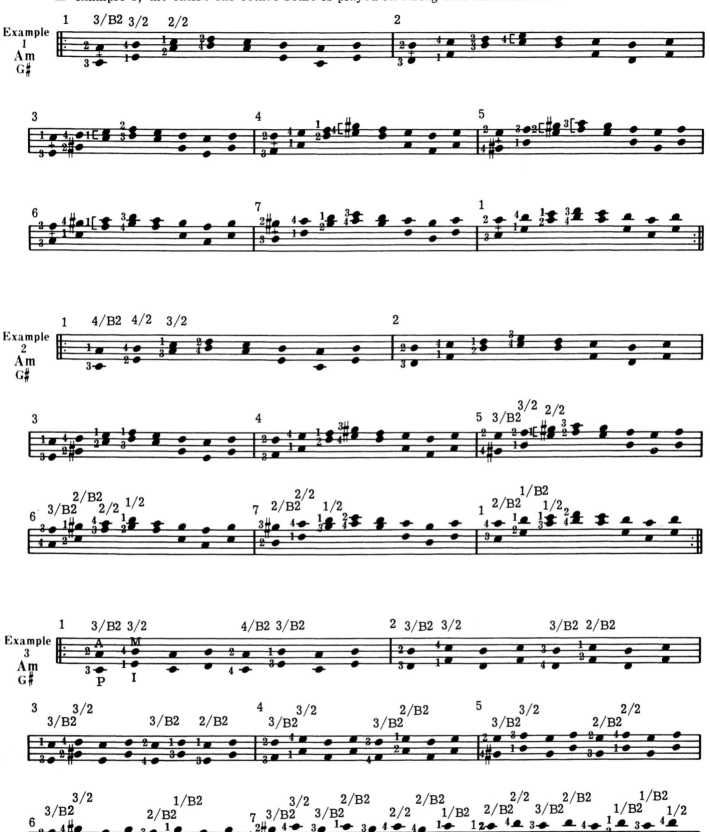

Apply these team principles to the melodic Minor - mixed Minor - Major etc.

SUPER AND SUB
HARMONIC VARIATIONS ON BASIC TRIAD SCALES

The following examples show a sixteen step independent chromatic upper voice against variations in the lower voices.

The eight intermediate triads that connect the normal steps employ the use of accidentals on notes in super and sub position—the normal steps are numbered.

Analyze the line of thought—experiment with the idea—then place them in all keys.

TRIAD VOICES SUPER AND SUB - contrary multi-voice motion - chromatic upper voice -
Super & Sub Notes Sharp & Flat

Major

Major

Major

Minor

Minor

End of the Super & Sub Series

256

GENERAL REMARKS

The art of accomplishing long reaches is based on relaxed power and control—not a large hand.

VISUALIZING

HARMONIC

SITUATIONS

Every harmonic/melodic situation has form, shape, a particular geographic appearance, as was mentioned in the foreword.

It is very important to recognize these shapes—use the eyes, train the mind's eye to distinguish the subtle differences in harmonic schematics, the vast variety of plans, the layout of the total fingerboard.

Many different harmonic modes occupy the same space, one on top of the other, in layers. Learn to see and hear them as though they were laid out in individual colors and tones.

THE MAGIC OF THE

CHROMATIC SCALE

The chromatic scale contains every known scale, arpeggio, chord, harmonic situation, theme, etc. in all twelve keys.

This is why I believe the chromatic scale is to music what the alphabet is to literature, and the colors to art.

Chromatics will be stressed frequently throughout my books because that is where the complete control of the instrument lies.

For the sake of clarity, many of the studies in these books are written using accidentals instead of key signatures because they don't belong to any particular key.

All accidentals, except key signatures, are canceled by a bar line, unless tied over. And of course, accidentals of one register do not apply to another register.

STRING CHART
EXPLANATION OF THE STRING SET SYMBOLS:

A vertical or angled line thus— / —means "Set"—
The number in front of it is the set number—
The number after it indicates the number of strings employed—

EXAMPLE:
When the 1st-2nd-3rd-strings are employed the symbol is:
1/3—The first set of three—etc.
When the 1st-2nd-3rd-4th-strings are employed the symbol is:
1/4—The 1st set of four—etc.

THE BROKEN AND THE DIVIDED SETS:
Example:
When the 1st-2nd-4th-strings are employed (skipping the 3rd string) it is termed a broken set —the symbol is:
1/B3—The first set of broken three—etc.
When the order is reversed, (skipping the 2nd instead of the 3rd string) the word "broken" is used first, thus:
B1/3—The broken first set of three—etc.

When the 1st-2nd-4th-5th-strings are employed it is termed a divided set—the symbol is:
D1/4—The divided first set of four— etc.
When the 1st-3rd-5th-strings are employed the symbol is:
1/D3—The first set of divided three—and so on—
When the 1st-4th-strings are employed the symbol is:
A 1—
When the 2nd-5th-strings are employed the symbol is:
A 2—etc.
When the 1st-5th-strings are employed the symbol is:
B 1—etc.

NOTE
A symbol for the 1st-3rd-4th-6th-strings is not necessary because it would encompass all of the strings, therefore, the very notation dictates where and on what strings the notes are located.

STRING SET CHART
SYMBOLS:—STRINGS EMPLOYED—

1/2 . . . . 1st-2nd-
2/2 . . . . 2nd-3rd-
3/2 . . . . 3rd-4th-
4/2 . . . . 4th-5th-
5/2 . . . . 5th-6th-

1/3 . . . . 1st-2nd-3rd-
2/3 . . . . 2nd-3rd-4th-
3/3 . . . . 3rd-4th-5th-
4/3 . . . . 4th-5th-6th-

1/4 . . . . 1st-2nd-3rd-4th-
2/4 . . . . 2nd-3rd-4th-5th-
3/4 . . . . 3rd-4th-5th-6th-

1/5 . . . . 1st-2nd-3rd-4th-5th-
2/5 . . . . 2nd-3rd-4th-5th-6th-

THE BROKEN AND DIVIDED SETS:

1/B2 . . . . 1st-3rd-
2/B2 . . . . 2nd-4th-
3/B2 . . . . 3rd-5th-
4/B2 . . . . 4th-6th-

1/B3 . . . . 1st-2nd-4th-
2/B3 . . . . 2nd-3rd-5th-
3/B3 . . . . 3rd-4th-6th-

B1/3 . . . . 1st-3rd-4th-
B2/3 . . . . 2nd-4th-5th-
B3/3 . . . . 3rd-5th-6th-

1/B4 . . . . 1st-2nd-3rd-5th-
2/B4 . . . . 2nd-3rd-4th-6th-

B1/4 . . . . 1st-3rd-4th-5th-
B2/4 . . . . 2nd-4th-5th-6th-

1D/3 . . . . 1st-2nd-5th-
2D/3 . . . . 2nd-3rd-6th-

1/D3 . . . . 1st-3rd-5th-
2/D3 . . . . 2nd-4th-6th-
D1/3 . . . . 1st-4th-5th-
D2/3 . . . . 2nd-5th-6th-
D1/4 . . . . 1st-2nd-4th-5th-
D2/4 . . . . 2nd-3rd-5th-6th-

A1 . . . . 1st-4th-
A2 . . . . 2nd-5th-
A3 . . . . 3rd-6th-

B1 . . . . 1st-5th-
B2 . . . . 2nd-6th-

01 . . . . 1st-6th-

CHROMATIC TRIADS—

1st–2nd–ROOT

The exercises in this group of studies, as in others, occasionally require some long left hand shifts. They are intentional—the intent being to show where the duplicates are located no matter how distant they may be.

The studies also contain smoother fingerings, string set changes, and locations. However, in practice the benefits derived from changing fingering, string sets, plus jumping great distances are manyfold.

There may be duplicates closer and easier to get to, but the only way to successfully make long difficult shifts is to intentionally practice them.

Practice of this nature teaches relationships, locations, orientation, duplication, alternatives, etc.

As in billiards, if one learns to handle the "hard shots," the easier shots almost take care of themselves.

Other reasons are: for agility, variety, dexterity, logics, and last but not least, challenge.

When performing it is desirable of course, to select logical locations and fingerings for tonal sonority, continuity of phrase, and overall smoothness.

These principles apply to everything in my books and the principles of one exercise should be applied to all of the others.

CHROMATIC TRIADS

PEDAL BASS

In this group of studies the basic triads chromatically go through a cycle against a pedal bass, where in one octave all possible relationships intervalwise of triad and bass result.

It doesn't matter what bass note is pedaled because in one chromatic octave all of the relationships are met.

Lowered fifths, sevenths, ninths, major and minor sevenths, pure majors and minors, etc. occur.

Because of range and reach it becomes necessary to change registers of both bass and triad at times.

Changing registers does not change the harmonic meaning nor does it spoil the progressional continuity or affect.

When the bass is raised an octave the voicing becomes more closed etc. The result is the same when the triad is raised or lowered an octave while the bass remains stationary.

All through my books the emphasis will be on "chromatics". Chromatics, chromatics, and more chromatics.

MAJOR & MINOR SERIES

CONTRARY MOTION, CHROMATICS

Chromatic triads with pedal bass "C" - 1 octave range

MAJOR

Chromatic triads with alternating bass -C-G- 1 octave

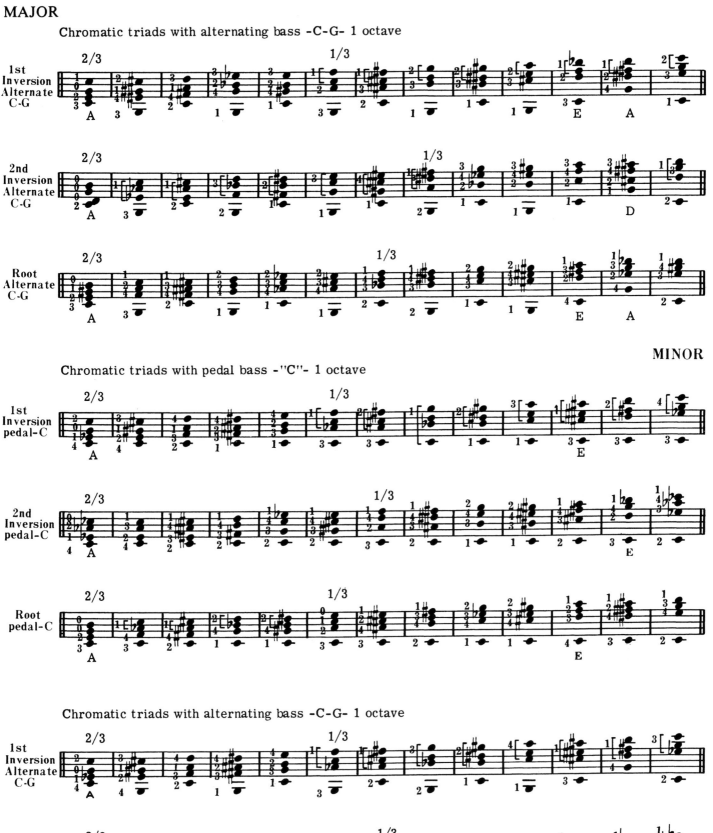

1st Inversion Alternate C-G

2nd Inversion Alternate C-G

Root Alternate C-G

MINOR

Chromatic triads with pedal bass -"C"- 1 octave

1st Inversion pedal-C

2nd Inversion pedal-C

Root pedal-C

Chromatic triads with alternating bass -C-G- 1 octave

1st Inversion Alternate C-G

2nd Inversion Alternate C-G

Root Alternate C-G

Chromatics - Triads - Root - 1st - 2nd inversion descending chromatically while the lower line descends thru the circle of fifths, the symbols to the left of the notes name the basic triads - the symbols above name the four note results, a minus sign and number indicates a missing interval.

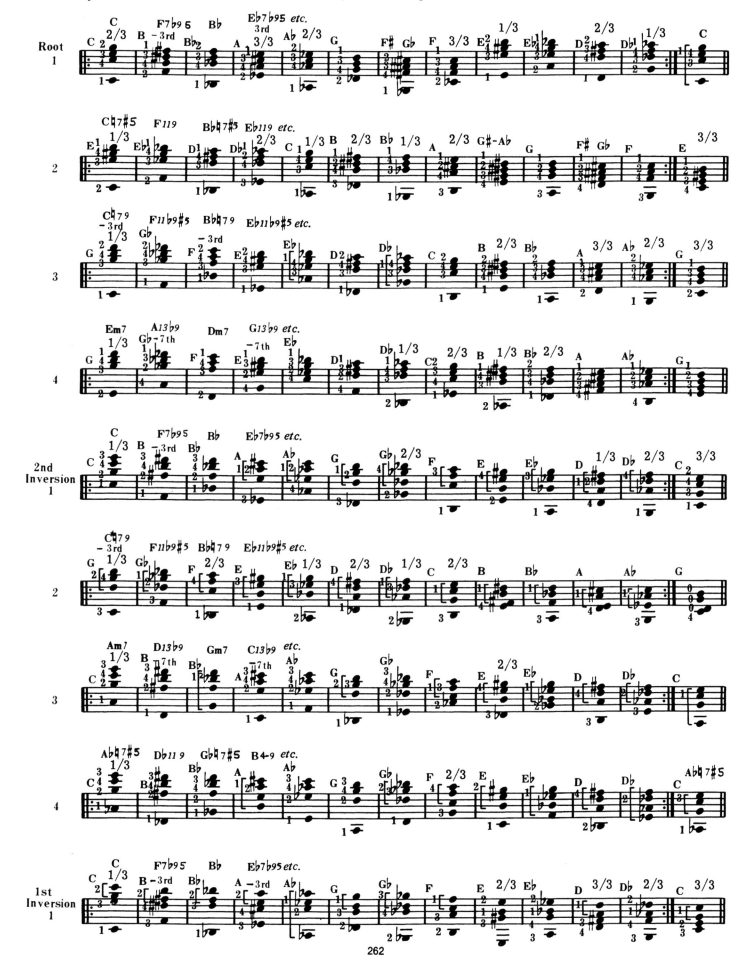

Chromatics - Triads -

Two inversions alternately - also variations

THE FIFTH FINGER PRINCIPLE

is the knack of sounding two notes simultaneously that are not located on the same fret, with one finger.

This is accomplished by angling the finger slightly across the fingerboard, so that the upper inside part of the third joint of the first finger sounds the upper note while the tip of the finger sounds the lower note.

The first finger must be arched slightly so that the fleshy inner part of the third joint can be gently pressed downward to depress the 1st string.

With practise the third joint of the first finger will be able to sound notes on the second string also.

Examples below;

Begin with figure one and three

Fig. 1

Fig. 2

Fig. 3

Fig. 4

Sustain the G & F
Fig. 5

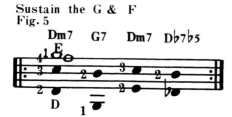

Fig. 6

264

Chromatics - Triads - Root - 1st-2nd inversions desending chromatically (While the lower line descends thru the circle of fifths) in two measure cycles

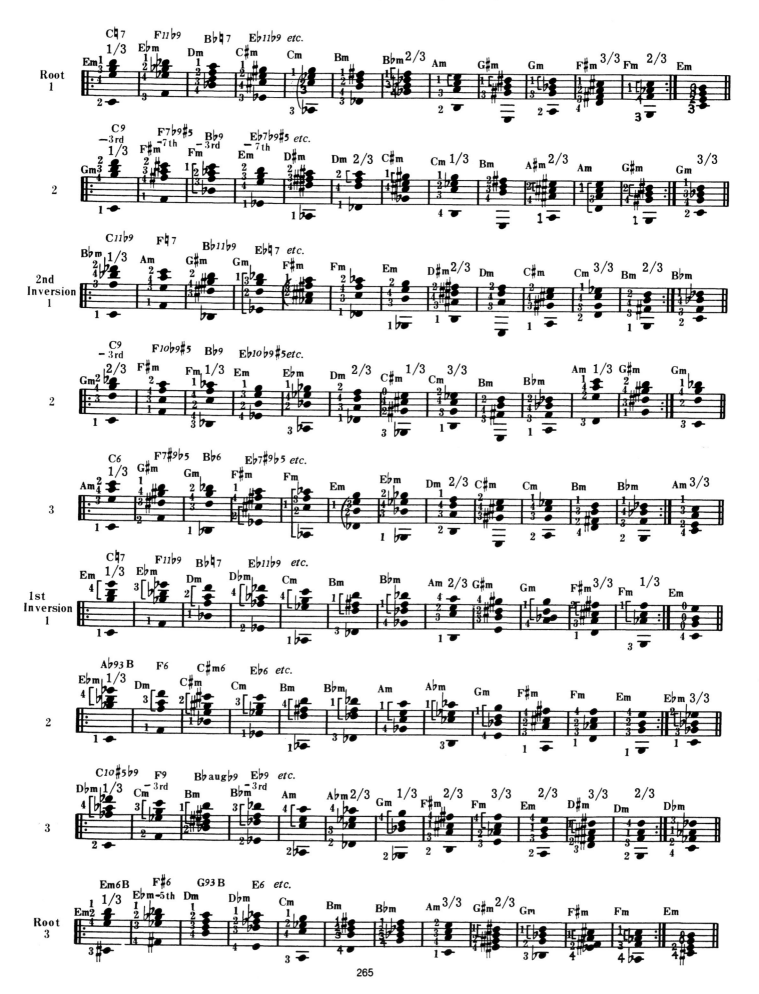

265

Chromatics Triads   -two inversions alternately-
Circle 5   -Minor-

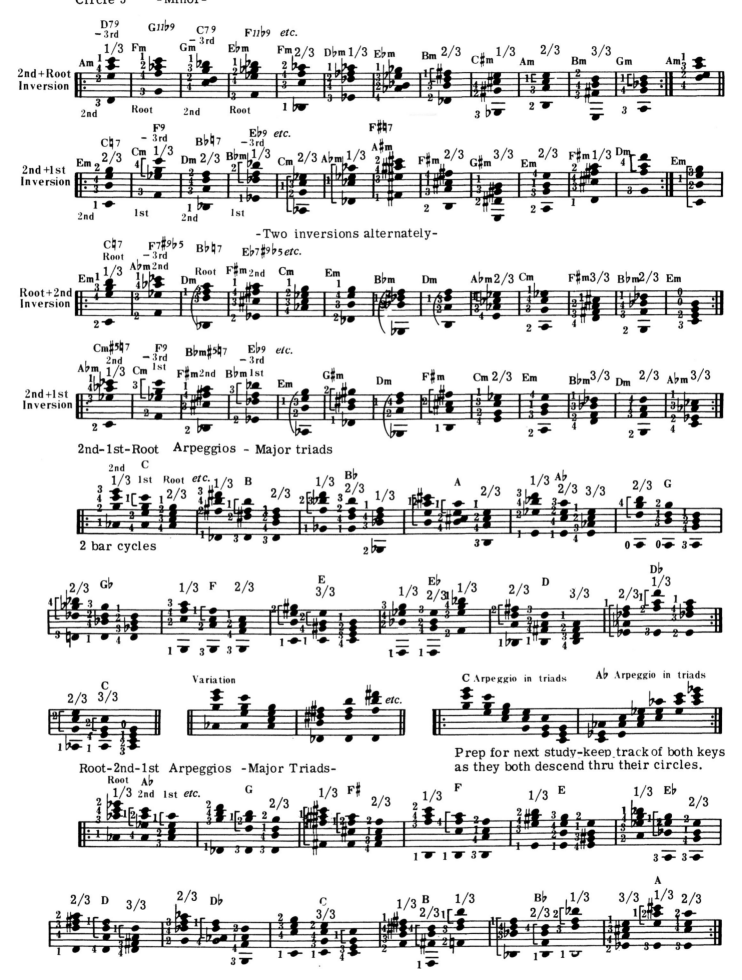

2nd-1st-Root   Arpeggios - Major triads

2 bar cycles

Prep for next study-keep track of both keys
as they both descend thru their circles.

Root-2nd-1st Arpeggios -Major Triads-

CIRCLE 5—

Triads are
in 2 Bar
Cycles
2nd 1st
Root
Root 2nd
1st   4 note chords are in 4 bar cycles

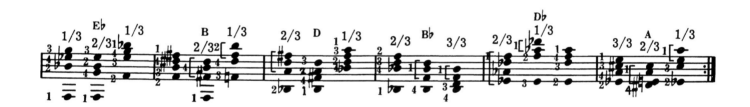

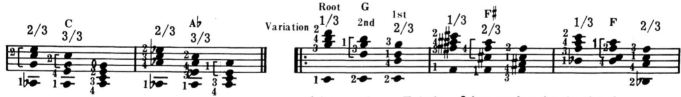

1 bar cycles = Triads - 2 bar cycles 4 note chord

Chromatics - Triads   2nd-Root-1st - in two keys with alternating bass -Major-
Circle 5

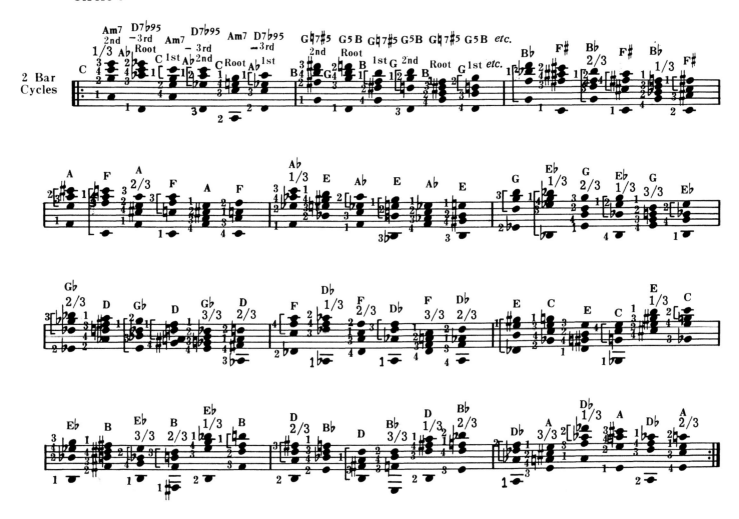

Variations

Reversed
Bass

Chromatic
Bass
starting
on B

Chromatic
Bass
starting
on B♭

Triad arpeggios descending chromatically forming progressions because of chromatic bass

3 bar cycles

Notice whole tone break in chromatic bass line in 2nd bar of each cycle to avoid unwanted dissonance

Cycle 5

Examples

Chromatics - Triads   1st-Root-2nd   Arpeggios - Minor triads -

MINOR

Circle 5

Chromatics - Triads   Root-2nd-1st   Arpeggios - Minor triads

Circle 5

CHROMATICS

This minor form is naturally dissonant in the fourth bar of each cycle because of the lowered thirds in the minor triads. However, the resulting information is necessary musically and technically.

Traditional configurations are well known; nontraditional configurations must be found, explored, analyzed, and well practiced.

The hands must be trained to be ready for the unusual. Experiment with the unusual formations; endeavor to carry the ideas further—extend the line of thought.

It is not good to shy away from dissonances. Let tones clash at times; continual consonant harmony soon becomes very boring.

Chromatics - Triads   2nd-1st-Root - Arpeggios   -Minor-
Circle 5

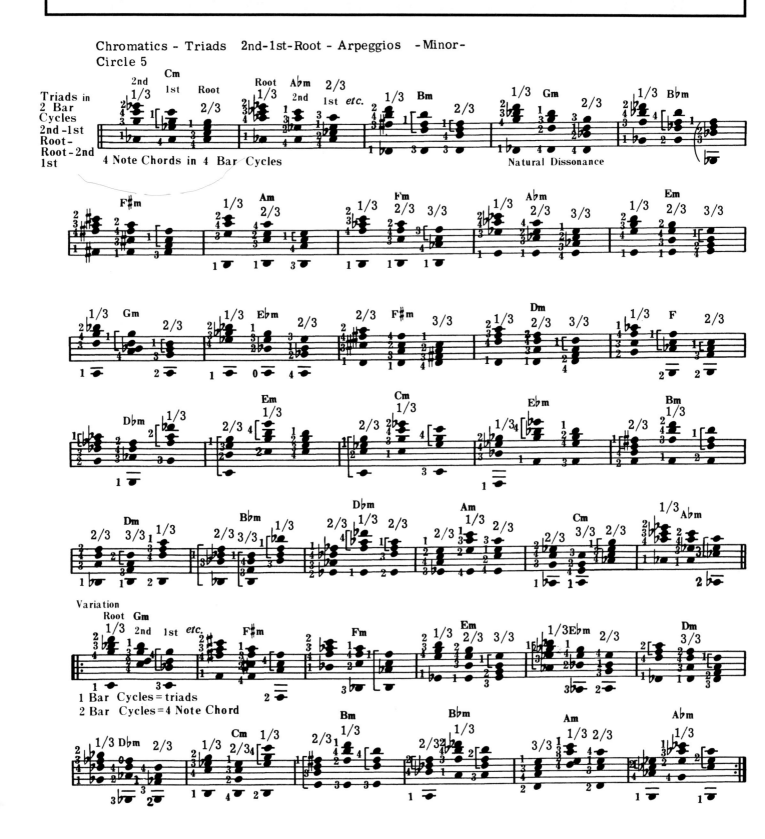

Chromatics - Triads   2nd - Root - 1st - Alternately in two keys with alternating bass - Minor -
Circle 5

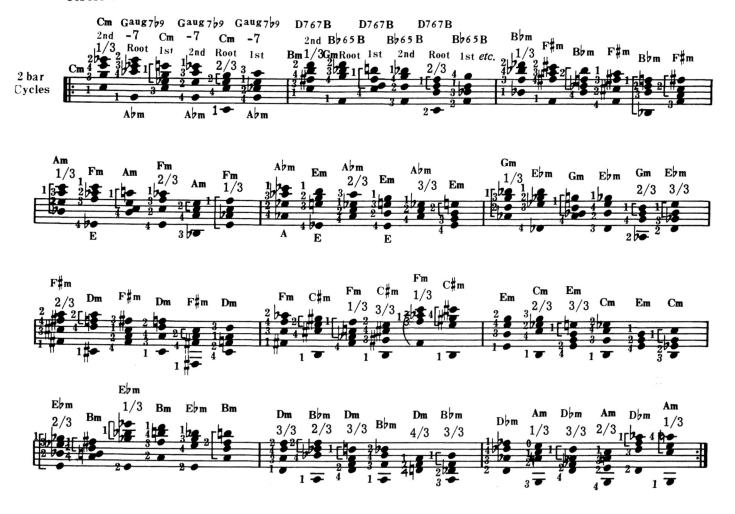

Variations

Chromatic
Bass
starting
on C

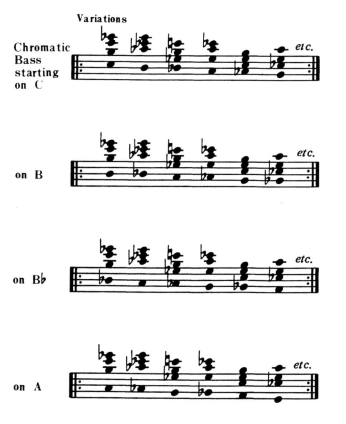

on B

on B♭

on A

Chromatics - Triads

Triad arpeggios descending chromatically - forming progressions because of the chromatic bass line

Examples

2nd Inversion
1st Chord Each measure

1st Inversion
2nd Chord of Each measure

Root Inversion
3rd Chord of Each measure

Chromatic Triads - Major and Minor - Mixed

Circle 5

Root Minor +Major 1st Inversion

Variations

Major Root+1st Inversion

Variations

CHROMATICS—TRIADS—
MAJOR & MINOR SERIES

This type of chordal movement is based on mathematical mechanical motion without regard for the harmonic result, which produces many interesting relationships, and provides very useful fingerboard knowledge. Notice the very interesting dissonances and progressions.

Extend all of the examples to cover all of the 12 keys.

Make up other patterns, select other keys, change the order of the triads, change the bass line also. Then, for the sake of discipline, don't deviate from that format. Stick to it, no matter how dissonant it sounds.

Later on, when the principle is understood more clearly, deviation should take place. The whole idea of this material is: to make scales, arpeggios, principles, and all findings work for you.

The bass lines are completely independent of the triads. The bass line is an independent fourth voice, therefore it will use its own accidentals and because of this, there will be a mixture of accidentals. This situation occurs when working with more than one key simultaneously because, one can't use multiple signatures.

Observe all the markings carefully because they contain many subtle changes.

MAJOR AND MINOR SERIES
CIRCLE–5

Chromatic triads 1st-2nd-root—alternately sharing a common bass line.

The purpose of this series on chromatic triads is to place them in as many varied relationships and positions to the bass as possible.

The three basic major and minor triads involved in this material can become quite complex when a fourth voice is added, even though they remain plain basic triads with no alterations. They may sound altered when the bass line is added, but the fact is that they have not been changed notationally. Harmonically they have been displaced into a different family that gives them another overall chordal sound. When analyzed in a displaced position, they take on another meaning.

Always think of the triad and bass as being separate isolated lines within an overall four note harmonic group of tones. It is very important that they keep their identities at all time while still becoming one overall sound.

Extend the harmonic principles presented in these studies to include open and closed voicings of all kinds.

The possibilities are endless when mutations and the inversions of mutations are introduced.

In this work the triads travel down one cycle of fifths while the bass follows another through the cycle keys, either a fifth down or a fourth up in one to four measure cycles.

The third and fourth measures, second cycle, in the major and minor series are harmonically identical to the first and second measures, first cycle, except that they are one whole tone lower.

(Other exercises in these examples may have a varying number of measures in each cycle.)

MAJOR AND MINOR SERIES

Notice how the triads gradually descend chromatically

In the first measure of the major series, the first triad is a C major. The first triad in the second measure is B major. In the third, it is B flat major etc.

The second triad in the first measure is an A flat major—in the third it is F sharp major, and so on.

All of the inversions go through the same cycle one at a time.

Because of using the three basic triads to build the four note chords each one is voiced three ways.

All of the explanations and thought lines apply to both the major and minor work—the only difference is harmonic.

A bass line descending through the cycle of fifths is neutral—neither major or minor—until other voices are introduced.

MAJOR AND MINOR SERIES
CHROMATIC TRIADS—
EXPLANATION OF SYMBOLS USED IN BOTH SERIES:

The letter "B" at the end of a chord symbol designates the bass note in the chord. Example:

If the bass is the third of the chord the last two figures would be the number three and the letter "B" = 3B etc.

The string set symbol is usually found above the chord. At times it will be found on the left, sometimes below the staff. It is easily recognized whereever it is located.
(Remember that the string set indicated remains in use until changed.)

In the example below the string set is first, the inversion second, the name of the triad third, and the name of the four note chord fourth.

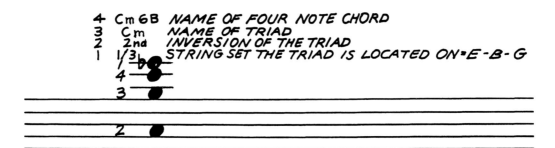

Occasionally the bass note may be sounded on two different strings without changing the fingering, in which case the string intended will be indicated by letter name.

In the above example, the string on which the "A" bass note is located was not marked because it can be sounded only on the fifth string when the set and finger markings are observed.

Major & Minor Series

Chromatics- Triads

The examples shown below will help in recognizing and naming all triad - bass relationships by using triad inversion (first, second, root) arpeggios ---
In other words, using the same notes re-distributed.

Number 1 shows a G flat root inversion triad with an A natural in the bass ---
The overall essence becomes a vague A 13th with a lowered ninth - but not easily recognized at first because the 13th (G♭) is just above the bass.

Number 2 becomes more recognizable just by placing the G♭ (13th) up one octave -- (the seventh is missing) - It is now a first inversion triad.

Number 3 shows a completely recognizable A 13th with the lowered ninth because of the added G natural above the bass -- which is the seventh.

Number 4 is simply another voicing of the same chord --- By moving the B♭ (lowered 9th) up one octave the triad on top becomes a second inversion.

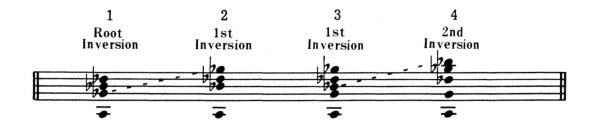

The inversion arpeggios help in finding the recognizable overall chords.

The thought lines used in these examples can be applied to all relationships, Major—Minor—diminished— all of the sevenths etc.

Some of the spellings are enharmonic because the triad and bass lines are completely independent of each other.

MAJOR SERIES
FIRST CYCLE—FIRST MEASURE

In the first measure two keys are represented, they are: "C" major and "A" flat major in triads. In both the major and minor series, the notes in the triads produce small chords that are separate from the bass line, but when combined they form a different four note chord. There are three basic triads in two different keys in each measure, plus six different four note chords, for a total of twelve chords. The first measure chords are:

Three "C" major triads = 2nd-1st-root- -1-3-5-
Three "A" flat major triads = root-2nd-1st- -2-4-6-
Three four note "A" flat major seventh, raised fifth chords -1-3-5-
Three four note pure "A" flat major chords -2-4-6-

This totals twelve, not counting their other callings.

All small chords have second, third, fourth (etc) callings under varied harmonic conditions, positions and situations. Here is a basic example:

The minor seventh chord has to contain the notes (open or closed) of one of the three pure major triads.
The major seventh chord has to contain the notes of one of the pure minor triads—in other words, major makes minor, and minor makes major.

The first four note chord in the first measure, besides being an "A" flat major seventh, raised fifth chord, is also an "F" minor ninth with the natural seventh on top and the third in the bass.

Natural seventh is a term commonly used for the leading tone of the scale which for instance would be "E" in the key of "F". It is written: ♮7.

FIRST CYCLE—SECOND MEASURE

In the second measure of the first cycle four keys are represented. They are:

"B" major and "G" major in triads. The bass in "D" flat plus the four note resulting Key of "G" sharp minor. The Key of "C" sharp cannot be included because enharmonically it is the same as "D" flat.

The second measure chords are:

Three "B" major triads = 2nd-1st-root- #1-3-5
Three "G" major triads = root-2nd-1st- #2-4-6
Three four note "G" sharp minor seventh chords with the fourth in the bass
Three four note "C" sharp seventh, flat ninth, flat fifth chords

Totaling twelve not counting their other callings.

Space does not permit listing all of the possible names and usages of each chord, because there are many.
They all can become parts of different harmonic situations in other keys. They are sometimes referred to as chameleons.

MAJOR SERIES
NAMING THE CHORDS IN THE MAJOR SERIES

The first four note chord in the first measure is a second inversion "C" major triad with the tonic, "A" flat in the bass. The "G" is the natural seventh, the "E" natural is the raised fifth, the symbol for this voicing is:

A♭ ♮7 ♯5

This chord is also an "F" minor ninth with the third, "A" flat, in the bass. The note "G" is the ninth, the "E" natural is the natural seventh—the symbol is: Fm9 ♮ 73B

The second four note chord in the first measure is an "A" flat major triad in root position with the tonic in the bass. Because it is pure the symbol is simply: A♭

The first four note chord in the second measure is a second inversion "B" major triad with "D" flat in the bass. The symbol is:

G♯ M74B

The "D" flat bass is the fourth. This chord is also a "C" sharp eleventh plus the ninth. It is also a "C" sharp suspended seventh; the "F" sharp is the eleventh and the suspended seventh.

The second four note chord in the second measure is a "G" major root position triad with the "D" flat tonic in the bass. The "D" natural is the flat ninth and the "G" is the flat fifth—the symbol is:

C♯7♭9♭5

This is also a "G" major chord with a lowered fifth, "D" flat in the bass.

MAJOR SERIES

The four note overall chords are named in the first cycle only, because thereafter only the keys change. They remain the same kind of chords through all of the keys, major and minor.

Example:
The first chord in the first cycle is an "A" flat natural seventh with a raised fifth—the symbol is:

A♭ ♮7 ♯5

The first chord in the second cycle is the same kind of chord except that it is one whole tone lower—and so on through the circle of keys.

Major Triads - 1st-2nd -Root inversions in two keys alternately descending chromatically in group form while employing a single bass line from one of those keys resulting in an altered effect.
The lower staffs show the reverse order which changes the resolution of each group. Analyze, and become familiar with them - note the patterns. Enharmonic spelling is used at times to isolate the keys and clarify the triad.
Major Series   -circle 5 chromatics - 2 measure cycles - ♮7 = Major 7th
Chords 1-3-5 of the 1st measure are A♭major 7#5 chords.   2-4-6 are pure A♭ major chords.
Chords 1-3-5 of the 2nd measure are G# minor 74B chords.   2-4-6 are C#7b9b5 chords.

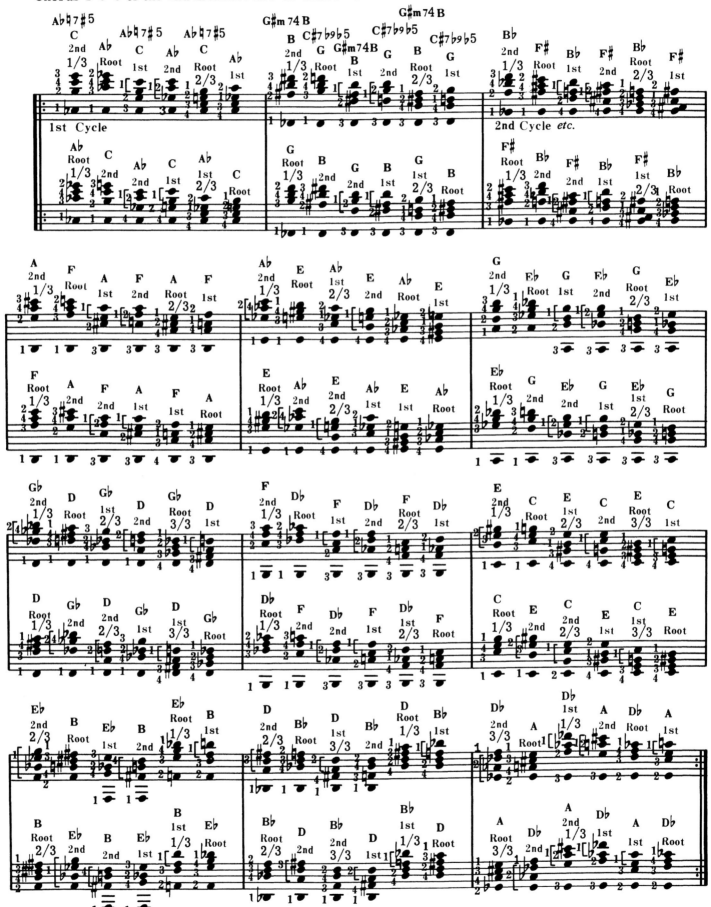

278

Chromatics - Triads - 2nd - Root - 1st - Employing various bass lines in a repeating harmonic situation
Major Series - these are but a few examples of the vast possibilities

Two Keys = C - A♭

Example
#4
Extended

This is example # four extended to show how it looks and sounds while going thru all 12 keys.

Extend the others also —

MINOR SERIES
FIRST CYCLE—FIRST MEASURE

In the first measure; four keys are represented. They are:
"C" minor—"A" flat minor—"B" major—"A" major

The first measure chords are:
Three "C" minor triads = 2nd-1st-root-   1-3-5
Three "A" flat minor triads = root-2nd-1st-   2-4-6
Three four note "C" minor six chords   1-3-6
Three four note "B" seven six chords with the seventh in the bass.

Total = twelve, not counting their other callings.

FIRST CYCLE—SECOND MEASURE

In the second measure of the first cycle, three keys are represented. They are the keys of:
"B" minor—"G" minor in triads—the bass in the Key of "D"

The second measure chords are:
Three "B" minor triads = 2nd-1st-root-   1-3-5
Three "G" minor triads = root-2nd-1st   2-4-6
Three four note "B" minor chords with the third in the bass
Three four note "G" minor chords with the fifth in the bass

Totaling twelve, not counting their other callings.

MINOR SERIES
NAMING THE CHORDS IN THE MINOR SERIES

The first four note chord in the first measure is a second inversion "C" minor triad with the sixth in the bass, "A" natural. The symbol is:

Cm6B

This chord is also an "F" ninth with the third, "A" natural, in the bass. The symbol is:

F93B

The "G" is the ninth of the chord.

The second four note chord in the first measure is an "A" flat minor triad in root position with an "A" natural in the bass—together they spell a basic "B" seventh chord containing the sixth, with the seventh in the bass. The "A" flat is the sixth of the chord and the symbol is:

B767B

This chord is also an "F" sharp minor ninth containing the sixth with the third, "A" natural in the bass. The symbol is:

F♯m963B

The "E" flat is the sixth of the chord.

The first four note chord in the second measure is a second inversion "B" minor triad with the third in the bass. The symbol is:

Bm3B

This is also a "D" major sixth chord minus the fifth, "A"

The second four note chord in the second measure is a "G" minor root position triad with fifth in the bass, "D"—the symbol is:

Gm5B

This is also a "B" flat major sixth chord with the third in the bass.

MINOR SERIES

Minor Triads - 1st - 2nd - Root inversions in two keys alternately, descending chromatically in group form while the bass line is in a third key. The lower staffs show the reverse order which changes the resolution of each group. Enharmonic spelling is used at times to isolate the keys and clarify the triad. Chords 1-3-5 in the 1st measure are Cm6B chords 2-4-6 are B767B chords. Chords 1-3-5 in the 2nd measure are Bm3B chords-2-4-6 are Gm5B chords. The letter B designates the bass position intervalwise.   -Circle 5 chromatics - 2 measure cycles-

282

Chromatics - Triads-2nd-Root-1st-Employing various bass lines in a repeating harmonic situation
Minor   These are but a few examples of the vast possibilities

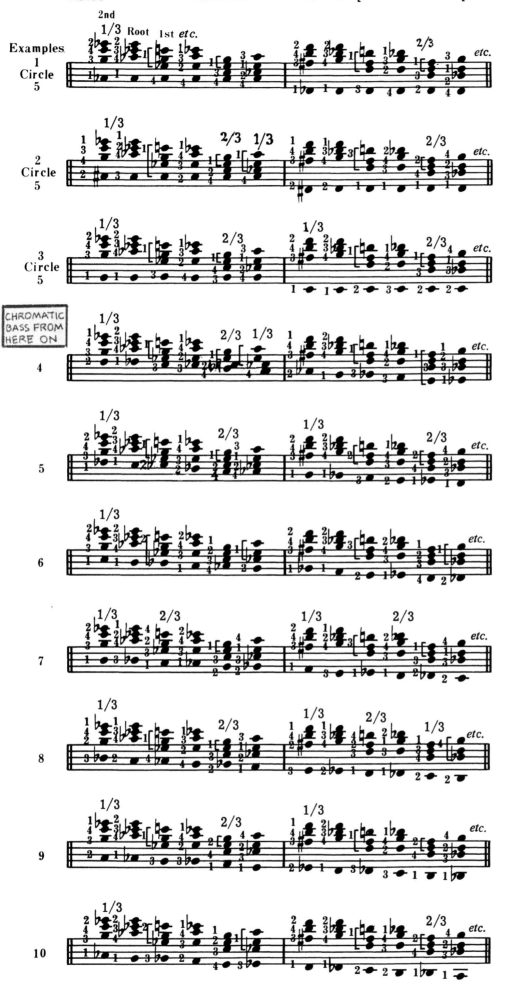

Chromatics - Triads 2nd-Root-1st-Alternately in two keys with the bass descending chromatically
Minor

Example
#4
Extended

GENERAL REMARKS

Dissonances are natural when working with chromatic contrary motion involving a chord line going one way and the bass line going another.

Also, in moving a chord chromatically up or down against a pedal bass note.

Relationshipwise, the result is the same --- in other words, is the bass standing still while the chord moves, or, is the chord standing still while the bass moves -- or both -----

The chords are the same in "A" and "B" but of course in different keys

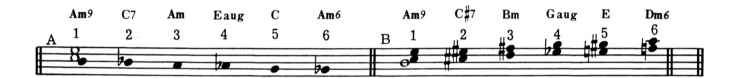

In example "C" they become more abstract

Notice the duplicate harmonic situations that appear when just the triad is in motion # 1- when just the bass is in motion #2 - then in contrary motion

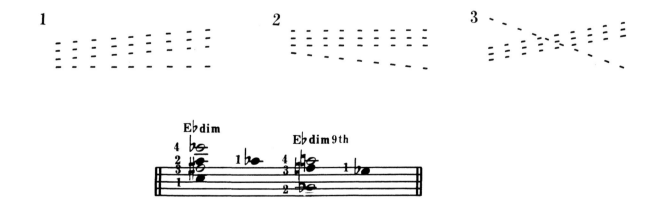

Chromatics - Triads   triad is ascending while the bass descends
Contrary Motion -Major-
The Dissonance is natural

1st Inversion

Reverse
Read
Backward
To return

2nd Inversion

Reverse

Root

Reverse

Triad ascends while top line descends
Contrary Motion -Major-

1st Inversion

Read
Backward
To return

2nd Inversion

Reverse

Root

Reverse

286

Chromatics - Triads - Triad ascends while bass descends
Contrary Motion -Minor-

Triad ascends while top line descends
Contrary Motion   -Minor-

CHROMATICS—TRIADS

EXPLANATION OF THE BLOCKOUTS

MAJOR & MINOR SERIES

A "blockout" is a graphic chart that shows a series of chords on the upper line of each cycle and an independent unrelated bass on the lower line.

Triads, both major and minor are employed in the following blockouts; root, first and second inversions are used. Their order of appearance may be consecutive majors, consecutive minors, mixed majors, mixed minors, or mixed majors and minors. But whatever the form, they are very interesting and informative in analysis.

Blockouts by their very nature will of course contain harmonic clashes and dissonances of many kinds because of the recurring chord and bass misalignment, but these dissonances are very helpful and necessary at times. It is useful information.

Certain parts and sections of each cycle will sound more pleasing to the ear than others, and this is perfectly natural and even desirable since it provides interest and variety to many ears.

Ears don't always hear or assimilate combinations of tones the same way, or at the same rate. Therefore, the different sections of the cycles provide interest to ears of many levels of taste, understanding and development.

After the basic thought line of the blockout principal is clearly understood, the unwanted dissonances may be altered or omitted by breaking away from the strict mathematical form of the principal. This can be achieved many different ways, such as: having just the chord repeat while the bass continues, having the bass note repeat while the chords continue, by having one or both skip a step or two in the cycles or by joining the more pleasing sections of the different cycles and forms together.

In other words, blend the cycles and forms
Change the triad order
Mix and blend the major and minor forms
Change major to minor and minor to major etc.
A chord symbol without an "M" is always major.
Always keep this fact in mind:
The bass line is one voice action
The three notes in the triads are independent voice actions
Sounding all four voices together produces various chords (singly)
When they are in motion as in the blockout cycles, a fifth action is intoduced which is, progressional motion.
Progression (voice motion) is one of the most important and necessary parts of all good music, regardless of the idiom of the moment.

It is important to remember that the upper symbols are the triad line and the lower line the bass notes, because they won't always be marked.

288

Chromatics-triads- Explanation of the Blockouts-

Major & Minor Series-

The first diagram below shows the bass line as one voice - the triad as one voice - then the combined result.

The second diagram shows the triad as three voices - then the result.

The third diagram provides a clearer view and breakdown of the first two diagrams.

Later, when aware and familiar with the movement of the voices in the triads, the progressional motion when going thru the cycles becomes easier to follow and understand.

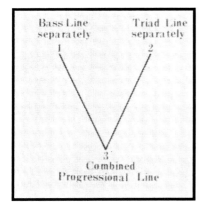
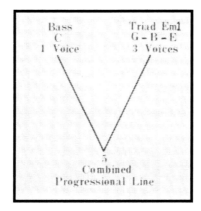
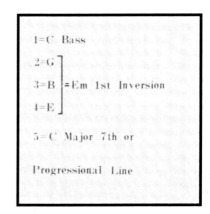

Harmonic breakdown of C bass - Em1 (1st inv.) Total = C Major 7th

Flats are used in the chromatic descending bass lines while the triads use their respective key accidentals which naturally will produce some enharmonic spellings which helps to keep the triad and bass lines separate and independent of each other - but at times will cause some of the intervals to appear wrong, however, the notes are correct even tho a third interval may look like a second etc. -- for instance:
When an "A" bass note lowers to an "A" flat against a "G" sharp in an "E" major triad it looks wrong -- but both are correct and the resulting enharmonic difference tends to isolate the two lines.

The principles involved in blockouts, whether these or others, must be followed very carefully until the thought lines become clearly established.

Rules and principles must be understood before they may be employed intelligently, in other words, strict adherance to the mathematical form is very important in the learning stage.

Understanding information gleaned from studying material of all kinds is very necessary to the ultimate goal - which is the art of improvisation/composition.

Notice the various subtle harmonic patterns that appear in all blockouts.
Analyze and compare them.

CHROMATICS—TRIADS—EXPLANATION OF THE BLOCKOUTS

(Continued)

When the three triad inversions are placed in a fixed uniform group that appears in exactly the same order over and over again, forming a pattern each measure or so thru the cycle, it is quite naturally termed a "repeat order."

It makes no difference which inversion is first, middle, or last in the group. The location of each inversion in the pattern does not change. The keys may change of course, but the inversions maintain their positions in the pattern.

Examples:

REPEAT ORDERS

1-2-R—1-2-R—1-2-R—1-2-R- R-1-2—R-1-2—R-1-2—R-1-2-

2-R-1—2-R-1—2-R-1—2-R-1—2-R-1 1-R-2—1-R-2—1-R-2—1-R-2- Etc.

The mixed order is a scrambling of the three inversions which generally makes a longer overall pattern that includes a whole cycle or more, but they eventually repeat. Some will take more than a hundred steps before repeating.

Mixed order example:

1-2-R—2-R-1—R-1-2—R-2-1- Etc.

The possibilities for varying the orders are vast. Make them up, block them out, and then adhere to the blockouts.

On a sectioned strip of paper that matches the spacing, superimpose other bass lines over the lines shown. Experiment with many different kinds of lines, also with many different keys for the triads.

GENERAL REMARKS ABOUT BLOCKOUTS

One of the main purposes of the blockouts is to be able to systematically investigate the progressional possibilities by following and studying the three basic Major and Minor triads in sequence, going thru a sequence, while locked in a set pattern against a completely independent bass line.

The chromatic bass lines provide the greatest variation in the triad bass relationships, but other types such as arpeggio (walkingbass) bass(etc.)
may be used with very good results, as is shown in one of the previous examples.

Another purpose of the blockouts is to provide fingerboard gymnastics formationwise -- some of the formations will of course be "old friends" while others will not be.

Notice how by changing the register (up or down) of the triad or the bass, or both, produces a different harmonic sound and result -- as the example shows --

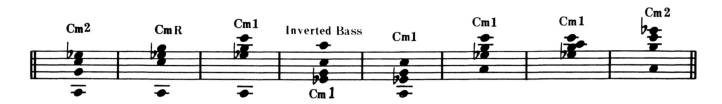

Each bar in the above example produces a different harmonic sound, and yet they are all alike in that they all contain C-G-E flat and "A" in varing positions, therefore they are all C minor sixth chords.
There are others, endeavor to find them.

BLOCKOUT CHARTS
CHROMATICS

This type of arithmetic layout may seem academic, mechanical, and contrived. It is very contrived, but by employing devices such as these, unusual relationships occur. They will produce progressional combinations and dissonances that normally might not come to mind. They also show the vastness of the possibilities.

Contrivance is not new to music—scales and arpeggios are contrived. They are devices all musicians must use.

Composers through the years have used many varied types of stimulating thought provoking devices and contrivances to lead the mind and ear; to help in the search for newness, freshness, to help find different harmonies, progressions, rhythms, and all sorts of sounds.

Music that withstands the test of time is the result of: inspiration, resourcefulness, imagination, inventiveness, etc. Emotions of the moment may conceive, but knowledge and knowhow has to put it all together into listenable logical form.

"Logical form" does not necessarily mean predictable. The melodic/harmonic form, whatever the idiom, can be full of surprises and yet in analysis be perfectly logical.

Musicians have to make musical things happen. Luck won't do it, and ignorance can't.

The mind must be trained to function like a cold, calculating machine, and then the ideas and findings must be tempered and warmed by the heart. Professional musicians can't take the time to just stare at the stars and wait for something wonderfully magic to happen—as I said before, "they have to make it happen."

The charts resulting from the blockouts can be read from the top down and the bottom up with very interesting results.

Bear in mind the fact that all the results in this series are from the basic major and minor triads: just imagine what can be done using other voicings and counterpoint, etc.; the possibilities are endless. Combining all of the concepts and principles, plus all of the possible combinations, would take forever by sheer numbers. This is an encouraging thought because it tells us that we have so far only scratched the surface.

Some register changes have been made to shorten the reaches. However, it is good practice to continue on as far as possible at first, and then later on make register changes where ever they sound more logical to you continuitywise.

The chordal relationships in the resulting progressions are easily named when the intervals dividing the selected keys are kept in mind. Notice that on certain steps the ear is fooled trying to follow the bass line. Sometimes the ear does not hear the bass half step clearly defined because of a clash in voices; this is audio illusion.

Treat each cycle as a separate exercise within a longer overall exercise.

CHROMATICS—TRIADS

MAJOR & MINOR SERIES

As has been stated many times before, it is very important to remember that a bar line cancels all previous accidentals. In many of these studies each chord is located by bar lines—this is done for the sake of clarity for it eliminates many accidentals as the examples demonstrate:

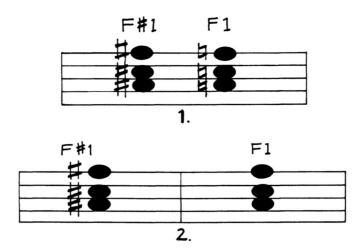

In Example #2 the natural signs are not needed.

The fingering and string set markings have been omitted in these blockout studies because all of the triad/bass relationships have been shown with both markings in previous material.

Another reason for the deletions is:
Blockouts are meant to be fingered and played in as many different locations and positions as possible.

BLOCKOUT PATTERNS
—TRIAD INVERSION = (repeat)
–MAJOR & MINOR SERIES–
CHROMATICS—TRIADS—
FORM A—(MAJOR)

HOW TO BLOCK OUT THREE KEYS: (see chart)

For example the keys of:

C-Ab-E-Major- (only for the first cycle of course)
They are major thirds apart descending—(any keys may be used). The order for the triad inversions will be: (repeat order). First=1-Second=2-Root=R- (any order may be used)

The bass will start on Ab descending chromatically (any step of the chromatic scale may be used to start because all of the bass-triad relationships will occur anyway, regardless of the starting note.

The relationships however, will not all be in the same keys, of course.

When the triads in each cycle are lowered chromatically thru the 12 keys, all of the relationships occur automatically, because the group of triads in the 12 chord cycles are lowering ½ tone each, while the bass line always returns to Ab, or to the note on which the bass was started.

Example:
The first chord in the first cycle is a C1—the first chord in the second cycle is a B1—in the third, it's a Bb1—in the fourth, it's an A1 and so on down the chromatic scale.

The second chord in the first cycle is an Ab2—the second chord in the second cycle is a G2—in the third cycle it's a Gb2—in the fourth it's an F2—and so on down the scale. The third chord in the first cycle an ER—in the second cycle it's an EbR—in the third it's a DR—and so on down the scale.

This principle applies to all of these forms, no matter whether repeated or mixed order is used.

In mixed order they won't be one below the other, but the principle is the same.

In this form as in all the others, when the bass line drops out of range, change registers; also change registers for reach reasons. The continuity will still be present.

The bass line can begin on any step of the chromatic scale desired. However, experimentation will show that some starting tones are more satisfying than others thru parts of each cycle.

Two lines opposing each other working chromatically will produce dissonances that may be avoided either by moving one of the lines a whole tone or more, or, by having one of them remain on a step for more than one beat. Later on, unwanted dissonances can be avoided when desired and wherever desired.

There are fingerings and positions for all of the relationships and harmonic situations in these examples by string set and/or register change. Change registers at times even when not necessary, and practice all fingerings both awkward and easy—in all positions.

All three inversions in all 12 relationships to the bass chromatically. Triad and bass assume the same relationship every 40 steps, but a minor third lower.

CHROMATICS-TRIADS-
FORM A (MAJOR)

-BLOCKOUT PATTERNS-
-TRIAD INVERSION ORDER=REPEAT
-MAJOR & MINOR SERIES-

Cycle												
Triad	C1	Ab2	ER	C1	Ab2	ER	C1	Ab2	ER	C1	Ab2	ER
1 **Bass**	Ab	G	Gb	F	E	Eb	D	Db	C	B	Bb	A
2	B1	G2	EbR	B1	G2	EbR	B1	G2	EbR	B1	G2	EbR
	Ab	G	Gb	F	E	Eb	D	Db	C	B	Bb	A
3	Bb1	Gb2	DR	Bb1	Gb2	DR	Bb1	Gb2	DR	Bb1	Gb2	DR
	Ab	G	Gb	F	E	Eb	D	Db	C	B	Bb	A
4	A1	F2	DbR	A1	F2	DbR	A1	F2	DbR	A1	F2	DbR
	Ab	G	Gb	F	E	Eb	D	Db	C	B	Bb	A
5	Ab1	E2	CR	Ab1	E2	CR	Ab1	E2	CR	Ab1	E2	CR
	Ab	G	Gb	F	E	Eb	D	Db	C	B	Bb	A
6	G1	Eb2	BR	G1	Eb2	BR	G1	Eb2	BR	G1	Eb2	BR
	Ab	G	Gb	F	E	Eb	D	Db	C	B	Bb	A
7	Gb1	D2	BbR	Gb1	D2	BbR	Gb1	D2	BbR	Gb1	D2	BbR
	Ab	G	Gb	F	E	Eb	D	Db	C	B	Bb	A
8	F1	Db2	AR	F1	Db2	AR	F1	Db2	AR	F1	Db2	AR
	Ab	G	Gb	F	E	Eb	D	Db	C	B	Bb	A
9	E1	C2	AbR	E1	C2	AbR	E1	C2	AbR	E1	C2	AbR
	Ab	G	Gb	F	E	Eb	D	Db	C	B	Bb	A
10	Eb1	B2	GR	Eb1	B2	GR	Eb1	B2	GR	Eb1	B2	GR
	Ab	G	Gb	F	E	Eb	D	Db	C	B	Bb	A
11	D1	Bb2	GbR	D1	Bb2	GbR	D1	Bb2	GbR	Db1	Bb2	GbR
	Ab	G	Gb	F	E	Eb	D	Db	C	B	Bb	A
12	Db1	A2	FR	Db1	A2	FR	Db1	A2	FR	Db1	A2	FR
	Ab	G	Gb	F	E	Eb	D	Db	C	B	Bb	A

Chromatics - Triads = 1st-2nd-Root inversions alternately
Blockouts - 3 keys in each cycle - 12 cycles - *Repeat order*

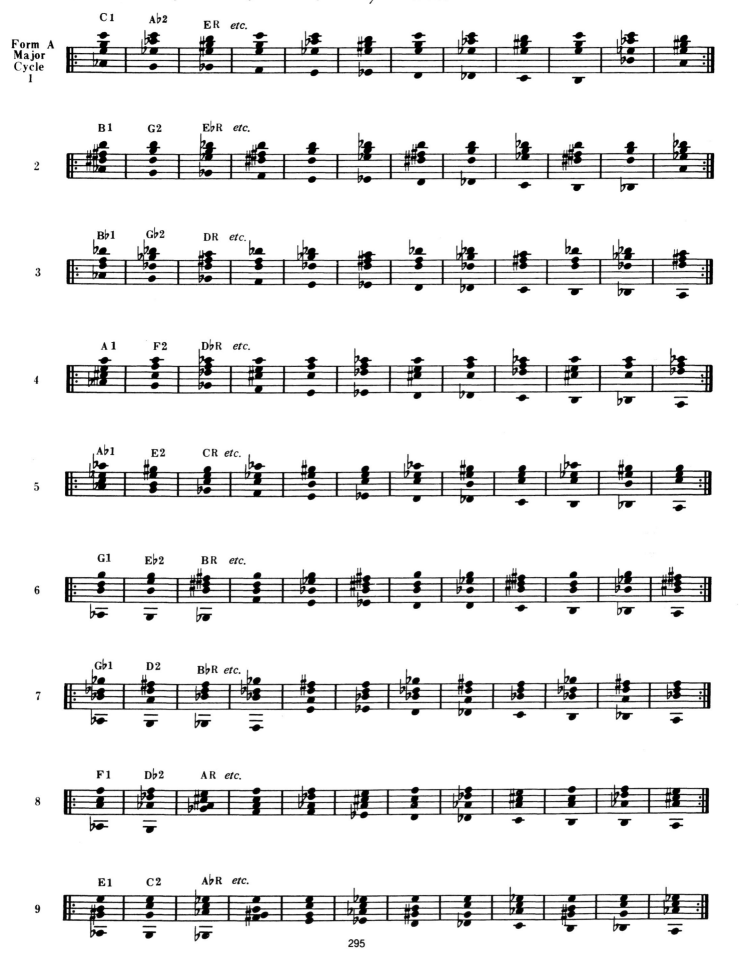

Bass-variation example using a repeat inversion order — bass line is descending, chromatic, inverted fifths—24 steps in the cycle — continue in all keys

This example uses all 1st inversion triads against the chromatic bass line starting on G—notice how the bass line becomes the lower note of the triad every 4 steps — continue in all keys

All 1st inversion triads with the chromatic bass starting on C

CHROMATICS—TRIADS—
FORM B (MAJOR)

How to block out three keys:
This example employs the same keys as Form A.
They are major thirds apart descending.
The order for the triad inversions will be:

1-2-R—2-R-1—2-1-R—1-R-2—R-2-1—R-1-2—

Then the order repeats, making an 18 step cycle for the inversion order.
For this example the chromatic bass will start on A natural, although any step of the scale may begin.
Notice how the triad order extends half way into the next cycle, which places the last 6 steps of the triad order one half tone lower. The reason for using an 18 step triad order against a 12 step bass is to show that in using an 18 against a 12, the result is a constantly changing 144 triad/bass combined cycle. In other words it takes 144 steps for the triad order to return to its original relationship to the bass line.

When the blockout concept becomes clearly understood, experiment with different key combinations in both major and minor and change their relationships.
Also experiment with other triad inversion orders.
Apply the previous rules to all blockouts.

CHROMATICS-TRIADS-
FORM B (MAJOR)
-BLOCKOUT PATTERNS-
-TRIAD INVERSION ORDER=MIXED
-MAJOR & MINOR SERIES-

Cycle

1	C1	Ab2	ER	C2	AbR	E1	C2	Ab1	ER	C1	AbR	E2
	A	Ab	G	Gb	F	E	Eb	D	Db	C	B	Bb

2	BR	G2	Eb1	BR	G1	Eb2	B1	G2	EbR	B2	GR	Eb1
	A	Ab	G	Gb	F	E	Eb	D	Db	C	B	Bb

3	Bb2	Gb1	DR	Bb1	GbR	D2	BbR	Gb2	D1	BbR	Gb1	D2
	A	Ab	G	Gb	F	E	Eb	D	Db	C	B	Bb

4	A1	F2	DbR	A2	FR	Db1	A2	F1	DbR	A1	FR	Db2
	A	Ab	G	Gb	F	E	E	D	Db	C	B	Bb

5	AbR	E2	C1	AbR	E1	C2	Ab1	E2	CR	Ab2	ER	C1
	A	Ab	G	Gb	F	E	Eb	D	Db	C	B	Bb

6	G2	Eb1	BR	G1	EbR	B2	GR	Eb2	B1	GR	Eb1	B2
	A	Ab	G	Gb	F	E	Eb	D	Db	C	B	Bb

7	Gb1	D2	BbR	Gb2	DR	Bb1	Gb2	D1	BbR	Gb1	DR	Bb2
	A	Ab	G	Gb	F	E	Eb	D	Db	C	B	Bb

8	FR	Db2	A1	FR	Db1	A2	F1	Db2	AR	F2	DbR	A1
	A	Ab	G	Gb	F	E	Eb	D	Db	C	B	Bb

9	E2	C1	AbR	E1	CR	Ab2	ER	C2	Ab1	ER	C1	Ab2
	A	Ab	G	Gb	F	E	Eb	D	Db	C	B	Bb

10	Eb1	B2	GR	Eb2	BR	G1	Eb2	B1	GR	Eb1	BR	G2
	A	Ab	G	Gb	F	E	Eb	D	Db	C	B	Bb

11	DR	Bb2	Gb1	DR	Bb1	Gb2	D1	Bb2	GbR	D2	BbR	Gb1
	A	Ab	G	Gb	F	E	Eb	D	Db	C	B	Bb

12	Db2	A1	FR	Db1	AR	F2	DbR	A2	F1	DbR	A1	F2
	A	Ab	G	Gb	F	E	Eb	D	Db	C	B	Bb

Chromatics - Triads - 1st-2nd-Root inversions alternately
Blockouts 3 keys each cycle - 12 cycles - *Mixed order*

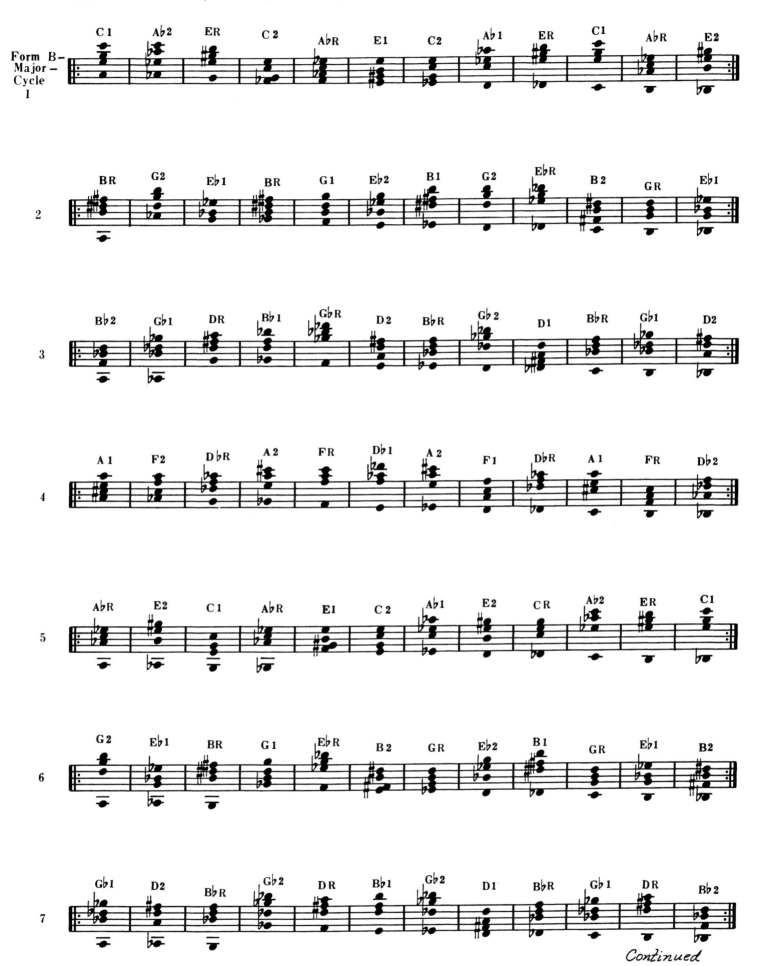

Continued

Continued

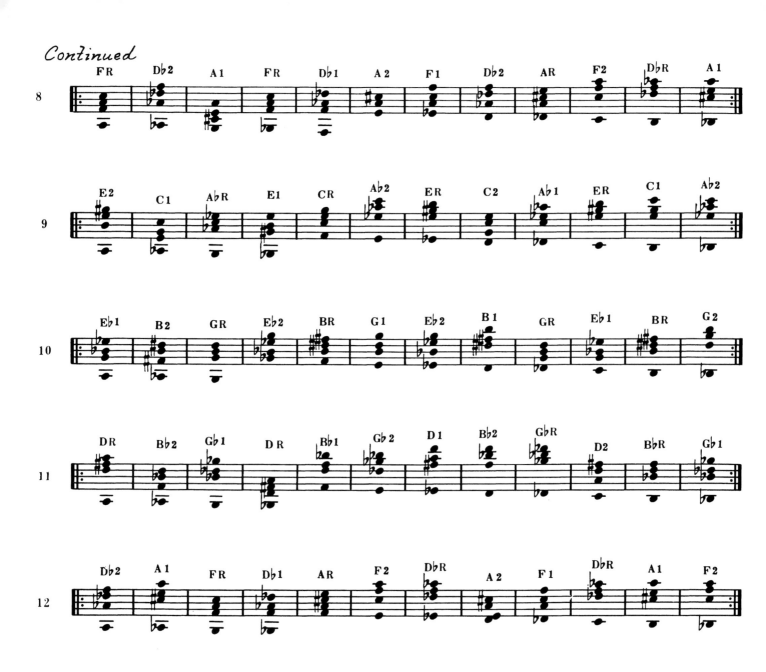

Example Variation - using a different mixed inversion order-continue in all keys-bass starts on A♮

Example - Variation using a double mixed inversion order - continue in all keys-bass starts on A♮

CHROMATICS-TRIADS-
FORM EXAMPLE

-BLOCKOUT PATTERNS-
-TRIAD INVERSION ORDER=MIXED
-MAJOR & MINOR SERIES-

C1	Ab2	ER	C1	Ab2	ER	C1	Ab2	ER	C1	Ab2	ER
G	Gb	F	E	Eb	D	Db	C	B	Bb	A	Ab

IN THE ABOVE EXAMPLE NOTICE THAT MOVING THE BAR LINES ONE STEP TO THE RIGHT TO FORM THREE GROUPS OF FOUR RESULTS IN A MIXED INVERSION ORDER THUS:

1-2-R-1---2-R-1-2---R-1-2-R-   (3 INTO 4)

IT ALSO PRODUCES A MIXED KEY ORDER THUS:

C-Ab-E-C---Ab-E-C-Ab---E-C-Ab-E-   (ALSO THREE INTO FOUR)

APPLY THIS THOUGHT LINE TO ALL BLOCKOUTS

BLOCKOUT PATTERNS
TRIAD INVERSION ORDER = MIXED
MAJOR & MINOR SERIES

CHROMATICS—TRIADS
FORM C (MAJOR)

How to block out four keys:
For this example the Keys of C-A-F♯-D♯ were selected.
They are minor thirds apart descending.
The order for the triad inversions will be:

1-2-R-1-

Using this order the first measure will read:
C1-A2-F♯R-D♯1—and then repeat.
Because there are but three basic triad inversions used and four keys to deal with, one of the inversions must be repeated. Any one of the three may be employed, therefore, the first inversion was selected only because it was next in line.

Mathematically this produces a three into four situation—five keys would be three into five etc.

If there were but three triads used in each measure, the inversion order would be a repeat order. Since there are four triads in each measure (which was caused by moving the bar lines one step to the right), the result is a mixed inversion order, as shown in the preceding blockout sample.

CHROMATICS-TRIADS-
FORM C (MAJOR)

-BLOCKOUT PATTERNS-
-TRIAD INVERSION ORDER=MIXED
-MAJOR & MINOR SERIES-

Cycle

1											
C1	A2	F#R	D#1	C2	AR	F#1	D#2	CR	A1	F#2	D#R
G	Gb	F	E	Eb	D	Db	C	B	Bb	A	Ab

2											
B1	Ab2	FR	D1	B2	AbR	F1	D2	BR	Ab1	F2	DR
G	Gb	F	E	Eb	D	Db	C	B	Bb	A	Ab

3											
Bb1	G2	ER	Db1	Bb2	GR	E1	Db2	BbR	G1	E2	DbR
G	Gb	F	E	Eb	D	Db	C	B	Bb	A	Ab

4											
A1	Gb2	EbR	C1	A2	GbR	Eb1	C2	AR	Gb1	Eb2	CR
G	Gb	F	E	Eb	D	Db	C	B	Bb	A	Ab

5											
Ab1	F2	DR	B1	Ab2	FR	D1	B2	AbR	F1	D2	BR
G	Gb	F	E	Eb	D	Db	C	B	Bb	A	Ab

6											
G1	E2	DbR	Bb1	G2	ER	Db1	Bb2	GR	E1	Db2	BbR
G	Gb	F	E	Eb	D	Db	C	B	Bb	A	Ab

7											
Gb1	Eb2	CR	A1	Gb2	EbR	C1	A2	GbR	Eb1	C2	AR
G	Gb	F	E	Eb	D	Db	C	B	Bb	A	Ab

8											
F1	D2	BR	Ab1	F2	DR	B1	Ab2	FR	D1	B2	AbR
G	Gb	F	E	Eb	D	Db	C	B	Bb	A	Ab

9											
E1	Db2	BbR	G1	E2	DbR	Bb1	G2	ER	Db1	Bb2	GR
G	Gb	F	E	Eb	D	Db	C	B	Bb	A	Ab

10											
Eb1	C2	AR	Gb1	Eb2	CR	A1	Gb2	EbR	C1	A2	GbR
G	Gb	F	E	Eb	D	Db	C	B	Bb	A	Ab

11											
D1	B2	AbR	F1	D2	BR	Ab1	F2	DR	B1	Ab2	FR
G	Gb	F	E	Eb	D	Db	C	B	Bb	A	Ab

12											
Db1	Bb2	GR	E1	Db2	BbR	G1	E2	DbR	Bb1	G2	ER
G	Gb	F	E	Eb	Db	Db	C	B	Bb	A	Ab

Chromatics - Triads = 1st-2nd-Root-1st inversions alternately
Blockouts - 4 keys each cycle - 12 cycles Mixed inversion order

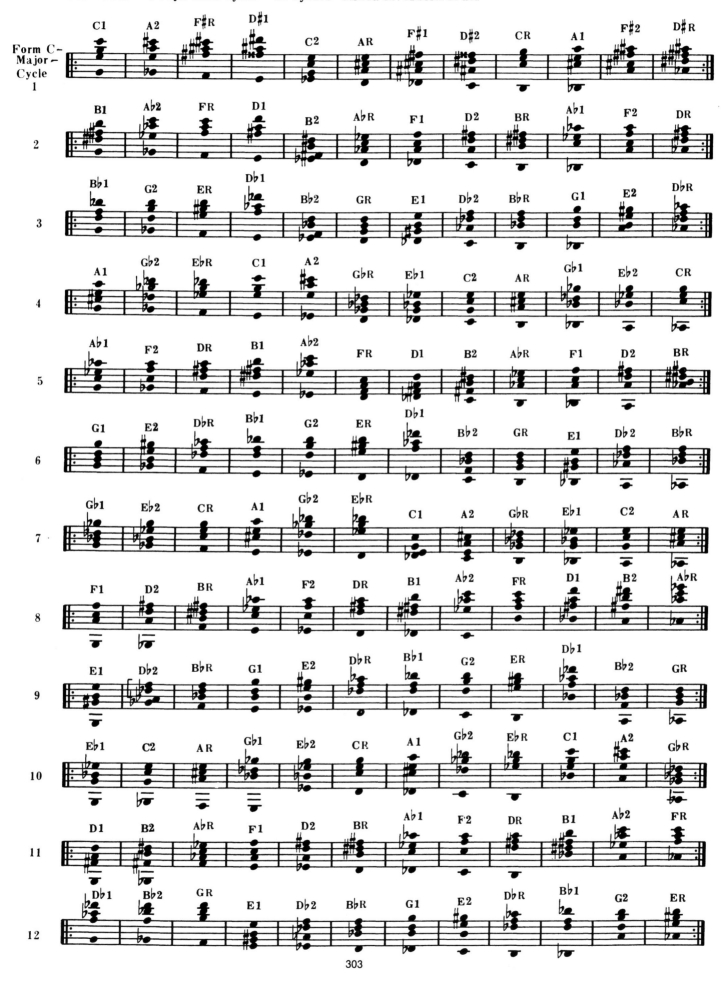

CHROMATICS-TRIADS-
FORM D (MAJOR)

-BLOCKOUT PATTERNS-
-TRIAD INVERSION ORDER=REPEAT
-MAJOR & MINOR SERIES-

Cycle

1

C1	Ab2	ER	C1	Ab2	ER	C1	Ab2	ER	C1	Ab2	ER
A	A♯	B	C	C♯	D	D♯	E	F	F♯	G	G♯

2

B1	G2	EbR	B1	G2	EbR	B1	G2	EbR	B1	G2	EbR
A	A♯	B	C	C♯	D	D♯	E	F	F♯	G	G♯

3

Bb1	Gb2	DR	Bb1	Gb2	DR	Bb1	Gb2	DR	Bb1	Gb2	DR
A	A♯	B	C	C♯	D	D♯	E	F	F♯	G	G♯

4

A1	F2	DbR	A1	F2	DbR	A1	F2	DbR	A1	F2	DbR
A	A♯	B	C	C♯	D	D♯	E	F	F♯	G	G♯

5

Ab1	E2	CR	Ab1	E2	CR	Ab1	E2	CR	Ab1	E2	CR
A	A♯	B	C	C♯	D	D♯	E	F	F♯	G	G♯

6

G1	Eb2	BR	G1	Eb2	BR	G1	Eb2	BR	G1	Eb2	BR
A	A♯	B	C	C♯	D	D♯	E	F	F♯	G	G♯

7

Gb1	D2	BbR	Gb1	D2	BbR	Gb1	D2	BbR	Gb1	D2	BbR
A	A♯	B	C	C♯	D	D♯	E	F	F♯	G	G♯

8

F1	Db2	AR	F1	Db2	AR	F1	Db2	AR	F1	Db2	AR
A	A♯	B	C	C♯	D	D♯	E	F	F♯	G	G♯

9

E1	C2	AbR	E1	C2	AbR	E1	C2	AbR	E1	C2	AbR
A	A♯	B	C	C♯	D	D♯	E	F	F♯	G	G♯

10

Eb1	B2	GR	Eb1	B2	GR	Eb1	B2	GR	Eb1	B2	GR
A	A♯	B	C	C♯	D	D♯	E	F	F♯	G	G♯

11

D1	Bb2	GbR	D1	Bb2	GbR	D1	Bb2	GbR	D1	Bb2	GbR
A	A♯	B	C	C♯	D	D♯	E	F	F♯	G	G♯

12

Db1	A2	FR	Db1	A2	FR	Db1	A2	FR	Db1	A2	FR
A	A♯	B	C	C♯	D	D♯	E	F	F♯	G	G♯

Chromatics - Triads = 1st-2nd-Root inversions alternately with an ascending chromatic bass
Blockouts - 3 keys each cycle - 12 cycles - repeat order

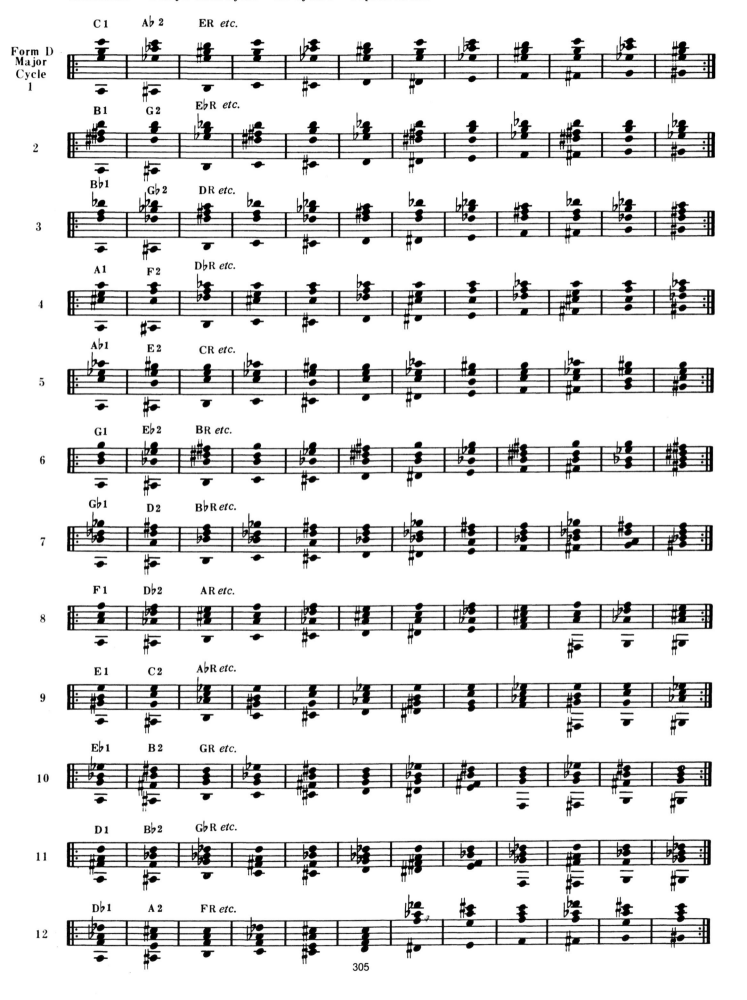

CHROMATICS-TRIADS-
FORM E (MAJOR)

-BLOCKOUT PATTERNS-
-TRIAD INVERSION ORDER=REPEAT
-MAJOR & MINOR SERIES-

CHROMATIC BASS = FIVE HALF TONES DOWN- FOUR UP ETC.

Cycles

1   **2**

CR	AbR	ER	C1	CR	AbR	ER	C1	CR	AbR	ER	C1	CR	AbR	ER	C1
C	B	Bb	A	Ab	A	A♯	B	B	Bb	A	Ab	G	G♯	A	A♯

3   **4**

CR	AbR	ER	C1	CR	AbR	ER	C1	CR	AbR	ER	C1	CR	AbR	ER	C1
Bb	A	Ab	G	Gb	G	G♯	A	A	Ab	G	Gb	F	F♯	G	G♯

5   **6**

CR	AbR	ER	C1	CR	AbR	ER	C1	CR	AbR	ER	C1	CR	AbR	ER	C1
Ab	G	Gb	F	E	F	F♯	G	G	Gb	F	E	Eb	E	F	F♯

7   **8**

CR	AbR	ER	C1	CR	AbR	ER	C1	CR	AbR	ER	C1	CR	AbR	ER	C1
Gb	F	E	Eb	D	D♯	E	F	F	E	Eb	D	Db	D	D♯	E

9   **10**

CR	AbR	ER	C1	CR	AbR	ER	C1	CR	AbR	ER	C1	CR	AbR	ER	C1
E	Eb	D	Db	C	C♯	D	D♯	Eb	D	Db	C	B	C	C♯	D

11   **12**

CR	AbR	ER	C1	CR	AbR	ER	C1	CR	AbR	ER	C1	CR	AbR	ER	C1
D	Db	C	B	Bb	B	C	C♯	Db	C	B	Bb	A	A♯	B	C

Chromatics - Triads = Root & 1st inversion -
Blockouts - 3 keys in each cycle - 12 cycles   *Repeat order*

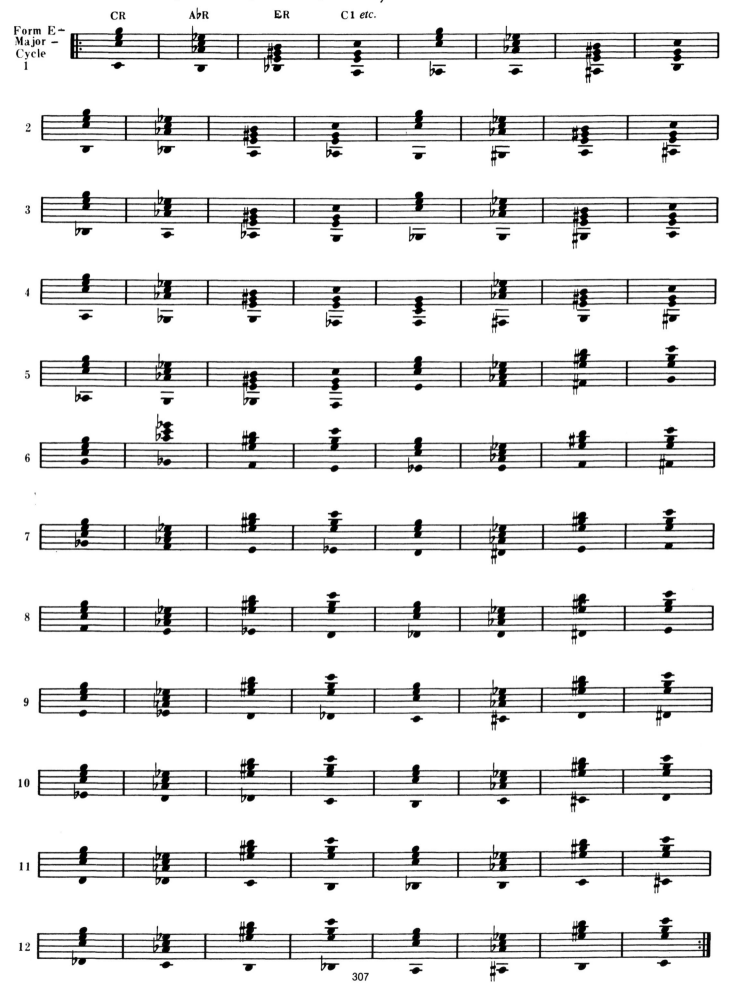

CHROMATICS-TRIADS-
FORM F ((MAJOR)

-BLOCKOUT PATTERNS-
-TRIAD INVERSION ORDER=REPEAT
-MAJOR & MINOR SERIES-

THIS FORM IS A VARIATION OF FORM E

Cycles

1				2				3				4			
CR	AbR	ER	C1	CR	AbR	ER	C1	CR	AbR	ER	C1	CR	AbR	ER	C1
C	B	Bb	A	Ab	A	A♯	B	Bb	A	Ab	G	Gb	G	G♯	A

5				6				7				8			
CR	AbR	ER	C1	CR	AbR	ER	C1	CR	AbR	ER	C1	CR	AbR	ER	C1
Ab	G	Gb	F	E	F	F♯	G	Gb	F	E	Eb	D	D♯	E	F

9				10				11				12			
CR	AbR	ER	C1	CR	AbR	ER	C1	CR	AbR	ER	C1	CR	AbR	ER	C1
E	Eb	D	Db	C	C♯	D	D♯	D	Db	C	B	Bb	B	C	C♯

Chromatics - Triads = Root & 1st inversion
Blockouts - 3 keys each cycle - 12 cycles *Repeat order*

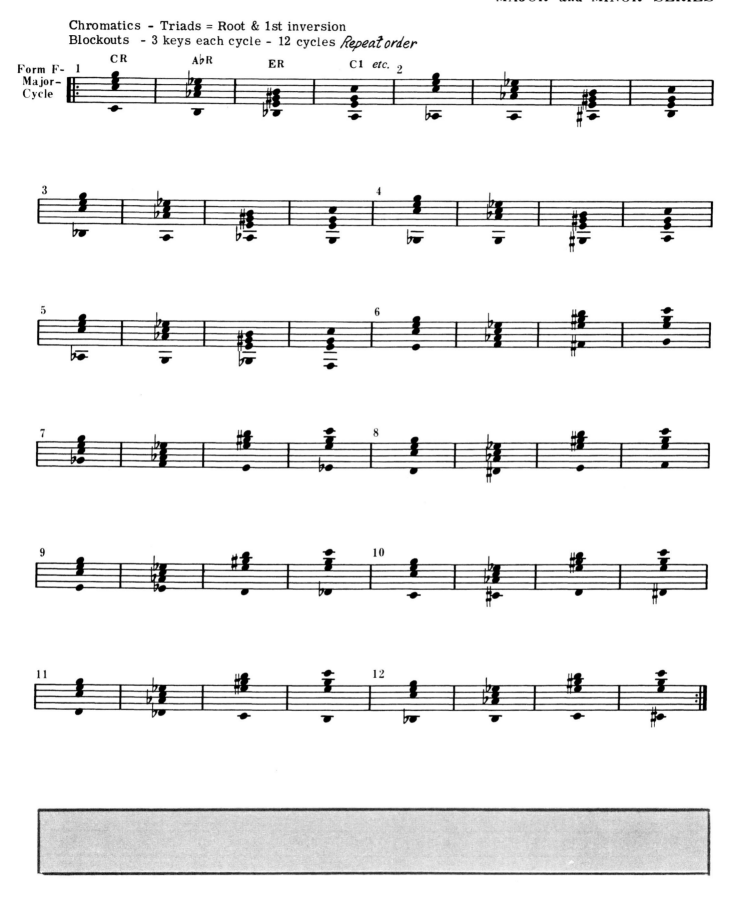

BLOCKOUT PATTERNS

CHROMATICS - TRIADS
Form G (Major)

TRIAD INVERSION ORDER = MIXED

Major & Minor Series

Cycle												
1	C1	F#2	Ab1	DR	E1	Bb2	C1	F#2	Ab1	DR	E1	Bb2
	Ab	G	Gb	F	E	Eb	D	Db	C	B	Bb	A
2	B1	F2	G1	DbR	Eb1	A2	B1	F2	G1	DbR	Bb1	A2
	Ab	G	Gb	F	E	Eb	D	Db	C	B	Bb	A
3	Bb1	E2	F#1	CR	D1	Ab2	Bb1	E2	F#1	CR	D1	Ab2
	Ab	G	Gb	F	E	Eb	D	Db	C	B	Bb	A
4	A1	Eb2	F1	BR	Db1	G2	A1	Eb2	F1	BR	Db1	G2
	Ab	G	Gb	F	E	Eb	D	Db	C	B	Bb	A
5	Ab1	D2	E1	BbR	C1	F#2	Ab1	D2	E1	BbR	B1	F#2
	Ab	G	Gb	F	E	Eb	D	Db	C	B	Bb	A
6	G1	Db2	Eb1	AR	B1	F2	G1	Db2	Eb1	AR	B1	F2
	Ab	G	Gb	F	E	Eb	D	Db	C	B	Bb	A
7	F#1	C2	D1	AbR	Bb1	E2	F#1	C2	D1	AbR	Bb1	E2
	Ab	G	Gb	F	E	Eb	D	Db	C	B	Bb	A
8	F1	B2	Db1	GR	A1	Eb2	F1	B2	Db1	GR	A1	Eb2
	Ab	G	Gb	F	E	Eb	D	Db	C	B	Bb	A
9	E1	Bb2	C1	F#R	Ab1	D2	E1	Bb2	C1	F#R	Ab1	D2
	Ab	G	Gb	F	E	Eb	D	Db	C	B	Bb	A
10	Eb1	A2	B1	FR	G1	Db2	Eb1	A2	B1	FR	G1	Db2
	Ab	G	Gb	F	E	Eb	D	Db	C	B	Bb	A
11	D1	Ab2	Ab1	ER	F#1	C2	D1	Ab2	Bb1	ER	F#1	C2
	Ab	G	Gb	F	E	Eb	D	Db	C	B	Bb	A
12	Db1	G2	A1	EbR	F1	B2	Db1	G2	A1	EbR	F1	B2
	Ab	G	Gb	F	E	Eb	D	Db	C	B	Bb	A

Chromatics - Triads - 1st-2nd-Root-inversions
Blockouts - 6 keys each cycle - 12 cycles -*Mixed order*

CHROMATICS-TRIADS-
FORM H (MINOR)

-BLOCKOUT PATTERNS-
-TRIAD INVERSION ORDER=REPEAT
-MAJOR & MINOR SERIES-

Cycle

1	Ĉ1	Âb2	ÊR	Ĉ1	Âb2	ÊR	Ĉ1	Âb2	ÊR	Ĉ1	Âb2	ÊR
	Ab	G	Gb	F	E	Eb	D	Db	C	B	Bb	A

2	B̂1	Ĝ2	ÊbR	B̂1	Ĝ2	ÊbR	B̂1	Ĝ2	ÊbR	B̂1	Ĝ2	ÊbR
	Ab	G	Gb	F	E	Eb	D	Db	C	B	Bb	A

3	B̂b1	Ĝb2	D̂R	B̂b1	Ĝb2	D̂R	B̂b1	Ĝb2	D̂R	B̂b1	Ĝb2	D̂R
	Ab	G	Gb	F	E	Eb	D	Db	C	B	Bb	A

4	Â1	F̂2	D̂bR	Â1	F̂2	D̂bR	Â1	F̂2	D̂bR	Â1	F̂2	D̂bR
	Ab	G	Gb	F	E	Eb	D	Db	C	B	Bb	A

5	Âb1	Ê2	ĈR	Âb1	Ê2	ĈR	Âb1	Ê2	ĈR	Âb1	Ê2	ĈR
	A	G	Gb	F	E	Eb	D	Db	C	B	Bb	A

6	Ĝ1	Êb2	B̂R	Ĝ1	Êb2	B̂R	Ĝ1	Êb2	B̂R	Ĝ1	Êb2	B̂R
	Ab	G	Gb	F	E	Eb	D	Db	C	B	Bb	A

7	Ĝb1	D̂2	B̂bR	Ĝb1	D̂2	B̂bR	Ĝb1	D̂2	B̂bR	Ĝb1	D̂2	B̂bR
	Ab	G	Gb	F	E	Eb	D	Db	C	B	Bb	A

8	F̂1	D̂b2	ÂR	F̂1	D̂b2	ÂR	F̂1	D̂b2	ÂR	F̂1	D̂b2	ÂR
	Ab	G	Gb	F	E	Eb	D	Db	C	B	Bb	A

9	Ê1	Ĉ2	ÂbR	Ê1	Ĉ2	ÂbR	Ê1	Ĉ2	ÂbR	Ê1	Ĉ2	ÂbR
	Ab	G	Gb	F	E	Eb	D	Db	C	B	Bb	A

10	Êb1	B̂2	ĜR	Êb1	B̂2	ĜR	Êb1	B̂2	ĜR	Êb1	B̂2	ĜR
	Ab	G	Gb	F	E	Eb	D	Db	C	B	Bb	A

11	D̂1	B̂b2	ĜbR	D̂1	B̂b2	ĜbR	D̂1	B̂b2	ĜbR	D̂1	B̂b2	ĜbR
	Ab	G	Gb	F	E	Eb	D	Db	C	B	Bb	A

12	D̂b1	Â2	F̂R	D̂b1	Â2	F̂R	D̂b1	Â2	F̂R	D̂b1	Â2	F̂R
	Ab	G	Gb	F	E	Eb	D	Db	C	B	Bb	A

Chromatics - Triads = 1st-2nd-Root-inversions alternately
Blockouts - 3 keys each cycle - 12 cycles -*Repeat order*

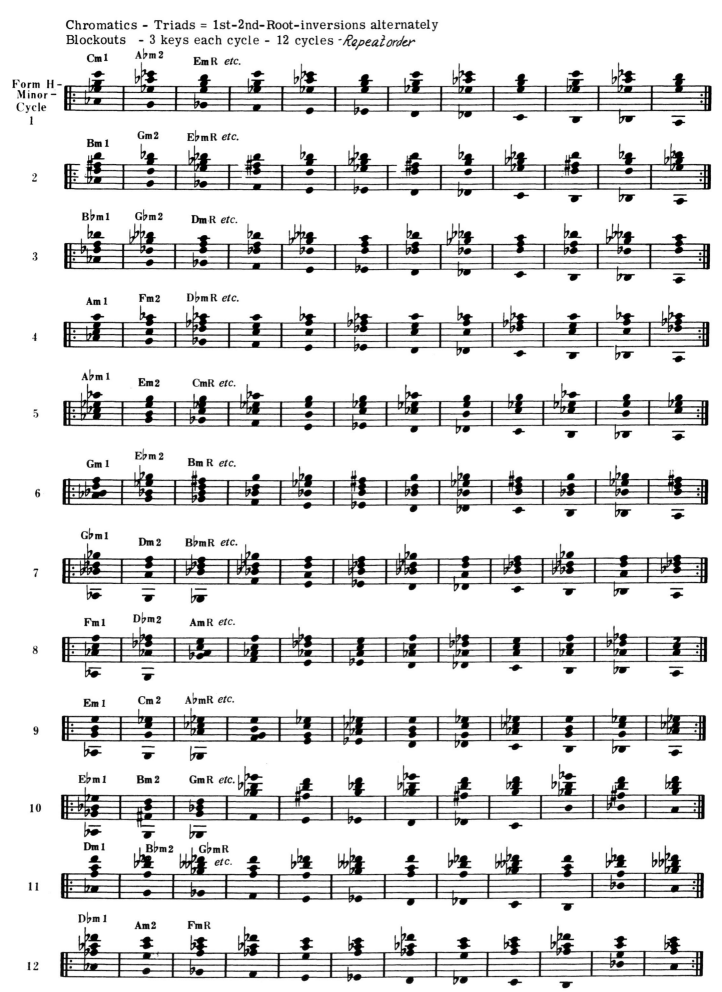

CHROMATICS-TRIADS-
FORM I (MINOR)

-BLOCKOUT PATTERNS-
-TRIAD INVERSION ORDER=REPEAT
-MAJOR & MINOR SERIES-

Cycle

1

C̆1	A♭̆2	ĔR	C̆1	A♭̆2	ĔR	C̆1	A♭̆2	ĔR	C̆1	A♭̆2	ĔR
C	B	B♭	A	A♭	G	G♭	F	E	E♭	D	D♭

2

B̆1	Ğ2	E♭̆R	B̆1	Ğ2	E♭̆R	B̆1	Ğ2	E♭̆R	B̆1	Ğ2	E♭̆R
C	B	B♭	A	A♭	G	G♭	F	E	E♭	D	D♭

3

B♭̆1	G♭̆2	D̆R	B♭̆1	G♭̆2	D̆R	B♭̆1	G♭̆2	D̆R	B♭̆1	G♭̆2	D̆R
C	B	B♭	A	A♭	G	G♭	F	E	E♭	D	D♭

4

Ă1	F̆2	D♭̆R	Ă1	F̆2	D♭̆R	Ă1	F̆2	D♭̆R	Ă1	F̆2	D♭̆R
C	B	B♭	A	A♭	G	G♭	F	E	E♭	D	D♭

5

A♭̆1	Ĕ2	C̆R	A♭̆1	Ĕ2	C̆R	A♭̆1	Ĕ2	C̆R	A♭̆1	Ĕ2	C̆R
C	B	B♭	A	A♭	G	G♭	F	E	E♭	D	D♭

6

Ğ1	E♭̆2	B̆R	Ğ1	E♭̆2	B̆R	Ğ1	E♭̆2	B̆R	Ğ1	E♭̆2	B̆R
C	B	B♭	A	A♭	G	G♭	F	E	E♭	D	D♭

7

G♭̆1	D̆2	B♭̆R	G♭̆1	D̆2	B♭̆R	G♭̆1	D̆2	B♭̆R	G♭̆1	D̆2	B♭̆R
C	B	B♭	A	A♭	G	G♭	F	E	E♭	D	D♭

8

F̆1	D♭̆2	ĂR	F̆1	D♭̆2	ĂR	F̆1	D♭̆2	ĂR	F̆1	D♭̆2	ĂR
C	B	B♭	A	A♭	G	G♭	F	E	E♭	D	D♭

9

Ĕ1	C̆2	A♭̆R	Ĕ1	C̆2	A♭̆R	Ĕ1	C̆2	A♭̆R	Ĕ1	C̆2	A♭̆R
C	B	B♭	A	A♭	G	G♭	F	E	E♭	D	D♭

10

E♭̆1	B̆2	ĞR	E♭̆1	B̆2	ĞR	E♭̆1	B̆2	ĞR	E♭̆1	B̆2	ĞR
C	B	B♭	A	A♭	G	G♭	F	E	E♭	D	D♭

11

D̆1	B♭̆2	G♭̆R	D̆1	B♭̆2	G♭̆R	D̆1	B♭̆2	G♭̆R	D̆1	B♭̆2	G♭̆R
C	B	B♭	A	A♭	G	G♭	F	E	E♭	D	D♭

12

D♭̈1	Ä2	F̈R	D♭̈1	Ä2	F̈R	D♭̈1	Ä2	F̈R	D♭̈1	Ä2	F̈R
C	B	B♭	A	A♭	G	G♭	F	E	E♭	D	D♭

Chromatics - Triads -first-second Root- alternately
Blockouts - 3 keys each cycle - 12 cycles - *Repeat order*

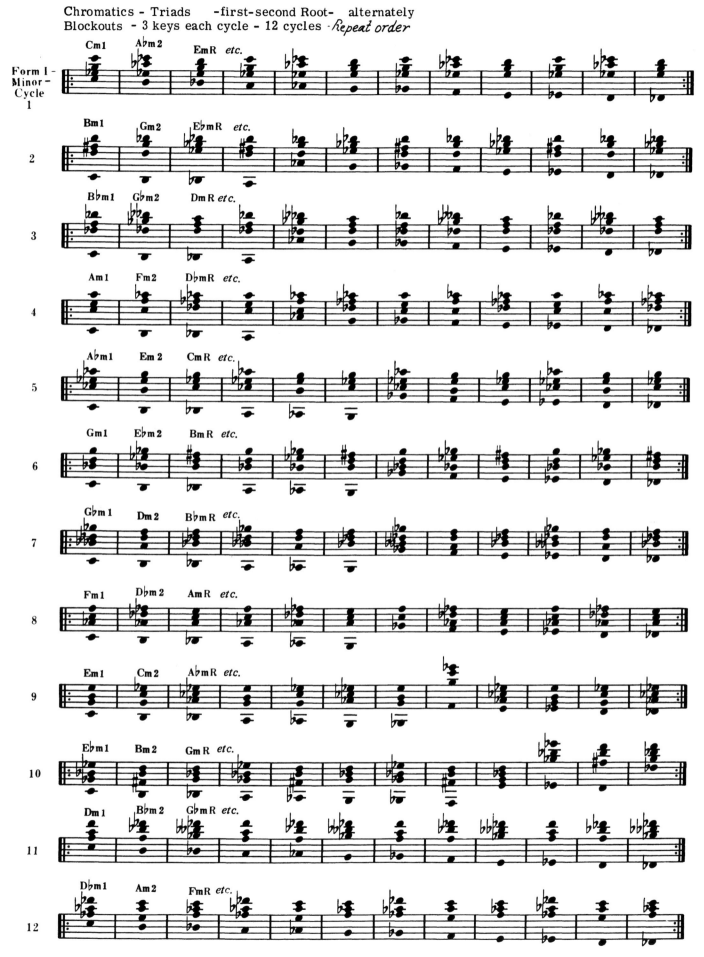

BLOCKOUT PATTERNS

TRIAD INVERSION ORDER = MIXED

Major & Minor Series

Cycle

1

Cm1	Ab m2	EmR	Cm2	Ab mR	Em1	CmR	Ab m1	Em2	Cm2	Ab m1	EmR
A	Ab	G	Gb	F	E	Eb	D	Db	C	B	Bb

2

Bm1	Gm2	Eb mR	Bm2	GmR	Eb m1	BmR	Gm1	Eb m2	Bm2	Gm1	Eb mR
A	Ab	G	Gb	F	E	Eb	D	Db	C	B	Bb

3

Bb m1	Gb m2	DmR	Bb m2	Gb mR	Dm1	Bb mR	Gb m1	Dm2	Bb m2	Gb m1	DmR
A	Ab	G	Gb	F	E	Eb	D	Db	C	B	Bb

4

Am1	Fm2	Db mR	Am2	FmR	Db m1	AmR	Fm1	Db m2	Am2	Fm1	Db mR
A	Ab	G	Gb	F	E	Eb	D	Db	C	B	Bb

5

Ab m1	Em2	CmR	Ab m2	EmR	Cm1	Ab mR	Em1	Cm2	Ab m2	Em1	CmR
A	Ab	G	Gb	F	E	Eb	D	Db	C	B	Bb

6

Gm1	Eb m2	BmR	Gm2	Eb mR	Bm1	GmR	Eb m1	Bm2	Gm2	Eb m1	BmR
A	Ab	G	Gb	F	E	Eb	D	Db	C	B	Bb

7

Gb m1	Dm2	Bb mR	Gb m2	DmR	Bb m1	Gb mR	Dm1	Bb m2	Gb m2	Dm1	Bb mR
A	Ab	G	Gb	F	E	Eb	D	Db	C	B	Bb

8

Fm1	Db m2	AmR	Fm2	Db mR	Am1	FmR	Db m1	Am2	Fm2	Db m1	AmR
A	Ab	G	Gb	F	E	Eb	D	Db	C	B	Bb

9

Em1	Cm2	Ab mR	Em2	CmR	Ab m1	EmR	Cm1	Ab m2	Em2	Cm1	Ab mR
A	Ab	G	Gb	F	E	Eb	D	Db	C	B	Bb

10

Eb m1	Bm2	GmR	Eb m2	BmR	Gm1	Eb mR	Bm1	Gm2	Eb m2	Bm1	GmR
A	Ab	G	Gb	F	E	Eb	D	Db	C	B	Bb

11

Dm1	Bb m2	Gb mR	Dm2	Bb mR	Gb m1	DmR	Bb m1	Gb m2	Dm2	Bb m1	Gb mR
A	Ab	G	Gb	F	E	Eb	D	Db	C	B	Bb

12

Db m1	Am2	FmR	Db m2	AmR	Fm1	Db mR	Am1	Fm2	Db m2	Am1	FmR
A	Ab	G	Gb	F	E	Eb	D	Db	C	B	Bb

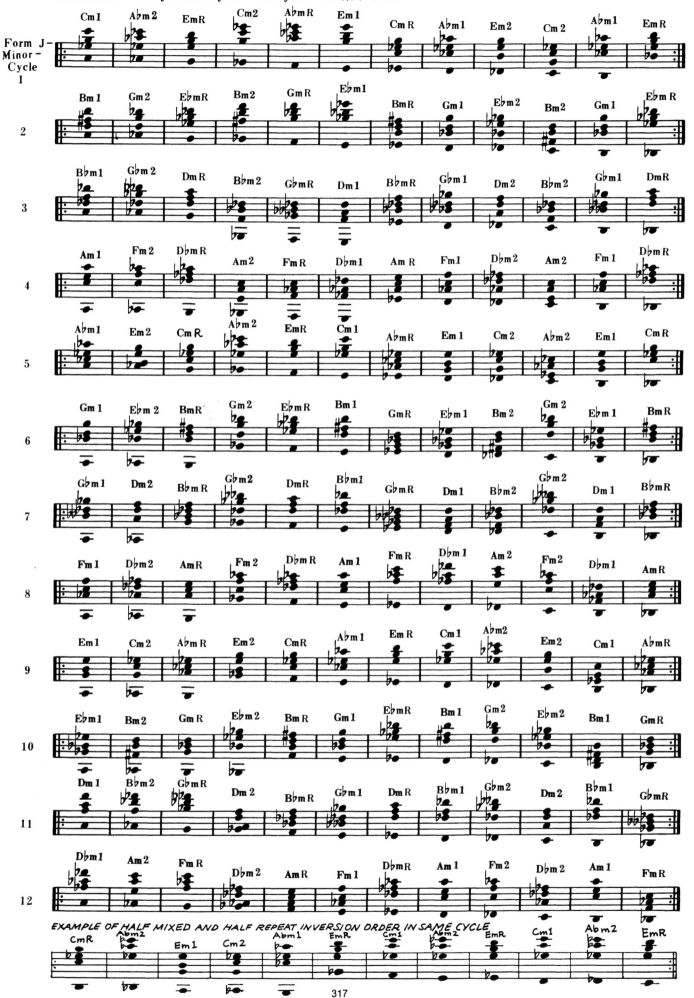

EXAMPLE OF HALF MIXED AND HALF REPEAT INVERSION ORDER IN SAME CYCLE

CHROMATICS-TRIADS-
FORM K (MAJOR & MINOR)

-BLOCKOUT PATTERNS-
-TRIAD INVERSION ORDER=REPEAT
-MAJOR & MINOR SERIES-

(Note: a small caret ^ appears over certain chord symbols in the original; indicated below as a trailing ^.)

Cycle

1

C1	Ab2^	ER	C1^	Ab2	ER^	C1	Ab2^	ER	C1^	Ab2	ER^
Ab	G	Gb	F	E	Eb	D	Db	C	B	Bb	A

2

B1	G2^	EbR	B1^	G2	EbR^	B1	G2^	EbR	B1^	G2	EbR^
Ab	G	Gb	F	E	Eb	D	Db	C	B	Bb	A

3

Bb1	Gb2^	DR	Bb1^	Gb2	DR^	Bb1	Gb2^	DR	Bb1^	Gb2	DR^
Ab	G	Gb	F	E	Eb	D	Db	C	B	Bb	A

4

A1	F2^	DbR	A1^	F2	DbR^	A1	F2^	DbR	A1^	F2	DbR^
Ab	G	Gb	F	E	Eb	D	Db	C	B	Bb	A

5

Ab1	E2^	CR	Ab1^	E2	CR^	Ab1	E2^	CR	Ab1^	E2	CR^
Ab	G	Gb	F	E	Eb	D	Db	C	B	Bb	A

6

G1	Eb2^	BR	G1^	Eb2	BR^	G1	Eb2^	BR	G1^	Eb2	BR^
Ab	G	Gb	F	E	Eb	D	Db	C	B	Bb	A

7

Gb1	D2^	BbR	Gb1^	D2	BbR^	Gb1	D2^	BbR	Gb1^	D2	BbR^
Ab	G	Gb	F	E	Eb	D	Db	C	B	Bb	A

8

F1	Db2^	AR	F1^	Db2	AR^	F1	Db2^	AR	F1^	Db2	AR^
Ab	G	Gb	F	E	Eb	D	Db	C	B	Bb	A

9

E1	C2^	AbR	E1^	C2	AbR^	E1	C2^	AbR	E1^	C2	AbR^
Ab	G	Gb	F	E	Eb	D	Db	C	B	Bb	A

10

Eb1	B2^	GR	Eb1^	B2	GR^	Eb1	B2^	GR	Eb1^	B2	GR^
Ab	G	Gb	F	E	Eb	D	Db	C	B	Bb	A

11

D1	Bb2^	GbR	D1^	Bb2	GbR^	D1	Bb2^	GbR	D1^	Bb2	GbR^
Ab	G	Gb	F	E	Eb	D	Db	C	B	Bb	A

12

Db1	A2^	FR	Db1^	A2	FR^	Db1	A2^	FR	Db1^	A2	FR^
Ab	G	Gb	F	E	Eb	D	Db	C	B	Bb	A

Chromatics - Triads = 1st - 2nd - Root inversions - Major & Minor Mixed alternately

Blockouts - 3 keys each cycle - 12 cycles - *Repeat order*

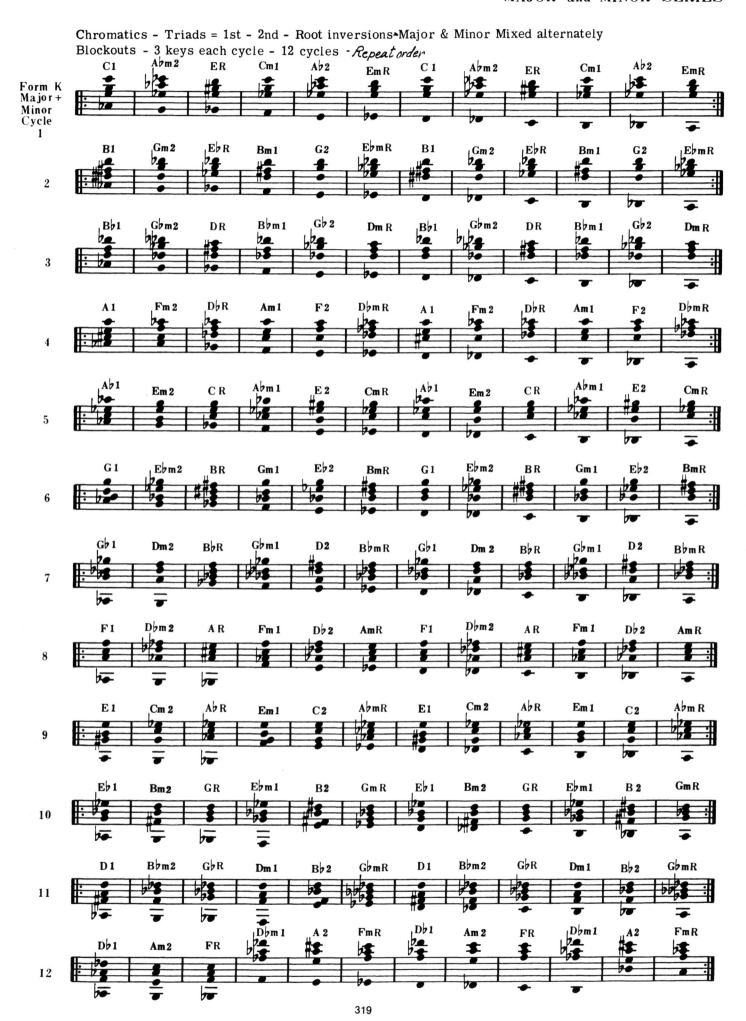

Form K
Major +
Minor
Cycle

319

CHROMATICS-TRIADS-
FORM L (MAJOR & MINOR)

-BLOCKOUT PATTERNS-
-TRIAD INVERSION ORDER=MIXED
-MAJOR & MINOR SERIES-

Cycle

1

^C1	F#2	^Ab1	DR	^E1	Bb2	^C1	F#2	^Ab1	DR	^E1	Bb2
Ab	G	Gb	F	E	Eb	D	Db	C	B	Bb	A

2

^B1	F2	^G1	DbR	^Eb1	A2	^B1	F2	^G1	DbR	^Eb1	A2
Ab	G	Gb	F	E	Eb	D	Db	C	B	Bb	A

3

^Bb1	E2	^F#1	CR	^D1	Ab2	^Bb1	E2	^F#1	CR	^D1	Ab2
Ab	G	Gb	F	E	Eb	D	Db	C	B	Bb	A

4

^A1	Eb2	^F1	BR	^Db1	G2	^A1	Eb2	^F1	BR	^Db1	G2
Ab	G	Gb	F	E	Eb	D	Db	C	B	Bb	A

5

^Ab1	D2	^E1	BbR	^C1	F#2	^Ab1	D2	^E1	BbR	^C1	F#2
Ab	G	Gb	F	E	Eb	D	Db	C	B	Bb	A

6

^G1	Db2	^Eb1	AR	^B1	F2	^G1	Db2	^Eb1	AR	^B1	F2
Ab	G	Gb	F	E	Eb	D	Db	C	B	Bb	A

7

F#1	^C2	D1	^AbR	Bb1	^E2	F#1	^C2	D1	^AbR	Bb1	^E2
Ab	G	Gb	F	E	Eb	D	Db	C	B	Bb	A

8

F1	^B2	Db1	^GR	A1	^Eb2	F1	^B2	Db1	^GR	A1	^Eb2
Ab	G	Gb	F	E	Eb	D	Db	C	B	Bb	A

9

E1	^Bb2	C1	^F#R	Ab1	^D2	E1	^Bb2	C1	^F#R	Ab1	^D2
Ab	G	Gb	F	E	Eb	D	Db	C	B	Bb	A

10

Eb1	^A2	B1	^FR	G1	^Db2	Eb1	^A2	B1	^FR	G1	^Db2
Ab	G	Gb	F	E	Eb	D	Db	C	B	Bb	A

11

D1	^Ab2	Bb1	^ER	F#1	^C2	D1	^Ab2	Bb1	^ER	F#1	^C2
Ab	G	Gb	F	E	Eb	D	Db	C	B	Bb	A

12

Db1	^G2	A1	^EbR	F1	^B2	Db1	^G2	A1	^EbR	F1	^B2
Ab	G	Gb	F	E	Eb	D	Db	C	B	Bb	A

Chromatics - Triads - 1st - 2nd - Root - inversions alternately - mixed Major & Minor
Blockouts - 6 keys each cycle - 12 cycles - Observe changing Major & Minor order -*Mixed order*

BLOCKOUT PATTERNS
MAJOR & MINOR SERIES

CHROMATICS—TRIADS—
BLOCKOUT PATTERNS

In the following blockout patterns, notation has been eliminated because the triads and the bass are to be played in as many different registers and positions as possible.

The minor triads have been marked with the usual letter "M"—all others are major, but they are merely suggestions and later on their locations should be changed.

In other words, not only experiment with different orders for the inversions but mix the majors and minors, turn all of the various blockouts inside out, outside in, upside down, backwards etc.

BLOCKOUT PATTERNS

TRIAD INVERSION ORDER = ALL FIRST INVERSIONS

CHROMATICS-TRIADS
Form   —Major—
(Example)

Major & Minor Series

1 is a basic blockout line -- #3 illustrates eliminating the unison in the fourth step by reducing to three voices so as not to double the bass line but still keep the continuity of that line -- #3 illustrates using three voices also in step # 4-8 12 -- #4 shows the use of the open triad voicings in steps # 4-8- and 12 --

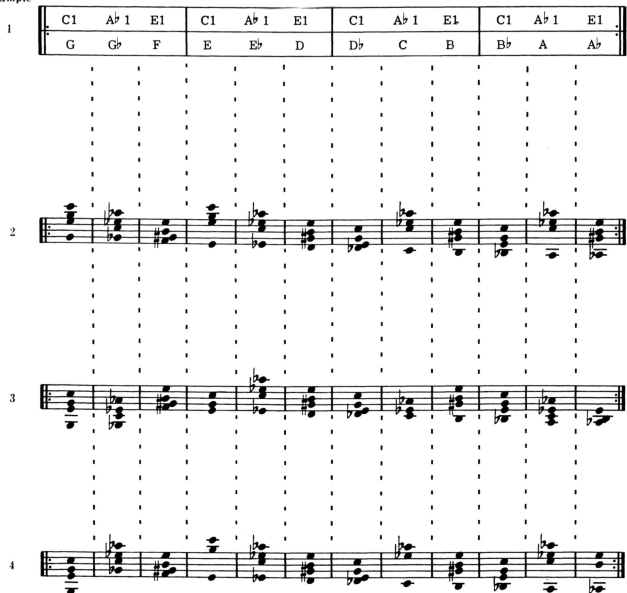

Example

C1	A♭ 1	E1	C1	A♭ 1	E1	C1	A♭ 1	E1	C1	A♭ 1	E1
G	G♭	F	E	E♭	D	D♭	C	B	B♭	A	A♭

As was previously stated, the progressions resulting from the blockout principle are not necessarily meant to be used by rote, they are meant to stimulate, to perhaps provide some progressional ideas --- It is all food for thought.

CHROMATICS-TRIADS-
FORM 1 (MAJOR/MINOR)

-BLOCKOUT PATTERNS-
-TRIAD INVERSION ORDER=OPTIONAL
-MAJOR & MINOR SERIES-

EMPLOY FIRST INVERSIONS THRU OUT- THEN SECOND INVERSIONS- THEN

ROOTS- IN BOTH MAJOR AND MINOR--THEN MIX THEM

Cycle 1				2				3				4			
C	Ab	E	C	B	G	Eb	B	Bb	Gb	D	Bb	A	F	Db	A
C	C#	B	C	C	C#	B	C	C	C#	B	C	C	C#	B	C

5				6				7				8			
Ab	E	C	Ab	G	Eb	B	G	Gb	D	Bb	Gb	F	Db	A	F
C	C#	B	C	C	C#	B	C	C	C#	B	C	C	C#	B	C

9				10				11				12			
E	C	Ab	E	Eb	B	G	Eb	D	Bb	Gb	D	Db	A	F	Db
C	C#	B	C	C	C#	B	C	C	C#	B	C	C	C#	B	C

APPLY ALL PREVIOUS RULES

CHROMATICS-TRIADS-
FORM 2 (MAJOR/MINOR)

-BLOCKOUT PATTERNS-
-TRIAD INVERSION ORDER=MIXED
-MAJOR & MINOR SERIES-

EMPLOY MAJOR AND MINOR TRIADS- MIX THEM-

Cycle 1				2				3				4			
C1	Ab2	ER	C1	Ab2	ER	C1	Ab2	ER	C1	Ab2	ER	C1	Ab2	ER	C1
C	C#	B	C	B	C	A#	B	Bb	B	A	Bb	A	Bb	G#	A

5				6				7				8			
Ab2	ER	C1	Ab2	ER	C1	Ab2	ER	C1	Ab2	ER	C1	Ab2	ER	C1	Ab2
Ab	A	G	Ab	G	A	F#	G	Gb	G	F	Gb	F	F#	E	F

9				10				11				12			
ER	C1	Ab2	ER	C1	Ab2	ER	C1	Ab2	ER	C1	Ab2	ER	C1	Ab2	ER
E	F	D#	E	Eb	E	D	Eb	D	D#	C#	D	Db	D	C	Db

APPLY ALL PREVIOUS RULES

CHROMATICS-TRIADS-
FORM 3 (MAJOR/MINOR)

-BLOCKOUT PATTERNS-
-TRIAD INVERSION ORDER=REPEAT
-MAJOR & MINOR SERIES-

EMPLOY MAJOR AND MINOR TRIADS- MIX THEM

Cycle 1				2				3				4			
C1	Ab2	ER	C1	B1	G2	EbR	B1	Bb1	Gb2	DR	Bb1	A1	F2	DbR	A1
C	D	B	C	C	D	B	C	C	D	B	C	C	D	B	C

5				6				7				8			
Ab1	E2	CR	Ab1	G1	Eb2	BR	G1	Gb1	D2	BbR	Gb1	F1	Db2	AR	F1
C	D	B	C	C	D	B	C	C	D	B	C	C	D	B	C

9				10				11				12			
E1	C2	AbR	E1	Eb1	B2	GR	Eb1	D1	Bb2	GbR	D1	Db1	A2	FR	Db1
C	D	B	C	C	D	B	C	C	D	B	C	C	D	B	C

APPLY ALL PREVIOUS RULES

CHROMATICS-TRIADS-
FORM 4 (MAJOR/MINOR)

-BLOCKOUT PATTERNS-
-TRIAD INVERSION ORDER=OPTIONAL
-MAJOR & MINOR SERIES-

ALL FIRST INVERSIONS- THEN SECOND INVERSIONS- THEN ROOT

EMPLOY MAJOR AND MINOR TRIADS - MIX THEM

DESCENDING TRIADS - ASCENDING BASS LINE

Cycle 1				2				3				4			
C1	Ab1	E1	C1	B1	G1	Eb1	B1	Bb1	Gb1	D1	Bb1	A1	F1	Db1	A1
C	D	Db	C	C#	D#	D	Db	D	E	Eb	D	D#	F	Fb	Eb

5				6				7				8			
Ab2	E2	C2	Ab2	G2	Eb2	B2	G2	Gb2	D2	Bb2	Gb2	F2	Db2	A2	F2
E	F#	F	E	F	G	Gb	F	F#	G#	G	F#	G	A	Ab	G

9				10				11				12			
ER	CR	AbR	ER	EbR	BR	GR	EbR	DR	BbR	GbR	DR	DbR	AR	FR	DbR
G#	A#	A	G#	A	B	Bb	A	A#	C	Cb	A#	B	C#	C	B

APPLY ALL PREVIOUS RULES

CHROMATICS-TRIADS-
FORM 5 (MAJOR/MINOR)

-BLOCKOUT PATTERNS-
-TRIAD INVERSION ORDER=OPTIONAL
-MAJOR & MINOR SERIES-

ALL FIRST INVERSIONS- THEN SECOND- THEN ROOT

EMPLOY MAJOR AND MINOR TRIADS- MIX THEM

Cycle

1				2				3				4			
C1	Ab2	ER	C1	B1	G2	EbR	B1	Bb1	Gb2	DR	Bb1	A1	F2	DbR	A1
C	D	Db	C	C	D	Db	C	C	D	Db	C	C	D	Db	C

5				6				7				8			
Ab1	E2	CR	Ab1	G1	Eb2	BR	G1	Gb1	D2	BbR	Gb1	F1	Db2	AR	F1
C	D	Db	C	C	D	Db	C	C	D	Db	C	C	D	Db	C

9				10				11				12			
E1	C2	AbR	E1	Eb1	B2	GR	Eb1	D1	Bb2	GbR	D1	Db1	A2	FR	Db1
C	D	Db	C	C	D	Db	C	C	D	Db	C	C	D	Db	C

APPLY ALL PREVIOUS RULES

CHROMATICS-TRIADS-
FORM 6 (MAJOR/MINOR)

-BLOCKOUT PATTERNS-
-TRIAD INVERSION ORDER=REPEAT
-MAJOR & MINOR SERIES-

A VARIATION OF FORM 5 -

EMPLOY MAJOR AND MINOR TRIADS - MIX THEM

Cycle

1				2				3				4			
CR	Ab1	E2	CR	BR	G1	Eb2	BR	BbR	Gb1	D2	BbR	AR	F1	Db2	AR
C	D	Db	C	C	D	Db	C	C	D	Db	C	C	D	Db	C

5				6				7				8			
AbR	E1	C2	AbR	GR	Eb1	B2	GR	GbR	D1	Bb2	GbR	FR	Db1	A2	FR
C	D	Db	C	C	D	Db	C	C	D	Db	C	C	D	Db	C

9				10				11				12			
ER	C1	Ab2	ER	EbR	B1	G2	EbR	DR	Bb1	Gb2	DR	DbR	A1	F2	DbR
C	D	Db	C	C	D	Db	C	C	D	Db	C	C	D	Db	C

APPLY ALL PREVIOUS RULES

CHROMATICS-TRIADS-
FORM 7 (MAJOR/MINOR)

-BLOCKOUT PATTERNS-
-TRIAD INVERSION ORDER=REPEAT
-MAJOR & MINOR SERIES-

EMPLOY MAJOR AND MINOR TRIADS-MIX THEM

Cycle 1

C1	ER	Ab2	CR	C1	ER	Ab2	CR	C1	ER	Ab2	CR	C1	ER	Ab2	CR
C	D	Db	C	B	C#	C	B	Bb	C	Cb	Bb	A	B	Bb	A

5 · 6 · 7 · 8

C1	ER	Ab2	CR	C1	ER	Ab2	CR	C1	ER	Ab2	CR	C1	ER	Ab2	CR
Ab	Bb	A	Ab	G	A	Ab	G	Gb	Ab	G	Gb	F	G	Gb	F

9 · 10 · 11 · 12

C1	ER	Ab2	CR	C1	ER	Ab2	CR	C1	ER	Ab2	CR	C1	ER	Ab2	CR
E	F#	F	E	Eb	F	Fb	Eb	D	E	Eb	D	Db	Eb	D	Db

APPLY ALL PREVIOUS RULES

CHROMATICS-TRIADS-
FORM 8 (MAJOR/MINOR)

-BLOCKOUT PATTERNS-
-TRIAD INVERSION ORDER=REPEAT
-MAJOR & MINOR SERIES-

EMPLOY MAJOR AND MINOR TRIADS-MIX THEM

Cycle 1

C2	Ab2	ER	C1	C2	Ab2	ER	C1	C2	Ab2	ER	C1	C2	Ab2	ER	C1
C	D	Db	C	B	C#	C	B	Bb	C	Cb	Bb	A	B	Bb	A

5 · 6 · 7 · 8

C2	Ab2	ER	C1	C2	Ab2	ER	C1	C2	Ab2	ER	C1	C2	Ab2	ER	C1
Ab	Bb	A	Ab	G	A	Ab	G	Gb	Ab	G	Gb	F	G	Gb	F

9 · 10 · 11 · 12

C2	Ab2	ER	C1	C2	Ab2	ER	C1	C2	Ab2	ER	C1	C2	Ab2	ER	C1
E	F#	F	E	Eb	F	E	Eb	D	E	Eb	D	Db	Eb	D	Db

APPLY ALL PREVIOUS RULES

CHROMATICS-TRIADS-
FORM 9 (MAJOR/MINOR)

-BLOCKOUT PATTERNS-
-TRIAD INVERSION ORDER=
-MAJOR & MINOR SERIES-

CONTINOUS DESCENDING BASS LINE - CHANGING REGISTERS(OF COURSE-)
EMPLOY MAJOR AND MINOR TRIADS - MIX THEM

Cycle 1

C2	AR	Gb1	Eb2	CR
Ab	G	Gb	F	E

2

C2	AR	Gb1	Eb2	CR
Eb	D	Db	C	B

3

C2	AR	Gb1	Eb2	CR
Bb	A	Ab	G	Gb

4

C2	AR	Gb1	Eb2	CR
F	E	Eb	D	Db

5

C2	AR	Gb1	Eb2	CR
C	B	Bb	A	Ab

6

C2	AR	Gb1	Eb2	CR
G	Gb	F	E	Eb

7

C2	AR	Gb1	Eb2	CR
D	Db	C	B	Bb

8

C2	AR	Gb1	Eb2	CR
A	Ab	G	Gb	F

9

C2	AR	Gb1	Eb2	CR
E	Eb	D	Db	C

10

C2	AR	Gb1	Eb2	CR
B	Bb	A	Ab	G

11

C2	AR	Gb1	Eb2	CR
Gb	F	E	Eb	D

12

C2	AR	Gb1	Eb2	CR
Db	C	B	Bb	A

APPLY ALL PREVIOUS RULES

CHROMATICS-TRIADS-
FORM 10 (MAJOR/MINOR)

-BLOCKOUT PATTERNS-
-TRIAD INVERSION ORDER=REPEAT
-MAJOR & MINOR SERIES-

CONTINUOUS DESCENDING BASS LINE.
EMPLOY MAJOR AND MINOR TRIADS-MIX THEM-
12 TRIAD CYCLES EQUAL 1 OVERALL CYCLE-IN OTHER WORDS,IT TAKES 12
TRIAD CYCLES BEFORE THE TRIAD AND BASS RETURN TO THEIR BEGINNING
RELATIONSHIP.

Cycle 1

C2	AR	Gb1	Eb2	CR
C	B	Bb	A	Ab

2

C2	AR	Gb1	Eb2	CR
G	Gb	F	E	Eb

3

C2	AR	Gb1	Eb2	CR
D	Db	C	B	Bb

4

C2	AR	Gb1	Eb2	CR
A	Ab	G	Gb	F

5

C2	AR	Gb1	Eb2	CR
E	Eb	D	Db	C

6

C2	AR	Gb1	Eb2	CR
B	Bb	A	Ab	G

7

C2	AR	Gb1	Eb2	CR
Gb	F	E	Eb	D

8

C2	AR	Gb1	Eb2	CR
Db	C	B	Bb	A

9

C2	AR	Gb1	Eb2	CR
Ab	G	Gb	F	E

10

C2	AR	Gb1	Eb2	CR
Eb	D	Db	C	B

11

C2	AR	Gb1	Eb2	CR
Bb	A	Ab	G	Gb

12

C2	AR	Gb1	Eb2	CR
F	E	Eb	D	Db

APPLY ALL PREVIOUS RULES

CHROMATICS-TRIADS-
FORM 11

-BLOCKOUT PATTERNS-
-TRIAD INVERSION ORDER = REPEAT
-MAJOR & MINOR SERIES-

OBSERVE CHANGING MAJOR AND MINOR MIXED ORDER - ALSO ENHARMONICS -

6 KEYS EACH CYCLE - WHOLE TONES APART DESCENDING -

A REMINDER: THOSE MARKED WITH AN "M" ARE MINOR - ALL OTHERS ARE MAJOR

(Chords marked (m) carry the minor "M" symbol above them.)

Cycle 1

CR(m)	Bb1	Ab2(m)	GbR	E1(m)	D2	CR(m)	Bb1	Ab2(m)	GbR	E1(m)	D2
Ab	G	Gb	F	E	Eb	D	Db	C	B	Bb	A

Cycle 2

BR(m)	A1	G2(m)	FR	Eb1(m)	Db2	BR(m)	A1	G2(m)	FR	Eb1(m)	Db2
Ab	G	Gb	F	E	Eb	D	Db	C	B	Bb	A

Cycle 3

BbR(m)	Ab1	Gb2(m)	ER	D1(m)	C2	BbR(m)	Ab1	Gb2(m)	ER	D1(m)	C2
Ab	G	Gb	F	E	Eb	D	Db	C	B	Bb	A

Cycle 4

AR	G1(m)	F2	EbR(m)	Db1	B2(m)	AR	G1(m)	F2	EbR(m)	Db1	B2(m)
Ab	G	Gb	F	E	Eb	D	Db	C	B	Bb	A

Cycle 5

AbR(m)	Gb1	E2(m)	DR	C1(m)	Bb2	AbR	Gb1(m)	E2	DR(m)	C1	Bb2(m)
A	A#	B	C	C#	D	D#	E	F	F#	G	G#

Cycle 6

GR	F1(m)	Eb2	DbR(m)	B1	A2(m)	GR	F1(m)	Eb2	DbR(m)	B1	A2(m)
A	Ab	G	Gb	F	E	Eb	D	Db	C	B	Bb

Cycle 7

GbR	E1	D2	CR	Bb1	G#2(m)	F#R	E1	D2	CR	A#1	Ab2
B	C	C#	D	D#	E	F	F#	G	G#	A	A#

Cycle 8

FR(m)	D#1	C#2	BR(m)	A1	G2(m)	FR(m)	Eb1	Db2(m)	BR(m)	A1	G2(m)
Ab	G	Gb	F	E	Eb	D	Db	C	B	Bb	A

Cycle 9

ER	D1(m)	C2	BbR(m)	Ab1	Gb2	ER(m)	D1	C2(m)	A#R	Ab1	F#2(m)
G#	A	A#	B	C	C#	D	D#	E	F	F#	G

Cycle 10

D#R(m)	Db1	B2	AR	G1(m)	F2	EbR(m)	Db1	B2(m)	AR(m)	G1	F2
Ab	G	Gb	F	E	Eb	D	Db	C	B	Bb	A

Cycle 11

DR	C1(m)	A#2	G#R(m)	F#1	E2(m)	DR	C1(m)	Bb2	AbR(m)	Gb1	E2(m)
G#	A#	C	D	E	F#	G#	A#	C	B	Bb	A

Cycle 12

DbR(m)	B1	A2(m)	GR	F1(m)	Eb2	C#R(m)	B1	A2(m)	GR	F1(m)	Eb2
Ab	G	Gb	F	E	Eb	D	Db	C	B	Bb	A

APPLY ALL PREVIOUS RULES